Tales of Old L

Other counties covered by the *Tales* series include

Buckinghamshire
Cambridgeshire
Cornwall
Cumbria
Derbyshire
Devon
Essex
Hampshire
Kent
Lincolnshire
Middlesex
Northamptonshire
Northumberland
Oxfordshire
Somerset
Staffordshire
Warwickshire
Wiltshire
North Yorkshire

Tales of
Old Lancashire

Elizabeth Ashworth

With illustrations by Clive Stevens

COUNTRYSIDE BOOKS
NEWBURY, BERKSHIRE

First published 2007
© Elizabeth Ashworth, 2007

COUNTRYSIDE BOOKS
3 Catherine Road
Newbury, Berkshire

To view our complete range of books,
please visit us at
www.countrysidebooks.co.uk

To view the author's website,
please go to
www.elizabethashworth.com

ISBN 978 1 84674 041 1

Produced through MRM Associates Ltd., Reading
Typeset by Jean Cussons Typesetting, Diss, Norfolk
Printed by Cambridge University Press

*All material for the manufacture of this book was sourced from
sustainable forests*

Contents

N

Grange
over Sands

LANCASTER

Sunderland
Point

Gisburn

CLITHEROE

Mitton   Pendle   Wycoller
          Hill

BLACKPOOL

Woodplumpton

Preston   Samlesbury

Lytham
St Annes   Blackburn

Hoghton

SOUTHPORT

Martin Mere   Rochdale

BOLTON

WIGAN

Ashton-under-Lyne

Ashton-in-
Makerfield   MANCHESTER

Liverpool   Winwick

Hale

The Prisoner in the Golden Cellar

The first Clegg Hall, near Rochdale was a house constructed in Norman times by either Bernulf de Clegg or his daughter Quenilda and her husband Adam; history is rather hazy about exactly who was responsible and some historians are unclear whether Quenilda was Bernulf's daughter or his wife. What is known for sure is that a new Hall was built beside it in 1618 by Theophilus Assheton. It was an altogether more ostentatious affair with four storeys and many fine rooms that overlooked the surrounding farmland and countryside.

The original building, part of which remained standing and was used for storing wood, had gained a reputation for being haunted. Locals believed that a boggart, or evil spirit, was trapped there by some unspeakably wicked act that it had done whilst still human flesh.

The first Clegg Hall would have been timber-framed with wattle and daub as only the powerful nobles would have been able to build stone castles, but it would probably have been a fortified manor house with a moat. It is from this time, around the 13th century, that the story of the boggart is said to originate. It is told that when the master of the house went away to fight in France he left his two sons in the care of their uncle as his wife had died five years before. His brother, keen

to gain possession of Clegg Hall, killed the two young heirs, fourteen-year-old Bertrand and his brother Randulph, a year younger, and threw their bodies into the moat. When the master returned his brother was waiting in a hidden passage to kill him as well, but he heard the children's voices calling out, 'Father beware!' which terrified the uncle so much that he ran away and plunged to his own death. Ever since the phantom boys have been heard issuing warnings. In another version this wicked uncle actually gained the inheritance for himself, but because of his wicked deeds his ghost was doomed to haunt Clegg Hall forever.

Following the death of Theophilus Assheton, who died unmarried and childless, Clegg Hall became the property of the Haworths of Haworth. One day a beggar came to the Hall and was allowed to sleep in one of the rooms of the old house. He became a regular visitor and although he told no one anything about himself, not even his name, he became known to the locals as Norman.

Now it was widely acknowledged that pulling down most of the old house hadn't got rid of the boggart and that it still haunted Clegg Hall, and it seemed to be especially disturbed by Norman's visits. Strange noises were heard coming from the lumber room where he slept and tapping was heard from underground whenever he was there.

Norman would relate tales of the boggart's visits to him in the night and the gullible servants believed that he was a wizard who had the power to conjure up ghosts. They refused to go near the lumber room and because they were so afraid of Norman and his powers he was pretty much allowed to come and go and use the old rooms as he pleased.

One person who believed in these good and bad spirits was the young daughter of the house, Lucy Haworth. She was also a great believer in romance and became almost obsessed by a handsome stranger she had seen on several occasions around the house and nearby woodlands.

Her romantic aspirations were also heightened by a strange event at a wedding she attended at nearby Stubley, when two

9

men dressed as Turks, with masked faces, came into the hall and performed a variety of conjuring tricks for the gathered guests. One of the men had a box and he asked Lucy Haworth if she would like it to be opened. She said yes and the man unlocked the box to reveal a mechanical peacock, so realistic that at first the guests thought it was a real bird. The peacock was put on the floor where it flapped its wings and spread its tail. Then, from its breast came a white dove; from the dove's breast came a nightingale, which fluttered its wings and sang; from the nightingale came a hummingbird, with a piece of paper in its beak which was given to Lucy. She read the note and quickly hid it in her dress whilst the two Turks gathered up their automated birds and packed them away.

The gathered guests congratulated their host, Robert Holt, on the fantastic entertainment, but he said he knew nothing of it and that the display must have been arranged by the bridegroom, though he too claimed it hadn't been set up by him.

Lucy, meanwhile, said nothing. She had recognised one of the Turks as her silent admirer and the note which she had hidden read 'Tomorrow at midnight, in the haunted chamber! If thou hast courage tarry there a while. Its occupant will protect thee. Peril threatens thy house, which thy coming can alone prevent. Shouldst thou reveal but one word of this warning, thy life, and those dear to thee, will be forfeit. From thine unknown monitor.'

The occupant was, of course, Norman, and when Lucy crept from her bed at midnight carrying a candle and entered the old lumber room, he immediately closed and bolted the door behind her. Suddenly her candle was blown out, her arms were seized by invisible hands and she was dragged down into some deep dank underground passages that ran beneath the house until she was thrust into an underground room and the door closed on her.

She wasn't left in total darkness though. There was an iron lamp hanging from the vaulted ceiling and by its light Lucy saw piles and piles of gold coins. Then the door opened and her handsome admirer appeared, professing his love for her and offering her all his wealth.

When the family discovered next morning that Lucy was missing they immediately began a search for her. Her brother, Nicholas, asked Norman if he knew what had happened to Lucy.

'Ask the little devils I saw yesternight,' he replied. 'I have told you of the terrible things that have visited me in the boggart chamber and how the ghost begged for a victim.'

Then, to prove that he was not in league with the boggart, Norman offered to cast out the spirit, but the suspicious Nicholas Haworth had Norman locked in the kitchen until the next day.

That night, the tapping and rattling of chains was heard, not just near the boggart's chamber in the lumber room, but all over Clegg Hall, though when Nicholas sent two terrified servants to check on Norman they found him sleeping soundly in the kitchen. Nicholas, filled with fear and anger, told Norman to rid the house of evil spirits at once or he would hand him over to the authorities, which would probably have resulted in him being hanged for witchcraft.

Norman agreed, but said that he must first be alone in the lumber room for a while. So he was locked in and a watch was kept to prevent his escape until he was ready to begin.

When Norman announced that he was ready he first drew a line on the floor in the dust and said that no one but him should cross it. He then began to mumble incantations which were answered by rumblings from below. He knocked on the floor and answering knocks came from underground. Then he began to conjure the spirit to ask what price must be paid for its departure. There were shrieks and yells and faint murmurings that Norman told the gathered family were the spirits of the two Clegg children who had been killed by their uncle so long ago. Then Norman announced the boggart's price.

11

'A living body must be sacrificed – and in four quarters it must be laid: then shall these wicked spirits not return hither until what is severed be joined together. With this hard condition we must be content.'

As Nicholas Haworth still suspected that the beggar had played some part in his sister's disappearance, he immediately suggested that Norman should be the sacrificial victim, but the man cried out that a human sacrifice was not necessary and a servant was sent to fetch a fowl from the barn. This was killed and cut into four quarters. One quarter was buried at Little Clegg in a field, the second at Beil Bridge, the third under the hearthstones in the Hall and the fourth under the floor in the barn.

When the last piece was buried there was a huge explosion which shook Clegg Hall on its foundations and smoke was seen pouring from one of the outbuildings on the other side of the moat.

With a cry of alarm Norman ran back to the lumber room, and moving a pile of wood, he revealed a trapdoor which he heaved open revealing a flight of steps down which he disappeared, with Nicholas Haworth in close pursuit. In the complete darkness Nicholas's only guide was the sound of Norman's footsteps ahead of him, but he ran on into the blackness, only speeding up when he heard his sister's voice shrieking somewhere ahead of him. He ran until he came to a door barring the way. Then the door was flung open and Norman came out, carrying an unconscious Lucy from a room filled with smoke and flames.

Having reached safety Norman turned to Nicholas and said 'There, at the peril of all I possess and of life too, I have rescued her. My hopes are gone – my schemes forever blasted – and I am a ruined, wretched old man, without a home or a morsel of bread.'

Busy attending to his sister, Nicholas didn't notice Norman leave the house. Afterwards people said that two men appeared on the avenue from the bowels of the earth and after being joined by Norman all three disappeared.

Later, Lucy told her family that she had been kept prisoner after refusing to be married to her secret admirer. Having shown her the cellar and its secrets the men dared not let her go in case she gave them away.

It transpired that Norman was in fact a descendant of the Clegg family. In his youth he had spent some time at Clegg Hall and was not only familiar with the story of the boggart but also knew about the old vaults and cellars, which had been originally excavated in the days of William the Conqueror when the Normans were sometimes forced to flee for their lives from the native Saxon armies. Norman houses were linked by these underground passages so that the families could escape from one to the other, though the entrances were kept a strict secret and passed down through the head of the family from one generation to the next. However, Norman knew where the secret entrances were, and having spent some time abroad in Spain, where he learnt the art of forging coins, he decided that Clegg Hall would provide an ideal hiding place for himself and his son to forge and store their counterfeit coins. The old tales of the boggart could be used to explain away any unusual sounds from underground.

When his son saw Lucy and fell in love with her, Norman saw a way of reclaiming Clegg Hall for the Clegg family and they believed that they would only have to show Lucy their vast treasure trove for her to immediately agree to a marriage. When she refused, they had no option but to keep her prisoner.

On further inspection, the vaults and cellars were found to extend under and out beyond the moat. The family had them walled up and also pulled down the remains of the original Clegg Hall. But it still wasn't enough to lay the ghost of the Clegg Hall boggart, and the locals continue to believe in him as fervently as ever.

The Smithills Hall Footprint

If you visit Smithills Hall, near Bolton, you will see, in a flagstone passageway just beyond the Great Hall, an indentation in the floor which is said to have been made by George Marsh when he stamped his foot in temper.

An inscription reads: 'Footprint of the reverend George Marsh of Deane, Martyr, who was examined at Smithills and burnt at Chester in the reign of Queen Mary.'

George Marsh was born in 1515 at Deane, which was then a separate village but is now a suburb of Bolton. He was a farmer who, after the death of his wife when he was about 30, left his children with his parents and went to Cambridge to study to be a priest.

He was ordained and appointed curate of All Hallows Church in Bread Street in the City of London, during the reign of Edward VI, who had become king in 1547, following the death of his father Henry VIII.

Edward was the son that Henry VIII had struggled for so long to produce. His first wife Catherine of Aragon had only given him a daughter, Mary, and desperate for a male heir he had had the marriage annulled and he moved away from the Roman Catholic faith to marry Anne Boleyn. But Anne also gave birth to a daughter, Elizabeth, and was beheaded three years later on charges of adultery. It was Henry's third marriage to Jane Seymour that produced Edward.

Edward had always been sickly and he died only six years after he became king. The Protestant nobles tried to follow his reign with that of Lady Jane Grey, who became known as the nine-day queen, but popular support for Mary Tudor was overwhelming so the monarchy passed to Mary, the daughter of Henry and of Catherine of Aragon, who had been so unfairly treated.

Mary Tudor, of course, was a devout Roman Catholic and she set about returning the country to that religion. But her zeal deteriorated into cruelty, especially after her marriage to Philip II of Spain, who had become fanatical in his desire to wipe out the Puritans.

She became known as 'Bloody Mary' because of the huge number of people – including the Archbishop of Canterbury, Thomas Cranmer – who were tortured and burned alive because they did not agree with the tenets of the Roman Catholic Church.

This persecution came to its zenith around 1554 when George Marsh, who had become outspoken about his beliefs, was brought before Sir Roger Barton at Smithills Hall for interrogation.

George Marsh had already attracted attention for his outspoken preaching in London. His rector, Reverend Sanders, had been killed and he was planning to leave the country and go into exile to save his own life. Before leaving he decided to visit Bolton to say goodbye to his parents and his children.

By some means the Earl of Derby came to learn of the visit and, as Justices of the Peace had been given permission to actively seek out heretics, he sent word to Sir Roger Barton, ordering him to find George Marsh and interrogate him.

At first George Marsh hid on nearby moorland but, when he learned that his mother and younger brother were being held responsible for his disappearance, he voluntarily went to Smithills Hall and gave himself up.

Although the outcome was a foregone conclusion, the law had to be seen to be observed and George Marsh was asked a series of set questions. One question in particular, whether or not he believed that the sacrament of the bread became the flesh of Christ, was asked as this was a fundamental difference between the two faiths. The Lady Elizabeth, later to become Elizabeth I, had also been asked this question but had answered in a clever enough way to save herself from the scaffold. But George Marsh was not such an educated man, and was unused to the subtleties of scholarly debates, so he answered simply and truthfully, saying what his belief was. He was then called on to recant and conform to the Roman Catholic religion to escape a cruel death. He refused saying: 'Between me and them let God witness. If my cause be just let this prayer of Thine unworthy servant be heard.'

And as he was led away he is said to have stamped his foot in anger, the imprint of which instantly appeared on the stone.

He was taken first to Lathom Hall where he was examined by the Earl of Derby, then to Lancaster Castle and was finally brought to the Ecclesiastical Court at Chester, where he was accused of 'preaching against the Pope's authority and the Catholic Church of Rome'. He was once again asked to recant, but refused. A few days later he was taken to his execution. He was chained to a post, covered in tar, and before the fire was lit around his feet he was given one last chance to turn to the Roman Catholic faith. He firmly refused, the fire was lit and George Marsh was burnt alive on 24 April 1555.

Later, the stone at Smithills Hall was moved and thrown out into the grounds, but all that night hideous noises were heard throughout the house and the following morning the stone was brought back inside. It is also said that the footprint becomes wet with blood every year at the time of George Marsh's interrogation. There is a memorial cross to George Marsh in the churchyard of the parish church of St Mary the Virgin in Deane.

Peg
O' Nell

Waddow Hall, near Clitheroe, is a 17th-century manor house and stands on the side of the river Ribble that used to be in Yorkshire until the 1974 boundary changes. It has been used by Girlguiding UK since 1927 as a training centre and camp.

In the grounds, by a disused well, there is a headless statue named Peg O' Nell, whose spirit is said to haunt the river and claim a life every seven years.

The statue probably originated from one of the local churches or monasteries. Traditionally it is thought to be a statue of St Margaret, which would account for the name of the ghost. Possibly taken from a church or monastery during the Reformation in the 16th century, when Henry VIII ordered the removal of all 'idols' from parish churches, the statue seems to have been used as a garden ornament by the Puritan Starkie family – and made to take the blame for anything that went wrong in the house.

Accidents and storms were all blamed on 'Peggy's work'. One night when Master Starkie returned home with a broken leg the blame was laid on Peggy although some said that the amount of ale he'd drunk after his day's hunting expedition could have been a contributory factor. Others maintained that Peggy had waylaid the master on his way home and 'caused his horse to fall'.

Another night, Mistress Starkie was expecting a visitor, a Puritan preacher who was on his way to visit the Hall. She had

sent for him to exorcise her youngest son, a boy of ten years old, who was being tormented by Peggy. As darkness fell and the winds and rain increased, she became increasingly alarmed and sent out servants to search for the man. He was pulled wet and half-drowned from the river and brought dripping to the Hall. He said that whilst he was crossing the river at the Brungerley 'hipping stones', a huge wave had rushed up the river Ribble and knocked him into the water. He declared that it had been caused by some evil spirit intent on preventing his arrival.

'It's Peggy's work!' cried Mistress Starkie, and clutching an axe, she rushed out into the storm in her best dress and chopped off the head of the statue. The body was left by the well as a warning to other evil spirits and the head was locked away in an attic room.

In his *Pictorial History of Lancashire* Dodd writes about visiting Waddow Hall in 1840 to see the statue. When he asked to see Peggy he was shown the stone head, which was kept in the pantry. 'I've lately brought her out of those gloomy rooms at the top of the house, washed her face, and now she lives in the larder,' the maid explained to him. When he asked about the body he was told that it was still in the field by the well.

'Does she ever plague you now?' he asked.

'No, sir. There is not a better girl in the parish. I fear she was much slandered,' said the maid.

The anniversary of her decapitation became known as Peg's Night and a legend grew up that her spirit haunted the river Ribble at the crossing at Brungerley and that she claimed a life every seven years. To appease her, locals used to offer a bird or a cat or dog in place of a human victim. Sometimes this satisfied Peg, but sometimes not. One night a stranger was riding to Waddow Hall when a maidservant at an inn where he'd stopped told him not to try to ford the rain-swollen river on his horse because it was Peg O'Nell's Night. The man ignored her and the following morning he was found drowned.

It is documented that men drowned in the river Ribble in 1894, 1901 and 1908 – a seven-year cycle.

An alternative legend records that Peg was a servant girl at Waddow Hall and, following a row with Master Starkie about going to draw water from the well near the river, he shouted after her, 'I hope you break your neck!' Unfortunately that was just what happened and the statue was placed where she died as a memorial to her, but she haunted the river and the Hall to spite the Starkies who had caused her death.

It is also believed that there is an upstairs room in the old part of the Hall which is haunted. A spectral mist appears and the air is chilled. Was this the bedroom of the maid Peggy who died? Is it the room where the head of the statue was previously kept? Who knows? But at one time they sacrificed a cock in here on Peg's Night to try to appease her lust for a victim.

Now, although the body of the statue still remains in the grounds of Waddow Hall, and the story adds a frisson of fear to the young campers who stay there, no one seems to know what happened to the head.

The Devil on
the Dun

M any years ago on the road that led from Clitheroe to Gisburn was a public house with the name the Dule Upo' Dun. On the pub sign was a picture of the devil riding bareback on a dun horse, his forked tail trailing behind him and his arms raised in fury. In the background was a picture of the same building that housed the pub, but at its door stood a small tailor, shaking his shears at the devil and grinning.

The tailor in the picture was Nicholas Gosford, the former owner of the building and legend tells that in his younger days he was very fond of his ale; so fond in fact that he spent all his money in the Spread Eagle pub and his wife, Matty, was forced to gather what little food and money she could to sustain them by selling firewood and doing odd jobs for the neighbours.

One night Nicholas had spent all his money on drink as usual and was bemoaning the fact that he didn't have money for more, when a stranger who was visiting the pub took him to one side to offer him a money-making scheme that he couldn't refuse.

This stranger is said to have been elderly and well spoken. He was very respectably dressed in a black suit and peaked hat and carried a cane that was as black as ebony with a yellow knob that glittered like gold. He told the tailor that there was a way for him to gain great riches and live in ease for the rest of his life.

'All you need to do is say the Creed and the Lord's Prayer backwards three times and the devil will appear and grant you three wishes,' he told the tailor.

So the next morning when his wife had gone out to work, Nicholas went to a solitary place on the banks of the river Ribble and decided to perform the incantation. He said the words of the Creed and the Lord's Prayer backwards three times and as he spoke the last word there was a terrific clap of thunder and a huge flash of lightning and the devil himself, attended by two imps, appeared before Nicholas.

'What do you want?' the devil demanded.

'Nothing,' whimpered the terrified tailor, but the devil flew into a rage and told Nicholas that he would punish him terribly if he didn't say why he had raised him. So Nicholas confessed that he wanted great riches and an easy life.

'Then I will grant you three wishes,' said the devil. 'The first three things that you or your wife wish for will be yours.'

Relieved at how easy it had all been Nicholas was beginning to feel rather pleased with himself until the devil presented him with a contract for his signature that agreed that after seven years his soul would belong to the devil. At this point he tried to back out of the deal but the devil told him that he could either sign and be carried to hell in 20 years' time or be taken immediately. So Nicholas, deciding that things might change in 20 years, complied with the devil's request and he pricked his finger and signed with his blood.

Worried and distraught about what he had done, Nicholas went home to his wife who had prepared a meal of oaten bread and a rasher of bacon that had been given to her by a kindly neighbour. In his misery he stared at his food and couldn't eat. His wife, trying to cheer him up said: 'I know it isn't much. I wish there were two rashers of bacon for you.'

No sooner had she uttered the words than another piece of bacon appeared, hot and steaming, on his plate beside the first one.

'Woman,' he cried, 'what have you done? I wish you would go away and leave me alone.' Instantly his wife disappeared and the tailor realised that two out of his three wishes had been wasted.

Over the coming weeks Nicholas was very careful about what he said. He tried to make amends by working hard and staying sober, but he missed his wife and the house grew dirty and untidy. One morning when he had to go out into the snow to get some wood to light a fire he was so miserable that he forgot the need to be cautious with his words. 'I wish Matty was here,' he said. And no sooner had the wish been spoken than his wife re-appeared, standing beside him – and he realised that his third wish was gone.

He confessed to her what he had done and swore that in the future he would stay away from the alehouse and work hard. Nicholas kept his word and, as the years passed, the couple became quite comfortably off, but as time went on he became more anxious and miserable as he was sure that the devil would return to claim him.

At noon on the twentieth anniversary of the signing of the contract there came the inevitable thunder-clap and the devil appeared. Despite his terror the trembling tailor tried to reason with him. He told him that he had been cheated and that despite the promise of wealth and riches the wishes had been worth nothing to him. And in fact he told the devil that he didn't think he had the power to grant such riches anyway.

Well, this questioning of his power made the devil so furious that he told the tailor that he would prove his prowess by granting him one more wish. 'Wish for anything you want, no matter how great and I will grant it,' he told him.

Nicholas was wondering how best to use this last wish when he noticed a dun horse grazing nearby.

'I wish that you were riding that dun horse back to hell and that you never come back to earth to cheat me or any other poor fool!' shouted Nicholas. And with a scream that is said to have been heard as far away as Colne, the devil was whisked through the air and placed on the back of the horse which set off at a wild gallop never to be seen again.

Nicholas and his wife lived on until old age and after their deaths their fortune was left to their poorer relatives, one of whom turned the house into a pub and named it the Dule upo' Dun to perpetuate the memory of Nicholas Gosford, the only man to have ever out-witted the devil.

Meg Shelton, the Fylde Witch

Meg Shelton lived in a cottage at Cuckoo Hall, near Wesham – and whilst that sounds quite idyllic it was described as being a 'wretched hovel'. She was in fact very poor and lived on a diet of boiled groats mixed with thyme and parsley and whatever else she could steal.

One day Meg heard that another cottage at nearby Catforth had come vacant and she very much wanted to move into it.

Now Meg had the ability to turn herself into a variety of living creatures as well as taking the shape of seemingly ordinary household implements – such as a broom for example, so she agreed a bargain with her landlord that she would turn herself into a hare and race the landlord's dogs from Wesham to Catforth. If she gave the dogs the slip and arrived at the cottage first, then it would be hers. Her only stipulation was that the ferocious black dog should not be sent after her but kept on its leash. However, after the hare had raced off, the landlord went back on his word and freed the black dog. It caught up with Meg outside the cottage door and managed to nip her on the heel before she got inside, and though Meg was left with a permanent limp she did get her new cottage.

Another legend that centres on Meg's ability to shape-shift tells of the time that a miller at Singleton suspected her of stealing his corn. Night after night he watched and saw her going into the mill, but when he rushed across to confront her there was no one there. Yet next morning it was clear that

he had been robbed. Then he came up with a cunning plan. He carefully counted how many sacks of grain he had stored and when he rushed in that night to a seemingly empty barn he counted them again and found there was one extra. So he seized a pitchfork and plunged it into each sack in turn until a squeal of rage betrayed Meg, who, with her arm bleeding from the wound, seized a nearby broom and flew off into the night, never to return and steal any more corn.

Another day a local farmer saw her flying low over his cows with a jug in her hand, but by the time he reached the field he could only find an old woman grazing her goose. But then he caught sight of a bead of milk on the goose's beak. He kicked the goose which shattered into the fragments of a broken jug in a pool of milk and an angry Meg flew off over the hedge.

Meg, who was also accused of misdeeds such as laming cattle and turning milk sour, was in fact a real person. Her name was Margery Hilton and in 1705 she was found dead in her cottage, crushed between a barrel and a wall. After her death, because she had been born a Christian and had never been 'examined as a witch' it was grudgingly agreed that she had the right to a Christian burial in holy ground.

So many people were unhappy with this that, as a compromise, she was buried at night, on 2 May by torchlight, in the churchyard of St Anne's at Woodplumpton. But Meg soon clawed her way back to the surface. She was buried a second time, but scratched her way out again. So a priest from Cottam Hall came to exorcise the place where she lay. Afterwards she was re-buried once more, head down so that if she began to dig again she would only dig herself deeper. The grave was topped by a huge boulder, probably one carried down on a glacier during the Ice Age, to keep her in. Hopefully, she remains there to this day, though it doesn't explain why a young boy, who was visiting with his family in 1933 and who went into the church ahead of the adults, came running out, terrified, saying that an old woman dressed in 'funny clothes' had chased him.

There is an old ritual associated with the grave, mostly performed by local children. You must walk around the grave three times then stand on the stone. Look north, then east, then south and finally west. Then you make a wish and run round the church three times, but if you see the devil through the keyhole of the church door, you'll run away even faster! It seems a visit to this churchyard isn't for the fainthearted. You have been warned.

The Healing Hand of Edmund Arrowsmith

In the Roman Catholic church of St Oswald at Ashton-in-Makerfield there is a revered holy relic. Pilgrims come to see it and miraculous cures have been attributed to it. Carefully wrapped in white silk and kept in a silver casket is the severed hand of Saint Edmund Arrowsmith.

Edmund Arrowsmith was the son of Robert and Margery Arrowsmith (née Gerard) and was born at Haydock in 1585. At his baptism he was given the name of Bryan, but took the name of Edmund at his confirmation. The family remained true to their Roman Catholic faith, even though this was a time of great persecution. His maternal grandfather, Nicholas Gerard, was a recusant and his father's father died a confessor in prison. His parents and their household were taken to Lancaster where they were held in gaol, leaving Edmund and his three siblings to be cared for by neighbours. Edmund was taken in and cared for by an old priest and as he grew up he professed a wish to be ordained to the priesthood himself. Of course, no priest could be ordained in England, so when he was 20 years old, Edmund went to the English College at Douai, in France, to study for his vocation. He was ordained at the age of 27 in Arras in 1611 and later, in 1624 he became a Jesuit.

In 1613 he returned to his home county of Lancashire. It was a brave and courageous thing to do as he would have known that the penalty for saying Mass was the death of a traitor by the gruesome custom of hanging, drawing and quartering. The prisoner would be first hung from the gallows, then, before he was dead, would be cut down and his heart and entrails drawn from his body before being thrown onto a fire. Then the body would be quartered with a butcher's knife and thrown into a cauldron of bubbling pitch before being displayed to the public.

Father Arrowsmith based himself in the Chorley area and one of the places where he stayed was in a secret attic room, concealed under the thatched roof of the Blue Anchor Inn near Hoghton. From here he travelled throughout the county, where most people still adhered to the old faith, visiting homes, farms and the Halls of the gentry to give comfort to the sick and the dying and to say Mass in secret places. And because he travelled such long distances he often rode on horseback with an attendant who would take the horses and hide them whilst the visit was in progress to avoid arousing suspicion. There was also a tradition that placing the figure of a cat on the windowsill indicated to the faithful that the priest was in the house.

Father Arrowsmith is believed to have said his last Mass at a house in Brindle on Gregson Lane, before being betrayed by a young woman who was angry with him for criticising her marriage.

The landlord of the Blue Anchor Inn, where he was staying, was named Holden and was a devout Roman Catholic, however one of his sons had married a first cousin, who was a Protestant. As the marriage had been performed by a Protestant minister and because the marriage of first cousins was not allowed by the Roman Catholic Church without a special dispensation, Father Arrowsmith regarded the wedding as null and void and believed that the couple were living in sin and that the son's soul was in danger. And because he felt so indebted to the Holden family for giving

30

him refuge and shelter, he determined to set things right by applying to the Pope for dispensation, persuading the girl to convert to the Roman Catholic faith and marrying them properly.

The girl did indeed become a Roman Catholic and the dispensation arrived from Rome, but rather than marrying them immediately Father Arrowsmith insisted that there should be a fourteen day separation before the wedding could go ahead. Whilst this might not seem too unreasonable it was one condition too many for the girl who had a message sent to the Justice of the Peace, a Captain Rawsthorn, telling him that Edmund Arrowsmith was a priest and that he was hiding out at the Blue Anchor Inn.

Now Captain Rawsthorn was a local man and he was a friend and neighbour of the Holdens. He didn't want any trouble so he sent a message to the landlord warning him to get rid of the priest before he and his men arrived to search the premises.

Father Arrowsmith quickly gathered his few possessions and set out on horseback with another man. It is thought that they intended to head for Wickenhouse Farm at Withnell, an isolated place where the priest sometimes said Mass and where he knew he could gain refuge. But they rode at first in the opposite direction to try to confuse their pursuers. A Mr Worden, who was a previous occupant of the house in Gregson Lane where Father Arrowsmith said his last Mass, later gave an account of the priest's flight and capture.

'They set off in a contrary direction to Withnell, going on the road towards Preston, but turned to the left past the Oak Tree Inn, and went up Gregson Lane. They passed over Jack Green by the Town House and then turned to the left towards Marsh Lane Head. They turned to the left again at the Well, where there is a farmhouse, then occupied by a family called Crook, and on past Windmill House onto Brindle Moss. Meanwhile the pursuer had got on the scent, and inquired at the farm at the Well which way the two horsemen had gone. Crook, the farmer, directed him, as he had observed the fugitives pass his house. The pursuer overtook them at the Moss and ran on our martyr with his drawn sword. Finding that his horse refused to jump the Moss Ditch, the Father dismounted and ran along its side, hoping to reach the place higher up where the ditch is much narrower.'

At his trial Father Arrowsmith gave his own account of what happened next,

'That very man [the justice's servant] rushed out upon me with a drawn sword. He was meanly dressed and upon horseback. I made what haste I could from him, but being weak and sickly was forced by him at last to the Moss, where I alighted, and fled with all the speed I was able – which yet could not be very great, seeing I was loaded with heavy clothes, boots, and other things. At length he came up to me at the Moss Ditch, and struck at me, though I had nothing to defend myself with but a little walking stick, and a sword which I did not draw. With the blow he cut the stick close to my hand and did me some little hurt. I then asked him if his design was to take my purse and my life. He answered that perhaps it was, and then I fled again from him, but was soon overtaken. Then came up this youth [the justice's son who was twelve years old] who has given evidence against me, with others to assist him. They used me with much indignity, and took me to an alehouse [the Boar's Head Inn in Hoghton Lane], and searched me to the skin, offering insults which modesty forbids me to relate, and which I resisted as far as I was able. That done, they fell to drinking, and spent nine shillings of my money in an hour. They told me that the Justice of the Peace, by whose warrant I was apprehended, was there in person, but that I would not believe. Upon this occasion, my Lord, I began to find fault with the man's wicked and rude behaviour who seemed to be the ringleader; and I besought him, for Jesus' sake, to give up his disordered life, drinking and foolish talk, and whatever might offend Almighty God. Upon my word and my life, this, or to this effect, is all I said to him. Let him look on me, and gainsay it, if he can. As for that youth, I deny not to have told him that

I hoped when he came to riper years, he would look better into himself, and become a true Catholic, for that, and that alone, would be the means to save his soul, to which he made no answer at all. And I hope, my Lord, that neither they nor any other can prove ill against me.'

But the outcome of the trial was assured before it even began. For saying the Roman Catholic Mass, Father Arrowsmith was condemned to a traitor's death. However, the priest was so revered by both Roman Catholics and Protestants that no one was willing to be his executioner. A butcher was paid £5 to perform the deed, but he told his servant to do it, and the servant refused and ran away, never to be seen again. Eventually a soldier, who was under the sentence of death himself for deserting his regiment, agreed to kill the priest in exchange for 40 shillings, the prisoner's clothes and his own freedom. The martyr's last words were, 'Nothing grieves me so much as this England which I pray God soon to convert.' He died with the words 'Bone Jesu', meaning O Good Jesus.

After his death in 1628, relics of the priest were sought from the warders at Lancaster Castle, and one of these, Edmund Arrowsmith's right hand, was kept by the Gerard family for many years before it was given to St Oswald's.

In 1737 it was recorded that a boy at Appleton-within-Widnes had been healed of a sickness after being touched by the hand, and Edmund Arrowsmith is now venerated as a Roman Catholic saint.

A small ivory statue of the Virgin Mary, holding Jesus in her arms, that the priest always carried with him, but dropped during his flight, was also later found. More relics of the martyr were discovered in 1841 when part of the wall in the house in Gregson Lane, where he said his last Mass, was blown down. A box was found containing two priest's vestments, a chalice and two altar stones. Miracles are also attributed to one of these vestments, fragments of which are held at St Joseph's Roman Catholic church in Hoghton where there is a portrait of the saint. In this room a curious phenomenon is said to sometimes appear, when a cross of light shines on the wall.

The Crook family, however, who assisted in the capture of Father Arrowsmith, are believed to have suffered some divine retribution. Crook was given the priest's cloak as a reward for the information he had given. He had the cloak altered by a tailor to fit his eleven-year-old son who was paraded in front of his family before being lifted onto a horse to take a triumphant ride. But the horse, which had always previously been placid, bolted and threw the boy who hit his head on a stone boulder and died instantly. The horrified family returned to the Roman Catholic faith and, although up until that time they had been noted for their good looks, future children were affected by deformities. In his book *Lancashire Stories*, Frank Hird recalls one of the family, James, known as 'Turk' who was a dwarf and was drowned in the river Darwen in 1862.

The Holy Hand of Edmund Arrowsmith was approved for public veneration in 1934, and the Roman Catholic High School at Ashton, near Wigan, is named after this local martyr.

The Last Wolf

Up until the boundary changes of 1974 the area to the north of Morecambe Bay was in Lancashire and was known as Lancashire Over Sands, as it could be reached by a perilous journey across ever shifting channels and quicksands – a shortcut that saved a full day's travel around the bay, before the construction of the Furness Railway in 1887.

As early as AD 79, a local resident led a Roman army commanded by Julius Agricola across the bay and in the 5th century the route was used by raiding parties of Scots. By the 14th century, King Edward III became so concerned by the loss of life in the bay that he asked the Abbot of Furness to enquire into it. On his recommendation the king appointed a guide to help travellers to safely negotiate the treacherous sands. The first guides were monks from Coniston and Cartmel priories but, after the dissolution of the monasteries in the reign of Henry VIII, the Duchy of Lancaster took responsibility for appointing the guide. Today the official Queen's Guide to the Sands is Cedric Robinson, who takes parties of walkers across the eight and a half miles of the bay in a journey of around three hours.

Just beyond Grange over Sands on the north shore is a high limestone cliff called Humphrey Head, which juts out into Morecambe Bay. It was here that legend records the killing of the last wolf in England.

In 1281, as sheep farming became an important part of the country's economy, King Edward I commissioned Peter Corbet of Alcester to kill every wolf in the counties of Worcestershire, Herefordshire, Gloucestershire, Shropshire and Staffordshire. It was quite a task, but he was successful,

possibly helped by the king offering a bounty for each wolf pelt that more than equalled the profit on a year's harvest, and he was knighted for his services. By the early 14th century wolves only remained in the north of England and Scotland, and the few that still lived in Cartmel Forest were gradually exterminated by the Harringtons of Wraysholme Tower.

During one of these wolf hunts, Sir Edgar Harrington lost sight of his companions and rode to the summit of Humphrey Head to look around for them. Whilst galloping through the forest he heard the terrified shrieks of a young girl, whom he found sheltering behind a rock as an enormous wolf barked and growled at her. Harrington killed the wolf with his hunting spear and rescued the girl, and, as in all the best legends, her gratitude turned quickly to love and they were soon married at a nearby chapel.

However there is an anonymous ballad that runs to 75 verses relating a slightly embellished version of the legend.

Sir Edgar Harrington of Wraysholme Tower had sworn to hunt out and kill every last wolf from Cartmel Forest. He had also promised that the man who killed the last wolf would receive the hand of his niece in marriage and half of his lands as well. His niece was a beautiful young girl named Adela who had been orphaned and was now Sir Edgar's ward. Many of the local men were keen to make her their wife, especially a knight named Laybourne, but Adela it seemed was in love with her cousin, Sir Edgar Harrington's son, John. Sir Edgar had disapproved of this attachment and following an argument his son had gone away to fight in a foreign war, but before he left the young couple had sworn to be faithful to one another.

It was thought that the young Harrington had been killed in battle, but the night before the wolf hunt a young knight, a stranger calling himself Delisle, came to Wraysholme Tower mounted on a white Arab stallion. The next day the huntsmen set out. Laybourne rode a large Flemish carthorse, of the type that could carry the weight of a knight in chainmail and metal armour. The stranger, Delisle, rode his fleet-footed Arab.

They hunted the wolf from its lair through a long and tiring day, chasing it all around Cartmel Forest and even across part of Windermere, before heading it off towards Humphrey Head late in the evening. Out of all the men who set out, now only Laybourne and Delisle remained in the hunt. They chased the wolf up the limestone crag but when they reached a gaping chasm in the rock Laybourne's heavy horse refused to jump across. Delisle was determined to win the hand of Adela and spurred his horse across the gap. It was too wide and the horse's hooves couldn't get a grip on the far side and it tumbled to its death, although Delisle managed to cling onto the ground and was unhurt. But meanwhile, the wolf had leapt at Adela who was watching from her horse nearby. It was barking and growling with bared teeth. She was terrified, thinking that she would be torn apart by the ferocious creature but Delisle drew his spear and flung it at the wolf, killing it. He then revealed his true identity as John Harrington – Sir Edgar's long-lost son and Adela's true love. Sir Edgar welcomed back his son and told him that he could have Adela as his bride as he had won her so bravely.

As father and son embraced, the Prior of St Mary passed by to drink at the nearby Holy Well. The monk was asked to marry John and Adela on the spot, to which request he complied and the cave where the wedding took place was known afterwards as Sir Edgar's Chapel.

The couple lived happily ever after, producing many healthy children, and used the image of the wolf on their crest. They are buried together in a quiet corner of Cartmel Priory, with their effigies cut in stone and a wolf carved at their feet. As there is no inscription it is difficult to authenticate this story, but the weathervane on top of Cartmel Priory is in the shape of a wolf's head and it is believed that Humphrey Head was the last place that a wolf was ever seen in England.

The Lost Lake
of Sir Lancelot

From the M6 motorway you can see the towering castle of
Camelot near Park Hall at Charnock Richard. Yes, it is
only a theme park, but not many people realise why the
theme was chosen.

Here, up until the end of the 17th century, there was a
huge lake, the largest in England, called Martin Mere. This
fresh water lake, surrounded by bogs and mosses and with
isolated islands, spreads over an area of 12 square miles, and
up to 18 square miles after a particularly rainy spell. Around
1692, Thomas Fleetwood of Bank Hall, Bretherton, proposed
to other landowners in the area that the lake should be
drained to provide agricultural land for pasture and crop
growing. The plan was to drain the water into the sea at the
mouth of the river Ribble. So a canal, 24 feet wide, was cut
from the Mere down to the coast but because the lake was ten
feet below the high water mark of the spring tides, a pair of
floodgates was installed to stop the seawater flowing inland.
Sluice-gates were built to allow water from the lake to drain
into the sea at low tide.

The mouth of the Ribble lies between Southport and
Lytham. It is a distance of about four miles and the opposite
coastline can be clearly seen from each town. Both coasts are
very flat and sandy, and over time sand and silt built up in
front of the sluice-gates and prevented water draining out. So
in 1714 the floodgates were raised by twenty inches, and
though this kept the sluices free from silt, it meant that the

water didn't drain as efficiently from the Mere and standing water remained throughout the winter. Despite other adjustments, the drainage was never perfect and when a particularly high tide in 1755 breached and washed down the floodgates they lay neglected for many years until the drainage of the Mere was taken up by Thomas Eccleston of Scarisbrick Hall in 1781. He asked his friend John Gilbert from Worsley, who had worked for the Duke of Bridgewater on his canals, to help him. This time three pairs of sluice-gates were built. The first pair to keep out the sea were the Sea Gates. The second pair, half a mile nearer to the Mere, as a back-up in case the sea broached the first pair of gates, were the Stop Gates. The third pair, built near the Sea Gates, but opening contrary to them, were the Flushing Gates. When the tide was out all three pairs of gates were kept open to allow water to drain from the Mere and when the tide rose the Sea Gates were closed. When the weather was dry, however, and not enough water was flowing from the Mere to prevent a build-up of sand and silt at the sluice, the tide was allowed to flow in as far as the Stop Gates and at high tide the Flushing Gates were closed to keep the sea water in the channel. When this water was released it rushed out and cleaned the sluices, so the system was kept clean and efficient.

By using this method Martin Mere was successfully drained and became valuable farmland for both growing crops and grazing animals. Today the area around Ormskirk is well known for its potatoes and other crops and what remains of Martin Mere has become a bird sanctuary.

But what about Camelot? Well, there is a story that Sir Lancelot's parents, King Ban of Benwick and his queen, Elaine, came to Lancashire to escape from their enemies in France, and when Elaine put down the baby Lancelot on the shore of the lake to go to help her husband who had fallen, the nymph Vivian took the baby and vanished into the lake with him. Vivian brought up Lancelot and when he went to King Arthur's court he was knighted as 'Lancelot of the Lake'.

So this is why the theme park at Park Hall is Camelot and tells many of the stories of King Arthur and his Knights of the Round Table. But there are other legends associated with Park Hall. It once belonged to Henry de Lea, who was a participant in the Banastre Rebellion. He was one of the knights who was captured and beheaded. His estates were passed to the de Hoghton family, who used the secluded house in Elizabethan times to shelter Roman Catholic priests. A priest hole and an underground passage were later found here.

Another story tells of how monks used to live and work here, quarrying stone on the shores of the lake and how a local girl fell in love with one of the monks and in despair drowned herself in the lake. In January 1967, Mr and Mrs Few, who owned Park Hall at the time, saw an apparition of intense whiteness rise from the middle of the lake by the hotel. She has appeared again since and is known as the Lady of the Lake. So is she the ghost of a girl who died from unrequited love? Or is she the spirit of the Arthurian legend?

As recently as 2002 there have been sightings and reports of a monster in the water at Martin Mere that was taking birds as large as swans. A group from Exeter, from the Centre for Fortean Zoology, came to investigate and concluded that the monster could be a Wels catfish – a huge fish, larger than a pike, that was thought to measure up to 16 feet in length and could have been born in the reign of Queen Victoria.

So, although much of what was once a shallow lake that was dangerous to cross has now been transformed into rich farmland, the legends about the lake, and its ethereal Lady, still persist.

Tales of Winwick

Winwick, just north of Warrington, was a residence of King Oswald, the first Christian king of Northumbria. He was involved in a lot of fighting in the area with the pagan king Penda of Mercia and was eventually killed here in AD 642. The place where he died was fenced off and marked by a large boulder after it gained a reputation as a holy place where any sick person who touched the ground was instantly restored to full health – and for these healing powers and his tireless fights against the pagans Oswald was later made a saint.

Many early churches were named in his honour, as was the parish church at Winwick, although there is a strange tale concerning the place where it was built. It had been decided that the church should be built near to the holy site, so that pilgrims could worship in the church and then visit the shrine to offer gifts and receive healing. Plans were agreed for a wooden building with stone doorways and windows and the layout was sketched into the ground.

Work soon got underway, with stones being gathered and trees felled in the nearby forest, when a wild boar strayed onto the site seeming to nose about for food. He stayed around for quite a while, grubbing and snuffling at the ground. He appeared to be very interested in the planned layout of the new church and the workers grew quite fond of him.

Eventually the time came for the actual building to begin and stones were laid out to mark where the walls and doorways would be, and at the end of a long and tiring day the men went home, pleased with their progress. But when they got up the next morning they were amazed to find that all their stones had been moved and rearranged around the boulder that marked the place of St Oswald's shrine. In the midst of the stones was the boar. At first the villagers thought he was sleeping in the sunshine, but when they looked more closely they saw that he had died.

The village elders gathered for a meeting and decided that the church should be built where the boar had placed the stones. They also decided that they should carve an image of the boar onto the stone that marked the shrine in his memory. And when the church was rebuilt from stone in the 14th century, an image of a boar was carved on one of the stones used to build the tower, where it can still be seen, on the west wall of the church.

However the truth is not so romantic. The small carving of a pig is next to a niche which contains the statue of a saint. The original statue was destroyed by Cromwell's men, who were stationed in the church after the Battle of Red Bank in 1648, and was probably that of St Antony of Egypt. St Antony was a founder of monasteries and would have been a significant saint to early Christians from the community of Iona in Northumberland from where Oswald came. Pigs belonging to St Antony's order were permitted to roam at liberty, and the pig eventually became the emblem of the saint.

New carvings of saints were added to the tower in 1973. Oswald is on the left, and St Antony, with his pig, is on the right.

About half a mile from the church there is a well which is also reputed to be holy and have healing powers. Another legend says that this is the place where Oswald died, the well having been formed when the blood of the dead king was scraped up from the ground. Up until the 19th century all the neighbouring Roman Catholic chapels drew their holy water from here and a man was paid a small annuity to keep the well clear of weeds so that it wouldn't become contaminated.

Winwick is also famous for a huge oak that once stood there. It is said that its branches spread so wide that they acted as a canopy for a dinner of 124 people. The dinner was given in honour of Captain Phipps Hornby, who had commanded the *Volage* at the Battle of Lissa in 1811 and captured a French flag. His father was the Rector of Winwick and when he returned, having been away fighting for five years, friends and family fêted him with a banquet under the oak tree.

The Winwick Oak stood in a field to the south of the church and covered an area 100 yards in circumference. The lower branches measured 99 ft from north to south and 87 ft from east to west. The girth of the trunk was 14 ft. Although its age isn't recorded it must have been very ancient, but sadly was blown down in a gale on 4 February 1850.

Miss M'Avoy
Sees by Touch

In the summer of 1817 in Liverpool there was huge excitement and the topic under discussion was whether or not Miss M'Avoy, a young girl of seventeen, could see by touch.

Miss M'Avoy had become blind the previous year through illness, and although she wore a bandage over her eyes to prove that she had no residual sight she could apparently recognise colours, describe scenes and even read print, by touching it with her fingers.

She began giving demonstrations of her skill, and every day her family home was besieged by crowds of people – all eager to witness her amazing gift. Many accounts were written about how she could detect the most delicate of colours, and how she could read the tiniest of print – even in the dark. And one doctor, a Dr Renwick, was so convinced of her powers that he published a pamphlet saying that not only did he believe her abilities were completely genuine, but that he believed she had a new and supernatural skill.

The M'Avoy family were respectable, middle-class people and no charge was made for their daughter's demonstrations of her skills, so at first very few people suspected it was a hoax, even when the girl began to claim that by placing her fingers behind her on a window, she could see the people in the churchyard across the road from her house. With her back to the window and her fingers on the glass she described the people and their clothes in vivid detail.

But finally public opinion began to change, as it often does, and there was talk that Miss M'Avoy was a fraud. People began to have their doubts about whether her powers really were supernatural or whether it was all some sort of trick. So when one man said that he would pay her twenty guineas if she could read one line of standard-sized print whilst wearing a mask that he had designed, and Miss M'Avoy would not agree to the test, it was widely believed that she had tricked them all.

Though why she wanted to trick them wasn't clear. No payments were charged for the demonstrations, and the family were reasonably well off, so it wasn't for money. Perhaps she did it for the attention. Who knows?

It was claimed that she had been able to see the people in the churchyard by looking into a mirror on the opposite wall and that she had been able to read and see colours as she wasn't really blind at all. Though no one ever managed to explain how she did it in the dark.

Like all seven-day wonders, Miss M'Avoy was quickly forgotten and no record exists of what happened to her.

Ned King, the Lancashire Highwayman

The crossroads at Mitton is just another rural junction these days, where you have to pause to check the signpost and to make sure there are no fast cars approaching around the sharp bend in the road. But in times gone by it was a place you would have wanted to cross quickly.

It was here that Ned King, Lancashire's highwayman, would leap from the trees, pistol in hand, shouting, 'Stand and deliver!' at passing coaches. Always dressed in the traditional highwayman's outfit of white-ruffled shirt, gold-trimmed scarlet coat, white breeches and knee-length black boots, he took jewellery and money from the passengers before allowing them to continue on their way.

One version of the story tells that the Blue Bell in Whalley, which was formerly an inn and is now a private house, was Ned's headquarters. John Briscoe was the landlord there and he was in league with the highwayman. Whenever a party of wealthy-looking passengers left the inn by coach, Briscoe would tip off Ned King, who would then mount his horse and race across country to reach the crossroads before them and then hold them up and rob them.

After robbing a total of seven coaches during 1752, people began to make a connection between the inn and the robberies. The Redcoats were sent for and they rode from

Fulwood Barracks at Preston to arrest John Briscoe, whom they tied to a chair and tortured with thumbscrews. The pain of having both his thumbs broken made him quickly confess and he named Ned King as the perpetrator of the robberies.

So the Redcoats disguised themselves as ordinary travellers, throwing black cloaks over their red uniforms, and took a coach to the crossroads where Ned King was waiting. With their muskets cocked and ready they waited for King to leap in front of them with his usual cry of, 'Stand and deliver!' upon which they opened fire, killing his horse and wounding him.

The Redcoats planned to arrest King and take him back to Preston for trial but, as he was bleeding profusely from his injuries, they decided to hang him before he died, and strung him up from an oak tree at the crossroads, where his ghost still haunts the road.

The nearby village of Hurst Green, thought to have provided part of the setting for JRR Tolkien's *The Lord of the Rings* trilogy, is also said to be haunted by the ghost of Ned King. His ghostly apparition has been frequently seen riding down the main street late at night, though whether this was before or after the witness had visited the Shireburn Arms is not recorded.

However it is a pub further down the road, the Punchbowl Inn, that is the second claimant to having been Ned's headquarters. It is said that it was from here that he watched travellers as they alighted from coaches, sizing up their jewellery and the thickness of their wallets, before going out to wait for them further down the road. One day the King's troopers cornered him in the hayloft at the Punchbowl. There was a shoot out and Ned King was taken in chains and hanged on the gallows in Gallows Lane, a short walk away, without ever being brought to trial.

It is said that for over 200 years the ghost of Ned King haunted the inn, with knocking and moaning noises and bottles crashing from shelves for no apparent reason. He was described as being a rather bad tempered ghost, though his activities here were reduced, if not entirely stopped, after an exorcism by a priest from nearby Stonyhurst College in 1942.

There have been many reported sightings of Ned King over the years, but there is one that seems credible enough not to be dismissed as a flight of fancy or the product of an overactive imagination.

During the long hot summer of 1976 there were many grass fires in the Ribble valley. One day a farmer contacted the Clitheroe Fire Brigade about a fire on his land, but when they arrived they found that the fire was raging out of control and a call went out to the Blackburn Fire Brigade to come and assist them. Racing down the narrow country lane near Mitton, lights flashing and sirens wailing, the firefighters were horrified to suddenly see a horse and rider in the middle of the road. Unable to brake in time, the fire engine ploughed into them. Now although firefighters on their way to a fire are not supposed to stop, on this occasion they did pull up to see what assistance they could give and found themselves staring in puzzlement at empty tarmac. What they had seen was the ghost of Ned King.

Mab's Cross

There is a legend that the baby daughter of a 14th-century Lancashire family called Norris, who lived at Haigh near Wigan, was kidnapped from her cradle. Whether this was for a ransom or because someone was desperate for a child no one knows. The story goes on to say that this girl was brought up in a poor, peasant family and grew to be very beautiful. One day, as she was drawing water from a well near her village, a young knight noticed her and finding her very attractive he stopped his horse and asked if she would give him a drink from the water she had drawn. The knight was captivated by her beauty and wanted to marry her, but he knew it would be frowned on by society if he married a peasant girl. However, he believed that someone so beautiful must be of noble birth and he managed to prove that the girl was the long lost daughter of Hugh Norris. As a reward for reuniting her with her true family, her hand was given in marriage and Sir William Bradshaw and Lady Mabel should have lived happily ever after.

Whether this story is true no one knows but it is a fact that Mabel Norris, heiress of Haigh and Blackrod, did marry Sir William Bradshaw.

The king at that time was Edward II, whom many people disliked. His father Edward I had had a vision of a united Britain and had spent much of his reign engaged in war with the Scots. When his son came to the throne in 1307 he showed little interest in war and allowed Robert Bruce to recapture much of Scotland. In 1314, Bruce defeated the English forces at the Battle of Bannockburn and ensured Scottish independence until the union of England and Scotland in 1707.

Edward II had a French male companion, Piers Gaveston, who his father had exiled because of his undue influence on young Edward, but who had come back when Edward II became king and was now in a position of power. Some barons were less than impressed by this and under the leadership of Edward's cousin, Thomas the Earl of Lancaster, they planned a revolt against the king. The first revolt took place in 1312 and Gaveston was murdered. The king wasn't removed from the throne but accepted restrictions of his power and agreed that Thomas, Earl of Lancaster, should share the responsibilities of government.

However, in Lancashire, Thomas was unpopular and Sir Adam Banastre, who owned lands around Standish, organised a local rebellion. One of his supporters was Sir William Bradshaw. This group of local knights met at Wingates, near Westhoughton in 1315 and vowed to live or die together after which they appear to have set out on a rampage across the county, killing and stealing in the name of the king, until they reached Preston where 300 of the Earl of Lancaster's men took under an hour to overcome them. Some were killed, some were captured later and beheaded, but Sir William was reputed to have fled the country.

Meanwhile the years passed and Lady Mabel waited for news of her husband only to find that a Welsh knight named Sir Osmund Nevill turned up and claimed that the king had given him Haigh Hall in return for his support. Sir Osmund told Lady Mabel that the only way she could protect herself and her children and save them from being turned out of their home to live as penniless beggars was to marry him. At first she refused, but when she saw that there was no alternative, and now believing Sir William to be dead, she eventually complied.

By this time King Edward II had a new French advisor,

Hugh le Despenser, who persuaded him to take on the barons again in 1322 when the king raised an army to meet the Earl of Lancaster in battle at Boroughbridge in North Yorkshire.

The king's commander, Sir Andrew Harclay, crushed the rebellion at Boroughbridge and Thomas, Earl of Lancaster, was executed along with 28 other barons and knights, and many more were exiled. It was following this that Sir William Bradshaw may have felt it was safe to return home to Haigh Hall.

One day when Lady Mabel was handing out bread and meat to the poor at Haigh Hall, a man came to her who is recorded as being dressed as a palmer. Now some historians have written that this means he was dressed as someone who had made a pilgrimage to Jerusalem which has led others to believe that he had been away fighting in the Crusades. But the last crusade ended in 1270, ten years before Sir William was born – and pilgrims actually wore a badge in the shape of a cross to show that they had been on pilgrimage. What Sir William may have worn was the habit of the Palmer's Guild, which was a religious guild set up after the end of the Crusades to raise money to pay for priests and chaplains and to help out members in distress. It is reasonable to think that he may have been a member of this guild and that he had gone to them for help and asylum after his escape from the Banastre Rebellion.

So, perhaps well aware of the situation that he would find his wife in, he had come in secret. But when he drew back his hood, Lady Mabel, who was convinced her husband was dead, was so startled by his resemblance to the man she thought had died ten years before that she simply burst into tears – the result of which was that Sir Osmund Nevill gave her a public beating.

Although probably tempted to floor the man on the spot, Sir William must have realised that he needed help and he went and made himself known to many of his tenants, who returned to Haigh Hall with their master to claim back both the estate and his wife. Nevill fled, and they chased him, catching up with him at Newton Park, where Sir William challenged him, fought him and killed him.

Yet the couple were still parted. For the killing of the Welsh knight, it was said that Sir William was banished for a year and a day before he could be re-united with his wife. And for her sin of bigamy, Lady Mabel was instructed by her confessor to walk, every week, bare foot and bare legged to a cross near Wigan as a penance.

Sir William and Lady Mabel were eventually reunited, but their troubles were not over.

Edward II was removed from the throne in 1327 after his wife, Queen Isabella, had begun an affair with Roger Mortimer, another baron who had become disaffected by Edward. Her brother was the French king Charles IV, who helped Isabella and Roger depose Edward and replace him with his son in 1327. Edward III was crowned king at the age of fourteen, although it was his mother and Roger Mortimer who had the real power. But three years later in 1330 Edward III instigated a revolt against his mother and assumed control of the country. He also wanted a better relationship with the barons and nobles, and Henry, Earl of Lancaster, brother of the executed Thomas, Earl of Lancaster, was his chief advisor.

Edward II was killed and Sir William Bradshaw was murdered in 1333. A total of 44 men were accused of being involved although John de Radcliffe seems to be the principal suspect, no doubt because one of his brothers had been murdered during the Banastre Rebellion, and it is likely that he still bore a grudge against Sir William.

On the road between Newton and Winwick there is a small boulder made of red sandstone. This is known as 'the bloody stone' and marks the place where Sir William Bradshaw was murdered. Though some claim that it marks the place where Sir William slew the Welsh knight.

In the parish church of All Saints at Wigan you will still find the Bradshaw Chapel, which was paid for by Lady Mabel as a memorial to her husband. Here Sir William and Lady Mabel lie side by side. Their marble effigies above the tomb show him dressed in a coat of chain mail, with his shield on his shoulder and his sword partially drawn from its scabbard. She is dressed in a long robe and her hands are joined in prayer. The sculptured panel at the head of the tomb is traditionally thought to depict Sir William slaying the Welsh knight, although it could, of course, be an image of Sir William's murder.

Originally sited on the other side of the road and moved during an upgrading of the road, the remains of Mab's Cross can now be found outside the Mab's Cross Community Primary School, in Standishgate at Wigan. It was to here from Haigh Hall that Lady Mabel walked barefoot as a penance.

Good or bad? True or false? The truth lies buried somewhere within the legend of Lady Mabel and Sir William Bradshaw, and the two have become so intertwined no one will ever know the truth. But Mab's Cross remains as a monument to Lady Mabel Bradshaw, who did much work for the poor and needy – and who loved her husband.

The Holy Hermit
of Clitheroe

The remains of the keep of Clitheroe Castle still stand guard over the town on a limestone outcrop. The castle was the smallest in England, but it was an important strategic defence against raids from the north by the Scots, who were still unhappy about the invasion of the country by the Normans in 1066.

The construction of the castle may have been begun by Roger de Poictou, who was given the land by William the Conqueror. But, in the reign of William's son, William Rufus, the whole of Blackburnshire, as well as the 'great fee' of Pontefract, passed to Ilbert de Lacy, a Norman knight who had also fought at the Battle of Hastings. Now owning Pontefract and Clitheroe and all the land in between, Ilbert de Lacy became one of the most powerful nobles in the north. In fact, it was said that the de Lacys could ride from Pontefract to Clitheroe and stay each night in a house that they owned.

The lands and the castle were passed down through the de Lacy family for four generations until they were inherited by Robert de Lacy, who in 1186 built the castle keep to protect the administrative centre of his vast estates and as a temporary retreat.

During the reign of Richard the Lionheart (1189 to 1199), it became a tradition that young noblemen should go to fight in the third crusade in the Holy Land to try to claim Jerusalem as a Christian city. Some were killed in battle; some returned either injured or ill.

Many of those who came back had contracted leprosy, and the disease became a scourge in England, creating widespread fear and panic as people were terrified of catching this infectious disease for which there was no cure. Lepers, no matter what their status or rights by birth, were all treated in accordance with the laws of Moses as laid down in the Old Testament. The leper was taken to the door of his local church and read the Mass of Separation. His clothes were taken and burned and he was given leper's clothes – a shirt, a tunic and a large black cloak with a hood. He then knelt before the priest as his funeral service was read. Now, as far as his family and friends were concerned, he was dead.

The leper was then escorted by the priest to a leper house, outside the town, where he was compelled to stay. If a leper did appear in public he was to conceal his face with the hood of his cloak and to sound a wooden clapper to warn people of his approach.

It was a leper like this who arrived one night at the house of the Dean of Whalley to beg for help. At that time the position of Dean of Whalley was hereditary, as it wasn't until 1215 that Roman Catholic priests were forbidden to marry. The position was a combination of priest and lord of the manor. The Dean sheltered and fed the leper and probably prayed with him for a cure. It could have been the Dean who directed the leper to wash in the sulphurous water of the holy well in Clitheroe.

Nearby the leper discovered a small cell cut into the stone of the hillside, and there he lived as a hermit, fasting and praying and washing daily at the well. He became known to the locals as the Holy Hermit of the Rock. No one knew where he had come from and he spoke to no one about his past life.

In the castle above him, the ageing Robert de Lacy and his wife Isabella remained childless and no doubt there was much speculation about just who would inherit the Clitheroe estates on Robert's death. The Dean of Whalley, who was a distant relative of Isabella, was hopeful that the lands would be bequeathed to him. The only other claimant was believed to be a cousin of Robert's called Albreda de Lisours who lived at Halton Castle in Cheshire. She was the widow of Richard Fitz Eustace and had had a son, John, who was killed in Palestine in 1190. John's sons were also thought to have fought in the Holy Land and the eldest, Roger, was feared dead.

Shortly after Robert de Lacy's death, armed men were seen approaching Clitheroe Castle from the south. Leading the way was Roger Fitz Eustace, come to claim the de Lacy estates on behalf of his grandmother, Albreda de Lizours. The procession made an imposing sight. Roger Fitz Eustace was clad in a light suit of armour; he wore a cylindrical helmet with the face guard thrown up and a violet coloured surcoat. His horse was also clad with decorations and on one side of his saddle was fastened a French stabbing sword and on the other side a battle axe. His armour bearer carried his huge broad sword. Behind him came an escort of archers and crossbowmen, and behind them horses laden with provisions, cooking utensils and furniture.

Roger Fitz Eustace was the Constable of Chester and had earned the nickname 'Helle' because of his ferocious temper and the pitiless way treated his prisoners. So there must have been some disquiet as he paraded up the hill to take possession of Clitheroe Castle. However, the Dean of Whalley decided that he was not going to be so easily thwarted, and after preparing a forgery of Robert de Lacy's will, which said that all the land should be left to the Dean of Whalley and his heirs forever, he called to see Roger Fitz Eustace.

When the Holy Hermit suddenly appeared at the meeting, the Dean warned Roger Fitz Eustace that he should be tied down to prevent him using his magical powers. But when a guard approached the hermit, he seized him and hurled him to the ground. Several guards managed to hold back the hermit and, as they did so, the Dean noticed a parchment concealed within the hermit's cloak and he grabbed it and thrust it into his own cloak. He didn't try to conceal his action, saying that the document must contain Robert de

Lacy's will which had been given to the holy man for safe keeping. However, the will he produced a moment later was the forgery. And although the hermit protested that this will was not the real one and urged that the Dean should be searched, Roger Fitz Eustace believed that the will was genuine. But the hermit broke free from his guards, leapt at the Dean and, as he held him down by his throat with one hand, he tore open his cloak with the other, to reveal the other parchment hidden within its folds.

He passed this to Roger Fitz Eustace, who unrolled it to find that it was the original copy of the will, which his grandmother had shown him. This will left the Clitheroe estates to the Fitz Eustace family, provided that they became known by the name of de Lacy.

He was now furious and demanded that the unscrupulous Dean should be hanged immediately. But the hermit intervened, saying that he had promised Robert de Lacy that he would protect the Dean. The furious Roger Fitz Eustace demanded to know how the hermit dared question his authority.

'I was an outcast, though heir to a vast heritage,' he replied. 'I vowed that if He, whose prerogative it is, should cleanse me from my stains, my life should thenceforth be His, and consecrate to heaven. I was a leper, but my prayer was heard. I washed in yonder holy well which gushes from the rock, whose virtues had been reported to me. Washing daily, with faith and prayer, I was healed.'

He went on to explain that from his small cell he had discovered other caves, secret chambers and passageways beneath the castle and had been able to visit Robert de Lacy, to whom he had become a friend and companion.

'It was at my desire that he left the whole of his domains to the Fitz Eustaces,' he said. 'But you are not the eldest born of thy father.'

Somewhat amazed by the hermit's words, Roger Fitz Eustace explained that his elder brother had contracted leprosy during the crusade and was dead. Then the hermit threw off his leper's cloak to reveal himself dressed in a full suit of armour, covered by a surcoat, on which was emblazoned the Fitz Eustace crest.

'I am Richard Fitz Eustace, your elder brother,' he said. He then explained that although he had been healed, he wasn't there to claim his birthright as he had dedicated his life to God. But he demanded that the terrified Dean be set free and that the Dean's son, Geoffrey de Whalley, should marry Roger Fitz Eustace's daughter.

Richard then retired to his cell and died shortly afterwards. The marriage, though, took place and, on the death of Roger Fitz Eustace de Lacy, a portion of his lands, including the manor of Towneley, was left to Geoffrey de Whalley. And it is from this marriage that the Towneley family of Towneley Hall at Burnley are descended.

Riding the Black Lad

M any ceremonies around the county are held to honour historical figures and events, but the ceremony of Riding the Black Lad, held in Ashton-under-Lyne, was begun to dishonour the memory of Sir Ralph of Assheton.

Sir Ralph was the Lord of the Manor of Ashton. He was married to the Middleton heiress Margaret Barton, and was knighted by King Richard III in 1483 and became lieutenant of the Tower of London and later Vice-Constable of England.

On his lands he re-introduced the ancient custom of 'guld-riding'. The 'guld' or corn marigold was a species of poisonous weed that grew in the cornfields and spoiled the harvest. At one time a law had been passed which entitled the Lord of the Manor to inspect the farmers' fields every spring and impose a fine of one wether sheep on anyone who hadn't completely cleared the weed from their fields – and if the fine wasn't paid the lord had the authority to punish transgressors by having them put in the stocks or even sending them to prison. But the custom had fallen into disuse over the years and there was a large swathe of low wetland near Ashton, known as Sour Carr (or Low Carr), that had become overrun with the corn marigold.

However, Sir Ralph seems to have decided that reviving this custom was an excellent idea so, in the spring he set out, dressed from head to toe in black armour, mounted on a huge charger and with a numerous retinue, to inspect the fields and levy the fines. At first the tenant farmers refused to pay up but Sir Ralph pursued his privilege without mercy and the farmers soon discovered that he did indeed have the power, not only to fine them, but also to imprison them and even send them to their deaths on Gallows Field if they didn't comply.

Sir Ralph is recorded as being a cruel tyrant who helped Richard III to stay in power by ridding the country of many of those who questioned his right to be the monarch. There is an account of his visit to a gentleman in Devonshire who, it was claimed, opposed King Richard. The gentleman in question regarded Sir Ralph's visit as a favour and entertained him lavishly with a sumptuous dinner. Afterwards Sir Ralph suggested that they take a walk around the fields and the gentleman agreed only to find that, a short distance from the house, Assheton's men had built a gibbet. The gentleman asked what its purpose was and Sir Ralph replied, 'It is for you.' The man was then hanged.

Each spring there was a reign of terror in Ashton as the Black Knight rode through on his yearly inspection, and the locals even had a special prayer for the occasion:

'Sweet Jesus, for Thy mercy's sake,
And for Thy bitter passion,
Save us from the Tower axe
And from Sir Ralph Assheton.'

There were those though, who championed Sir Ralph and argued that what he was doing was inspired by zeal to improve agriculture in the area, but his zeal certainly didn't endear him to any of his tenants. There is a story that it was his half-brother Sir Thomas Assheton who gave a sum of five shillings to pay for a ceremony each year to disrespect the tyrant after he had been executed following the defeat of Richard III at the Battle of Bosworth Field. In fact Sir Ralph wasn't killed and on 6 June 1486 and he was pardoned by King Henry VII.

However a tradition began that each year on Easter Monday a straw effigy, dressed in black, was paraded through the streets of Ashton on horseback and people would throw clods of mud at it, before it was shot to pieces.

The annual parade was kept up for almost 500 years – a long time to bear a grudge – though during the 19th century, the custom became rather chaotic, with rival Black Lad processions stopping for refreshment at every public house along the route.

By 1909 it had developed into The Black Knight Pageant, with the Black Knight being accompanied by a Pageant Queen and other figures attracting huge crowds to the town every Easter Monday. After that the custom fell into disuse, possibly because of the drunken brawling that began to accompany it, though it was briefly revived after the Second World War in 1947 when Ashton celebrated 100 years as a Borough. It lasted until 1954, after which there was a gap of 40 years before it was revived again in 1995 to celebrate the opening of The Arcades shopping centre in Ashton and has since become the focus of Ashton's yearly carnival.

Ophelia of
the Irwell

After completing her education at the Moravian boarding school in Manchester, Lavinia Robinson had set up a small school of her own in the house on Bridge Street where she lived with her sisters and brothers. She had recently become engaged to a young doctor and the wedding was set for January 1814. It was nearly Christmas and life looked good for young Lavinia as her wedding day approached. Lavinia deserved some happiness. Her mother had died when she was only twelve and her father when she was seventeen.

The winter of 1813-14 was one of the coldest on record. Most of the country was covered in a thick layer of snow, local rivers were frozen over and the icy weather was continuous for thirteen weeks from the middle of December until March.

It was during a partial thaw in the early days of these arctic conditions that it seems that Lavinia, expecting a visit from her fiancé opened the door to another young man who had heard of the impending marriage and who had come to plead with her not to go through with it. When she refused to listen to him he tried to force himself on her and this was the scene that met her fiancé. Jumping to the wrong conclusion, he accused Lavinia of unfaithfulness before storming off.

According to a witness Lavinia went after him, as far as the bridge near the New Bailey, where the argument intensified and ended with the fiancé slapping Lavinia as she pleaded with him to believe her.

In his statement to the police, the fiancé said that he had left Lavinia near the prison, thinking that she would make her own way home to Bridge Street. Whether Lavinia did return home that night remains unclear, although it seems that a note was later found on the parlour table in which she solemnly declared her innocence and her determination not to live under her fiancé's suspicions. When there was no sign of her the next morning and it was clear that her bed hadn't been slept in, her frantic family immediately thought that she may have committed suicide by throwing herself into the river. But the partial thaw that night had been followed by a heavy frost and the Irwell was solid from bank to bank.

A month passed and her family issued an advertisement, offering a reward of thirty guineas for her recovery 'living or otherwise'. She was described as 'of middle size, and good figure; of fair complexion with long light-brown hair; she had on a fawn-coloured twilled stuff dress; a pink and yellow shot figured silk handkerchief on her neck; a brown cloth mantle; a black beaver cottage bonnet; and her linen is marked L.R.'

The reward was later increased to 100 guineas by the town authorities, but as the weeks passed and the weather showed no sign of a thaw it was generally thought that the frozen river Irwell must be hiding the missing girl. So in early February, a large group of men – some of whom were paid by the town authorities, but who were mostly volunteers – set to work to break up the ice in the river.

Then on 7 February, almost eight weeks after her disappearance, a Mr Goodier who was at his mill at Mode Wheel, three miles outside Manchester, saw Lavinia's body 'reclining on a sandbank, environed by masses of ice, and with icicles gemming her hair in the place of orange blossoms'. The body of Lavinia, who came to be known to locals as the Ophelia of the Irwell, had been preserved by the icy cold water.

A message was sent to Manchester and members of her family came to identify the body before it was taken back to Bridge Street in a hearse.

Public opinion was that her fiancé would have to be answerable to the Coroner's court for his actions that night, but after much deliberation an open verdict was returned, acknowledging that Lavinia had drowned but that there was no evidence to show by what means she had entered the water. The fiancé meanwhile spoke of his 'bitter sorrow' at having accused Lavinia and accepted that the medical evidence proved his accusations wrong. But despite this and the conclusion of the court, the people of Manchester considered him guilty. They threw stones at his windows and at him too if he ventured outside and he was forced to leave Manchester and go into hiding.

Lavinia Robinson was buried on 8 February 1814 in St John's churchyard, Byrom Street, in the same grave as her parents. The gravestone is inscribed:

> 'Also LAVINIA, their daughter,
> Who departed this life 17th of
> December, 1813, aged 20 years.
>
> More lasting than in lines of art
> Thy spotless character's imprest;
> Thy worth engraved on every heart,
> Thy loss bewail'd in every breast.'

Thousands of people attended the funeral and money was given by public subscription to help the family pay the expenses they incurred in connection with her loss.

The Childe of Hale

In 1578, John Middleton was born in the small village of Hale, which lies on the banks of the river Mersey at the most southerly point of the County Palatine, in a pretty, whitewashed and thatched cottage which can still be seen today. He lived with his widowed mother and seemed at first to be a completely normal child – that is until he began to grow. He grew and grew until he reached the astonishing height of nine feet three inches.

Many people at the time attributed his huge size to magic. Others said that it happened after he drew an enormous giant in the sand at the edge of the Mersey, then fell asleep and woke to find that he had grown so large he filled the outline and had burst out of all his clothes. Though the real reason was probably that he suffered from gigantism, a defect caused by the over-secretion of growth hormones from the pituitary gland which causes the long bones to overgrow.

In 1617, when John would have been 39 years old, Sir Gilbert Ireland, the Lord of the Manor of Hale Hall – who was said to have employed John Middleton as a bodyguard – and some of his friends, decided to take the giant to London to challenge King James I's prize-fighter to a wrestling bout.

They decked John out in fine clothes: 'with ruffs about his neck and hands, a striped doublet of crimson and white, round his waist a blue girdle embroidered with gold; large white plush breeches powdered with blue flowers; green stockings; broad shoes of a light colour, having red heels, and

tied with large bows of red ribbon; just below his knees bandages of the same colour, with large bows; by his side a sword, suspended by a broad belt over his shoulder, and embroidered, as his girdle, with blue and gold, with the addition of a gold fringe upon the edge.' What an imposing sight he must have made when all this was topped off by a plumed hat. The party must have caused much comment and excitement on their journey to the capital for the fight with the king's champion.

Of course, you can only feel sorry for the poor champion, who up until then seems to have been the undefeated favourite of the king. I don't suppose he really stood a chance when faced with fighting someone who was probably almost twice his size, and neither would he have been able to refuse. He ended up well and truly beaten and with a dislocated thumb – and reports say that King James was furious at the defeat.

What happened to the king's wrestler isn't recorded, but John Middleton was given a prize of £20 – quite a lot of money then – and sent on his way.

On the journey home the party stopped off in Oxford, and Sir Gilbert Ireland who had graduated from Brasenose College and was a senior member there, took the giant to meet the students. John was welcomed and two life-size portraits of him were painted. One now hangs in Speke Hall at Liverpool and the other still hangs in Oxford where it provides inspiration to the Brasenose College Boat Club, who took the Childe of Hale as their mascot. The rowing club's first eight still wear the Childe of Hale colours of purple, yellow and red in his honour and each of their boats is named *The Childe of Hale.*

In 2002, twelve members of the club came to visit Hale to find out more about the man who provides their inspiration. They saw the life-size sculpture of John Middleton which was carved from a diseased elm tree, visited his grave in the churchyard opposite, and ended the visit with a meal and drink in the Childe of Hale pub.

Whether or not John Middleton continued to grow during his adult life isn't clear but, when he arrived back in Hale, it is told that he could only get inside his cottage by getting down on his hands and knees. Inside the cottage, he could only stand upright under the highest point of the roof where the ceiling had been cut away to accommodate his height. Legend also tells that when he went to bed he was obliged to sleep with his feet hanging out of the upstairs window.

One day, two burglars, who obviously weren't local or they would have known better, tried to break into the cottage. Faced with John, they thought the devil himself had caught them in the act and they fled, without stopping, all the way to the banks of the river Mersey.

John Middleton died six years after his trip to London, in 1623. For years his bones were kept at Hale Hall as a curiosity, before being given a decent burial. But even then John was not allowed to lie in peace. Arguments and doubts ensued about how big he had really been and his remains were exhumed in 1768, when a Mr Bushell, the parish clerk and local schoolmaster, attempted to verify the giant's height. Examination proved that he had been nine feet three inches tall. His thighbone was as long as a normal man's complete leg. His hand was seventeen inches long and the palm was eight and a half inches across.

John now rests in the churchyard at the parish church of St Mary. The inscription on the grave reads: 'Here lyeth the bodie of John Middleton. Nine foot three. Born A.D. 1578. Dyed A.D. 1623.'

There are now railings around his grave to keep John Middleton safe, and hopefully this gentle giant, who was tall enough to have looked Goliath in the eye, will rest peacefully in his huge grave in the village of Hale where the inhabitants are proud of their real-life giant.

The Ghostly Horseman of Wycoller

If you want to see the village of Wycoller, you have to park the car and walk. It isn't very far, the path is level and pleasant and as you approach you have time to appreciate the scenery rather than having just the quick glimpses of things that you get from a car. There is no through traffic because the road doesn't go anywhere; the only people who drive down are residents. As you walk it's like going back in time.

Although still in Lancashire, we're on the edge of Brontë country here. Walk up through the ancient village and over the packhorse bridge and you will see the ruins of Wycoller Hall built by the Hartley family at the end of the 16th century. It is said to have inspired Charlotte Brontë's description of Ferndean Manor in *Jane Eyre* and was used to illustrate the 1898 edition of the novel.

The twin-arched packhorse bridge is picturesque with its well-worn stones from the crossing of many feet and hooves. It dates from the 13th century and is still in constant use today, but once a year a ghostly visitor is said to gallop across it on a wild winter's night.

The horseman pulls his frothing mount to a halt by the front door of the Hall, jumps from the saddle, races in, and runs up the stairs that no longer exist to an upstairs room that is also long gone. A woman's voice is heard screaming. Then the horseman rushes out, remounts his horse and gallops away.

The ghost is thought to be one of the Cunliffe family who lived at the Hall for centuries. They were strong Royalists and lost their estates at Billington following the Civil War, which was when they moved to Wycoller. They were a family of country squires with a reputation for hard drinking and fast living. Nowadays it would probably be cars, but then it was reckless coach driving as well as cock fighting and hunting that made them notorious.

One day Simon Cunliffe was out hunting when the fox he was pursuing fled into the Hall seeking refuge. It ran up the stairs and into the bedroom of Mistress Cunliffe, followed not only by the pack of hounds who savaged it to death in front of her, but also by Simon who followed them up the stairs on horseback and rode into the bedroom. Mistress Cunliffe is said to have collapsed and died of shock. When the staircase was removed later, there were hoofprints on two of the steps.

This story could account for the ghostly visitations, but the more popular one is that in the 1670s, one of the Cunliffe family rode up to the Hall on a dark and stormy night and murdered his wife after discovering that she had been unfaithful to him. Before she died she cursed the Cunliffes, saying that the family was destined to become extinct. The prophecy came true in 1819 when the last squire died, reputedly as he was propped up in bed watching a cock fight laid on for his entertainment. Now it seems the spirit of the murderer is doomed to revisit his crime every year.

The Mexico Disaster

U p until Victorian times the stretch of coastline from Lytham St Annes to Blackpool was only sparsely populated. Though the water here often appears calm, with families enjoying the wide stretch of sands, the sea off the Fylde coast can become very fierce and has claimed many lives as well as ships.

Over the years the residents have profited from several wrecks. In 1755 came the wreck of the *Travers*, which provided homes with lace for many years. Then, in 1779, following a poor summer and meagre crops, a ship was wrecked off the Fylde coast carrying a cargo of peas and the Pea Soup Wreck helped to feed hungry families through that winter. In 1821 the *Fanny* kept the ladies in red and black flannel petticoats, though some Marton men had been sent to prison in 1839 after being caught taking silk from the wreck of the *Crusader*. And when the schooner *William Henry* was wrecked off South Shore in 1861 there were plenty of cheap tubs of lard for nearby housewives.

Of course local fishermen would always go out in their own boats to try to save the lives, as well as the cargoes, of those floundering at sea, but there were no lifeboats as such until Sir William Hillary co-ordinated the first lifeboat service in 1824.

In 1851, the Duke of Northumberland offered a prize of a hundred guineas to anyone who could build a boat capable of withstanding the roughest of seas. The prize was won by

Beechin and Son of Great Yarmouth who designed the first self-righting boat. A subscription was set up in Lytham to buy one of these new boats. But whilst watching the new boat being put through its paces off Southport, the crew of a nearby Merseyside boat were less than impressed and one man predicted that they would all drown the first time they took the boat out in rough seas.

However, when William Swann and his crew took the boat, *Eleanor Cecily*, out to sea to put her through her paces, they were confident. They set out rowing the boat and hoisted the sail when they reached the middle of the Ribble estuary. But the wind was freshening and a sudden gust caught the sail and the boat capsized. The captain and nine crew members were instantly thrown into the water. The rest managed to cling on to the boat. This happened at half past one in the afternoon and it was six o'clock before rescuers in small boats managed to reach them. During this time the exhausted sailors had, one by one, lost their grip and been taken by the waves. When the rescuers reached them there were only two survivors left – James Parkinson and Roger Gillett, who told them that his brother Thomas had lost his hold on the boat only fifteen minutes before. Over the next few days the bodies of the eight drowned men were washed up around the estuary from Lytham to Southport; eight women and twenty-six children were left bereaved.

If you walk along the seafront at St Annes, not far from the pier, you will notice a stone statue that depicts a lifeboat crewman. He is wearing an early version of a lifebelt, which consisted of corks – designed by RNLI Inspector Captain Ward in 1854 to give crews protection against the cold as well as buoyancy.

The statue is a memorial to the members of the St Annes lifeboat crew who were drowned on the night of Thursday 9 December 1886 whilst trying to rescue the crew of the *Mexico*.

The *Mexico* was a large barque from Hamburg which was

sailing from Liverpool to Guayaquil, Ecuador's largest city and main port, and signalled that it was in distress to the south-west of Lytham. At around ten o'clock the Lytham lifeboat, *Charles Biggs*, was launched in a moderate west-north-west gale with a very heavy sea. At this time the lifeboats had no engines, just oars and sails, and as the crew struggled to row against the heavy swell the boat filled with water four or five times and three of the oars were broken.

At eleven o'clock that same night the lifeboat from Southport, the *Eliza Fernley*, having been brought thirty-two miles along the coast was launched with a crew of sixteen.

The *Eliza Fernley* also battled against the wind and the sea and managed to come within about twenty yards of the *Mexico*, which was breaking up. Two of her masts had already gone, and her crew, lashed to various parts of the vessel, were shouting wildly for help. But a huge wave struck the lifeboat, tipping her upside down and all her crew were washed into the raging sea. Three members of the crew managed to get out from under the upturned boat and clinging to the underside were eventually washed ashore, although one of the men later died in hospital. The other ten bodies were washed ashore during the course of Friday morning.

At around half past ten the St Annes boat, *Laura Janet*, had also set out, under sail but she was quickly swept away. However, the boat from Lytham managed to reach the *Mexico*, plucking the captain and crew from the sinking vessel and bringing them safely to shore. Coxswain Thomas Clarkson was awarded the RNLI's Silver Medal for the rescue.

The lifeboat crew then went back into the raging sea to try to save the crew of the St Annes boat. But they were too late. All the crew of the St Annes boat drowned that night.

A total of twenty-seven lifeboatmen died at sea in the *Mexico* incident, and it was possibly the worst RNLI disaster on record. A fund was set up for the bereaved families and with contributions from Queen Victoria, the German Emperor and the Port of Hamburg a total of £50,000 was raised.

The disaster prompted a local businessman, Sir Charles

Macara, to found the Lifeboat Saturday Fund. The first event was held in 1891 in Manchester when 30,000 people attended and £5,500 was collected. The Fund continued for 20 years until it was taken over by the RNLI in 1910.

The St Annes lifeboat station was closed in 1925 and the Lytham lifeboat assumed responsibility for the area. In 1932 it was re-named Lytham St Annes. It celebrated its 150th anniversary in 2001. The Lytham station is just further up the promenade from the windmill at Lytham, where the small building behind the windmill was the original lifeboat house. It has an inflatable D-Class in-shore lifeboat, but because of the silting up of the Ribble estuary the larger sea-going lifeboat, a Mersey Class boat named *Her Majesty the Queen*, was moved back to St Annes in 1999. It was kept on the Beach Cafe car park before being moved to a new boathouse, just behind the swimming pool, in August 2003.

The White Lady of Samlesbury Hall

S amlesbury Hall, on the road between Preston and
Blackburn, looks distinctly Tudor with its façade of black
and white. Part of the building, however, dates back to as long
ago as 1325, when it was begun by Gilbert de Southworth after
the original house had been burned down by marauding
Scots.

It was added to by generations of the Southworth family
until 1679 when they sold it to the Bradylls. It later became an
inn for travellers and then a boarding school. By 1924 it was
almost derelict but was restored by public subscription and
today is open to the public.

Many visitors to the Hall, including a serviceman who was
walking home late one night having missed the last bus, claim
to have seen its famous White Lady. She is Lady Dorothy
Southworth, said to be the daughter of Sir John Southworth
who lived at Samlesbury Hall during the reign of Elizabeth I.
She fell in love with the son of a neighbouring Protestant
family, but because the Southworth family had kept to the
forbidden Roman Catholic faith her father forbade them to
marry, saying that 'no daughter of his should ever be united
to the son of a family which had deserted its ancestral faith'.

Her father's disapproval didn't stop the couple meeting
secretly in the woodland on the banks of the river Ribble.

Their secret was discovered, however, by Dorothy's brother who apparently overheard their plans to elope and, on the evening that Dorothy went to meet her lover, he followed her and murdered both the man and his attendant with a sword. Dorothy was sent away to a convent where she died, seemingly raving mad, with the name of her lover on her lips. She has haunted the grounds of Samlesbury Hall ever since.

According to the legend, she can be seen on clear, still evenings walking across the grounds to meet her lover, who receives her on his bended knee and accompanies her on her walk. When the figures reach a certain place they both utter a soft wailing sound, and then embrace each other before their forms slowly rise and melt away into the darkening sky.

Some years ago, during renovations, human skeletons were found buried in the grounds near this spot, giving credence to the story of the murder.

In February 1926, a letter appeared in the *London Morning Post* from a retired colonel of the 15th Yorks East Riding Regiment recalling the time he and a company of 50 soldiers were garrisoned at Samlesbury Hall during the cotton riots of 1878. The colonel had a bedroom off the long corridor which overlooks the garden and early one morning he was woken by the sound of anguished sobbing from a room above. He tried to find who it was, thinking that someone was in pain, but could discover no one, and when he related the story to his hosts at breakfast the following morning they told him the story of Lady Dorothy Southworth. In this version, Sir John Southworth's men ambushed her lover as he came to collect her to elope with him. They killed him below her bedroom window and the distraught Dorothy, who saw it happen, threw herself from the window and was also killed.

Interestingly a Mr Abram Sharples, who died aged 73 in 1926, told of when he was employed as a youth by Mr William Harrison, who lived with his sister Miss Harrison at Samlesbury Hall until May 1879. Whilst excavating land for a drain, he and another workman named Jacob Baron, unexpectedly broke into an enclosed brick chamber lying just outside the garden wall. Here they found the remains of two human bodies, which on being uncovered, crumbled away to bones and hair. Mr Harrison told them to clean and limewash the vault, replace the bodies and reseal it.

On the night of 10 January 1940, the resident caretaker, Mr Edward Smith, together with a male friend, kept a vigil near the rails of the staircase landing on the upper floor in Samlesbury Hall. They had sat there on several previous nights hoping to prove that the ghost did exist and at around half past eleven they saw a slight, grey, wraith-like form pass noiselessly along the side of the wall towards the great fireplace. Here the figure seemed to halt for a moment and then disappeared – dissolving before their eyes.

Shortly after the construction of the nearby Samlesbury Aerodrome during the Second World War, a Manchester Company of Pioneers was drafted to some huts which had been built close to the perimeter of the Hall's grounds. Late one evening two soldiers came outside for a last smoke before bedtime when they were joined by a third figure who walked silently beside them. Both men were terrified. One fled back to his hut and the other collapsed on the drive and had to be taken to hospital in an ambulance.

In October 1948 a play was being performed at the Hall called *The Tragedy of the House of Southworth* and some members of the cast saw a lady, dressed in white, pass by the window of their dressing room.

A couple walking their dog late at night were passed by a lady in a light coloured coat and afterwards wondered how she had passed so closely by the man, between him and the dog, without falling over the dog's lead. And a conductor on a late night Ribble bus had an argument with his driver who stopped at the bus stop for a passenger that the conductor could not see.

Other explanations for the White Lady centre on the fact that the Southworths were a Roman Catholic family who had secret visits from priests to say Mass. The house did have a priest hole and there is a story that a priest was pulled from this hiding place and killed in an upstairs room, and that the persistent bloodstains on the floor were so upsetting that the boards were replaced in Victorian times. But as the priests came and went by night and may have worn a light coloured cloak, a ghost story would have offered an explanation for any sightings, and many 'White Lady' stories do date from around this time.

This explanation doesn't account for all the later sightings, however. Maybe they were products of over-active imaginations, or maybe poor Dorothy Southworth is still seeking her lover.

King James
and Sir Loin

In August 1617 King James, 'the First of the Stuart kings who reigned over both England and Scotland', visited Lancashire on one of his journeys from Scotland to London.

He was entertained by various noblemen, but it was his lavish reception and stay at Hoghton Tower that outdid all the others. Sir Richard Hoghton literally rolled out the red carpet for the king.

After a huge banquet and civic reception in Preston, the king was escorted by the town's dignitaries as far as Walton. Sir Richard then escorted the king and his lengthy retinue of carriages, horses and baggage wagons back to Hoghton Tower along what is now Preston Old Road, where the king could see the magnificent fortified manor house, set high on the hill, as they approached. The mile-long up-hill avenue from the road to the Tower was covered in red velvet, and as the king's large and unwieldy coach was far too heavy to be drawn up the steep hill to the house, the king got down and was greeted by Sir Richard's son, Gilbert. Gilbert was recorded as being dressed in a cloak and hose glistening with embroidery, a vest of cloth of gold, enriched with rare and costly stones, shirt bands and ruffles worked with silver, and breathing out the choicest perfume.

The king then rode up to Hoghton Tower on horseback, accompanied by dukes and earls, baronets and knights and over a hundred Lancashire gentlemen – all dressed in

Hoghton livery, which had been sent out to them four days previously.

As the king approached the house there was loud cheering and two men, representing the Household Gods of Hoghton, appeared through the central gateway. The first, dressed in purple taffeta, carried a palm tree branch and wore a garland of palms on his head and was accompanied by a dog. He made a long and rambling speech of adulation and flattery. Then the second added to the flattery by being apparently struck dumb at the splendid sight of the king. It was clear that the Hoghtons knew exactly how to appeal to the king's vanity.

That evening the king went hunting. He killed a brace of stags, but then declared that the weather was too hot and went in for his supper. The next morning he went out hunting again, and it is said that although he was a bad shot and a bad rider, he was passionate about hunting and never missed an opportunity.

The third day of the visit was a Sunday, and in the morning the king heard a sermon preached by the Bishop of Chester. In the afternoon he was given a demonstration of the Lancashire custom of rushbearing.

This was originally a religious festival when villagers would hold a feast of dedication at their local parish church. All the old rushes that were strewn on the church's packed-earth floor were swept out and fresh ones were ceremoniously carried in. The rest of the day was then a holiday.

These holidays had been outlawed in 1579 in the reign of Elizabeth I because she disapproved of the drinking and revelling that took place in and around the churchyards. So after the demonstration, a petition was presented to King James, asking that these activities could be allowed once more. It was this petition that prompted King James to write his Book of Sports, recommending that 'diverting exercises' should take place after evening prayer on Sundays. But many people, who still associated these customs with the old Roman Catholic faith, were unhappy. They also believed that it would lead to a return of drunkenness and vice. And it was the republication of the book in the reign of Charles I, James' son, that gave the Parliamentarians the evidence they needed that led to the eventual execution of Charles and the implementation of Oliver Cromwell's stark, puritanical republic.

However, it was at the lavish supper that Sunday night at Hoghton Tower that King James, delighted with the hospitality and entertainment that he had been given, and maybe after sampling a little too many of the wines and ales from the Hoghton cellar, declared that the joint of beef he was served was so excellent that he would knight it. And drawing his sword he declared that the meat was Sir Loin – a cut of beef which we still refer to as sirloin to this day.

Sir Richard Hoghton though, had lavished so much money on this spectacle that he later spent several years in the Fleet Prison for debtors. Perhaps he should have taken his lead from a neighbour named Shuttleworth, who burned down his own house as a cheaper alternative to entertaining the king.

The Pendle
Witches

One of the most well-known Lancashire stories is that of the Pendle Witches. They were tried and hanged at Lancaster, though their fate seems to have been sealed by a combination of a falling out between neighbours and the death of Queen Elizabeth I.

When Elizabeth died she was succeeded by James I (James VI of Scotland). Like Elizabeth before him James was a Protestant monarch, and having survived the gunpowder plot by Catholic militants he was anxious and became obsessed with a fear of witchcraft.

Lancashire was a Catholic stronghold and a place where suspicions of plots against the king were rife. So when King James published his book *Daemonology* which told local magistrates what to look for when hunting down witches, a nobleman, Roger Nowell, possibly hoping to make a name for himself, decided to bring the local witches to justice and rid the county of their evil.

The Pendle witches came from two families who were feuding neighbours. Elizabeth Southerns, known as Old Demdike, lived at a place called Malkin Tower with her daughter, Elizabeth Device, and her grandchildren Alison, James and Jennet Device. Nearby, on land belonging to the Nutter family, lived Anne Whittle, known as Chattox, with her daughters Anne Redfern and Bessie Whittle. Both of these elderly women were widows and lived in abject poverty and squalor.

The two families had fallen out eleven years previously when the Demdikes believed that the Chattoxes had broken into their house at Malkin Tower and stolen food and clothing. It is thought that Bessie Whittle, Chattox's daughter, then turned up at church wearing some of the stolen clothing whereupon a huge argument ensued. The outcome was that John Device, Demdike's son-in-law, was so afraid that Chattox would bewitch him that he agreed to give the family a quantity of food each year to keep them safe, but when he was dying he claimed that he had been bewitched by Chattox because he had been unable to afford to give them food for the last year.

The road to their hanging at Lancaster began for these families on the day that Alison Device stopped a pedlar on the road to Colne and asked to buy some pins. The pedlar refused to stop and open his pack. Then a familiar spirit came to Alison in the shape of a black dog and told her to lame the pedlar. She put a curse on him and further along the road he became paralysed down his left side.

When Alison Device was brought before Roger Nowell who was the magistrate at Read, as well as confessing to witchcraft she also accused the Chattox family of being witches. The result was that after Roger Nowell had extracted confessions from Demdike and Chattox, as well as their daughters Alison Device and Anne Redfern, he had all four women transported to Lancaster Castle for trial.

The Clerk of the Assize Courts at the time was Master Thomas Potts from London and he made a full written record of the proceedings. The main witness was Jennet Device, Old Demdike's grandaughter, who was just nine years old and was stood on a table to give her evidence.

She told the court that on the Good Friday, a week after the four witches were taken to Lancaster, there was a meeting of witches at Malkin Tower, where a spell was cast that would not only cause the death of the jailer, Mr Covell, but would result in Lancaster Castle being blown up. As a result of the child's evidence a further eight people were sent to Lancaster accused of witchcraft – Elizabeth Device (Old Demdike's daughter), her son James, Katherine Hewitt (known as Mouldheels), John Bulrock and his mother Jane Bulrock, Isabel Robey, Margaret Pearson and Alice Nutter of Roughlee Hall, who was described by Potts as 'a rich woman who had a great estate, and children of good hope'. The only charges against Alice Nutter were that she was present at Malkin Tower on Good Friday and that she had bewitched to death an old man called Mitton because he had refused to give Old Demdike a penny.

As well as giving evidence against her mother and brother, Jennet Device gave evidence against her sister and grandmother. Who, or what, persuaded her to do so is, of course, not recorded.

The other evidence used to condemn the witches was their confessions given to Roger Nowell on the 2 April. Old Demdike, who was described by Potts as 'a very old woman, about the age of four score years', admitted to having been a witch for twenty years. She said that one day as she was coming home from begging, she met a devil or spirit in the shape of a boy. One half of his coat was black and the other half brown. The spirit said its name was Tib and it promised her power and riches if she surrendered her soul to him. The spirit then appeared to her for the next five or six years, usually about 'Daylight Gate', until it came one Sunday morning in the shape of a brown dog and drew blood from under her left arm whilst she was sleeping, causing her to become 'almost stark mad'. The only person she was accused of harming was the daughter of Richard Baldwyn. She had gone to see him with her daughter Alison Device, who had to lead her as she had become blind, to beg for money, but Baldwyn called them witches and drove them off. The spirit Tib appeared and told her to exact some revenge. Now although Demdike herself didn't confess to harming the man or any of his family, Alison Device told the court that the following day she heard that Baldwyn's daughter had fallen ill and that when she died a year later she believed that her grandmother had bewitched her to death.

The compunction with which the members of the family were so willing to give evidence against one another seems strange. Perhaps they were promised that their own lives would be saved. This was certainly true for young Jennet who was pardoned for giving evidence. Their quickness to confess doesn't appear to have been brought about by torture either. In these cases the confessions were given freely to the magistrate Roger Nowell at Read, though torture was not unheard of in other places. It may have been brought about by fear of going to hell when they died for not confessing their sins, as although they professed witchcraft, the ideas of religion, heaven and hell and forgiveness of sins would have been very real to them.

At the end of her confession Old Demdike described how she could take a life by making a clay image of the person she meant to kill. She would then prick the image with a thorn in the place she wanted to cause illness. When she wanted a part of the person to 'consume away' she would take that part of the image and burn it. If the whole of the image was burnt then the person would die.

When it was time for Chattox to be tried, she claimed that she was seduced into witchcraft by Old Demdike and that she had a familiar spirit named Fancie. She admitted to bewitching one man to death.

James Device also confessed to witchcraft. He said that his grandmother, Old Demdike, had sent him to church on Shrove Tuesday to receive the sacrament but told him not to eat the sacred bread, but to give it to a spirit he would meet on his way home. However, he didn't do it and when he met the spirit in the shape of a brown hare he called on the name of God and it disappeared. But a few days later the spirit returned in the shape of a brown dog and asked him for his soul. James Device told the spirit that his soul didn't belong to him but to Jesus Christ, though the spirit said it would be content with as much of his soul as he was free to give. A few days later, he went to Carr Hall to beg, but Mrs Towneley said that he and his mother had stolen some of her turf and told him to go away. The next morning, he said, he made a clay image of Mrs Towneley and every day he crumbled some of the image away. By the end of the week it was all gone and two days later Mrs Towneley died.

The strangest accusation though was levelled at Alice Nutter. The court heard that eighteen years before a young man named Robert Nutter had made advances to Anne Redfern. Six months later he died – and it was on this evidence that Anne Redfern was condemned to death as a witch. But could it have been because of this old family quarrel and Alice Nutter's attempts to help Chattox's family that her own relatives disowned her and were content to see her hanged?

On 20 August, one week after the three-day trial, Chattox, Anne Redfern, Elizabeth, James and Alison Device, Alice Nutter and Katherine Hewitt, were taken to Gallows Hill, near to where the Ashton Memorial now stands in Williamson Park at Lancaster. John Bulrock and Jane Bulrock were acquitted.

Prisoners on their way to execution were huddled into a cart with their backs to the horses and their coffins piled in behind them although they were allowed to stop at the Golden Lion for one last drink.

Old Demdike had already died in jail so, at eighty years of age, she was spared a public death. The spectacle watched by a jeering and jubilant crowd helped to give Lancaster the dubious honour of being known as the 'hanging city' where more prisoners were executed than in any other place in the country.

These days the Pendle Witches have become a tourist attraction, especially up at the village of Newchurch in Pendle, where the eye of God carved into the church tower is supposed to ward of evil and life-size models of some of the witches sit outside the souvenir shop. But it is worth considering, amongst all the hype, that this episode in history was perhaps not Lancashire's finest hour.

The Siege of
Lathom House

For many years Lancashire was divided by religion, but during the Civil War the county was also divided by politics.

By 1643 all the fortified towns and houses in Lancashire were in the hands of the Parliamentarians but James Stanley, the 7th Earl of Derby, remained a staunch supporter of King Charles I and he maintained his home at Lathom House as a Royalist stronghold.

At this time James Stanley received news that the Scots were planning to invade Lancashire in support of Parliament. He discovered that rather than risk marching an army south and being intercepted by a Royalist force they intended to send an army first to the Isle of Man and then to some secret landing place along the Lancashire coast. As the Isle of Man was part of his lands, James Lathom left his home in the care of his wife and sailed to the island to prevent any landing by the Scots.

Whilst he was away, the Parliamentarians saw the chance to take Lathom House, but they had not accounted for the determination of the Countess of Derby, Charlotte de Tremouille. She was the daughter of a high-ranking French nobleman and was related to William of Orange who later became king of England, and she had no intention of giving up her home without a fight.

At that time Lathom House was well fortified. It was surrounded by a strong wall two yards thick and along the wall were nine towers, each with six cannon. In the centre, on top of the house itself, was the Eagle Tower overlooking the surrounding land which also formed a natural defence.

Soon after Lord Derby's departure the Parliamentary Governor of Manchester, whose name was Holland, called on Lady Derby and asked her to yield up Lathom House. Of course she said no, but she did offer to place all Lord Derby's estates at their disposal on condition that she was left in peace. The Governor agreed to this and although the estates were sequestrated Lady Derby was allowed to stay in her home although she was confined to the gardens.

Then Alexander Rigby from Preston became a Colonel in the Parliamentary Army. He had a personal grudge against Lord Derby and was determined to take Lathom House. He began to send his troops to plunder the houses of Lady Derby's neighbours hoping to provoke her into going to their assistance, and in 1644 when some of her friends were taken prisoner she did send men to rescue them and Rigby complained to Sir Thomas Fairfax who decided that Lathom House must be surrendered.

On 28 February Sir Thomas Fairfax arrived at Lathom House and requested that Lady Derby surrender. Unknown to Sir Thomas, however, she had not been idle since her husband left and she had a garrison of 300 men to defend the house as well as a stockpile of plentiful supplies. Her reply was that she would take a week to consider his request. Fairfax refused and told her that she must come by coach to New Park, a house of Lord Derby's about a quarter of a mile away, to speak with him and his colonels. She replied with a message saying that she thought it was more fitting for Sir Thomas Fairfax to come to her.

After the exchange of several letters it was finally agreed that Lady Derby would receive Colonels Ashton and Rigby and she put on quite a show for them. The ramparts were manned, the cannon in the towers were ready for action with gunners beside them and the two Parliamentarians had to walk through a double line of soldiers on their way to the great hall where Lady Derby, seated on a dais with a daughter on either side of her and her ladies in attendance, graciously received them.

The men outlined Fairfax's proposals for her surrender, which she declined. They remonstrated with her, but she replied 'I shall know how to take care of my ways and those of my house.'

Negotiations continued for a further ten days and Fairfax sent her a letter that he had received from Lord Derby begging him to allow the Countess and her children to leave Lathom, but Lady Derby replied that he should discuss the matter with Lord Derby himself. Though it later transpired that Lady Derby was not making all these decisions alone but was in constant contact with her husband. He wrote letters that were sent in secret, sometimes written on linen and stitched into the clothes of a messenger, or written on small pieces of wax that could be rolled up and swallowed if the bearer was in danger of being discovered.

However, after Lady Derby's final refusal to comply, the household woke the following morning to find that their enemy had dug earthworks all around the house and they were under siege. Rigby, who is recorded as a cruel and ruthless man, had brought a mortar gun from London which he mounted on earthworks outside the walls of the house and used to shoot stone balls and other missiles into the house. But the besiegers didn't have an easy time. Although Rigby had a force of around 3,000 Roundhead soldiers and Lady Derby had a garrison of around only 300, small raiding parties would regularly burst out of the gates of the house, attack soldiers in the trenches outside and be back inside the castle walls before reinforcements arrived. They would also throw clay balls with lit matches in them over the wall and the soldiers, believing them to be bombs, would run in terror.

Eventually Rigby lost patience and sent a message to Lady Derby saying that if she didn't surrender he would burn the house down. She tore up his message within his sight and sent his messenger back with the reply that she would set it alight herself and allow herself and her daughters to perish in the flames rather than surrender it to him.

Yet Lady Derby knew she was in danger and that the only way to save herself was to stop Rigby using his mortar gun to bombard the house with the nail bombs he had recently acquired. So at four o'clock the following morning a party of men from the house came out of a gate, as they had done many times before, drove away the soldiers guarding the mortar gun and having tied ropes around it they dragged it inside the house walls.

Rigby sent for reinforcements but help was at hand for Lady Derby. Her relative, Prince Rupert, who was also a nephew of King Charles arrived and met up with Lord Derby who had returned from the Isle of Man. Together they entered Lancashire by Stockport Bridge on 25 May with an army of 10,000 men and, afraid of being surrounded, Rigby retreated.

Rigby believed that the army would march to York via either Blackburn or Lancaster so he retreated to Bolton to keep out of their way, but scarcely had he entered the town than he saw Prince Rupert's army coming over the moors at Deane.

The battle between the Royalists and Parliamentarians became known as the Bolton Massacre. That same night Lord Derby and Prince Rupert entered Lathom in triumph and of the 3,000 men led by Colonel Rigby, 1,500 were left dead, and 700 taken prisoner.

Shortly afterwards, Lady Derby went to live on the Isle of Man and during a second siege of Lathom House in the winter of 1645 the servants hung on bravely until, starving and exhausted, they were ordered by King Charles himself to give in, and the house was destroyed by the Parliamentarians.

After Cromwell's victory, James Stanley was hunted down and captured in Cheshire. After a three day trial, he was taken to Bolton, where he spent his last hours at Ye Olde Man and Scythe public house, before being beheaded in Churchgate on 15 October 1651.

'This brave and imp[...] those who have anyt[...] condition of those co[...] because of John Hosk[...] faced up to the career-wrecking consequences of the foolishness that put him in prison, and expressed his remorse to the wife of the victim of his lapse, and the courage with which he resisted all the pressures put upon him, in prison, not just by imprisonment but by individual criminals with whom he served his sentence. One must also salute the courage and humanity of the wife of his victim.

The public knows too little about what actually goes on in its prisons, being fed largely on a diet of sensation by the media. In inspection report after inspection report I draw attention to the effects of relentless cuts in education, work, probation staffs and proper preparation for release on prisoners. John Hoskison describes these, from the inside, far more effectively than I can, but our message is the same. In reading this book I hope that the Prison Service will take note of what he says about the inadequacy of his induction, the number of blind eyes that are turned to drug abuse and bullying and the effect that staff behaviour can have on families, one of the principal lifelines if anyone is to avoid re-offending on release. If they do, John Hoskison will have performed a public service. His book should be made required reading for all now serving in, and all joining the Prison Service in the future.'

Sir David Ramsbotham
HM Chief Inspector of Prisons (1995–2000)

John Hoskison was educated at St John's, Leatherhead. After a short time working in a bank he became a professional golfer and played the European tour until 1986. He was elected Surrey Professional Golf Association Captain and has twice represented Europe in PGA Cup matches against America. In 1992 he won the Club Professionals Grand Slam including the national title. He has regularly contributed to golf magazines.

INSIDE

One Man's
Experience
of Prison

JOHN HOSKISON

ORION

An Orion paperback
First published in Great Britain in 1998
by John Murray (Publishers) Ltd,
50 Albemarle Street, London W1X 4BD
This paperback edition published in 1999 by Orion Books Ltd,
Orion House, 5 Upper St Martin's Lane, London WC2H 9EA

ISBN: 0 75282 718 9

Printed and bound in Great Britain by
Clays Ltd, St Ives plc

Contents

Contents

Author's Note

It is with a great deal of anguish and uncertainty that I send this book off for publication. It is about an episode in my life that I am not proud of. As far as I and my family are concerned, the fewer people who know about the tragic event the better. However, there is hardly a day that passes without my reading or hearing that prison is a soft option. This may be so in some circumstances. It wasn't for me and it isn't for most. When people read this book I hope they understand why I could not simply turn my back and walk away.

Deep down I go where no light shines,
Through hidden caves of fear,
I thought that I'd explored my mind,
I thought I'd cried my tears.

But now I know I'll cry some more,
A new duct born through pain,
I know I'll cry more than before,
Whilst all the ghosts remain.

INSIDE

Prologue

There was a fight on my landing this morning. One of my neighbours was badly hurt. It was a gruesome sight, but one I have become used to. HMP Coldingley has been my home for the last year.

When I was driven through the gates for the first time last November, the branches of the prison tree were bare. I can see that tree from the exercise yard and I've been watching its golden leaves fall. If I can keep clear of trouble I should be leaving here when the leaves start to grow again. The seasons have always played a significant part in my life. Before I came to prison I was a professional golfer. For a number of years I played the European Tour, where I mixed and played with some of the best golfers in the world. I was elected captain of the Surrey Professional Golfers Association and twice I represented Europe in PGA Cup matches against the Americans. I was respected by my friends and colleagues.

When I left the tour to settle down, I became the head professional at one of the most beautiful courses in Surrey. The members became my friends. I lived in a flat on the course and in the early mornings I would often go out with my young son into its deserted bluebell woods where we would hide and watch the deer. Every morning I bounced out of bed, eager for the day to start. I truly had the most wonderful life. One day I smashed that world.

1

Prologue

*

It was a cold November afternoon and I went to play in a golf match with a friend. After we finished we went to the bar for a drink. I'd always been very careful not to drink and drive, a discipline I'd maintained over twenty years of travelling to tournaments, but that night I chose not to listen to my conscience. When I left the club I was over the limit but I still decided to take the risk and drive home. That short fateful journey took me down a dark country lane where I hit a cyclist, and he was killed. In my panic I didn't stop.

Overnight my world was shattered and I began a journey into a living hell. Two years later I still shrink from thinking about the devastating consequences for all concerned. I am still trying to come to terms with my actions that night. Just once I took the risk. It proved absolutely catastrophic.

The morning after the accident I offered my resignation to the golf club where I worked, to the golf magazine I wrote for, for which I had great plans, and to the Professional Golfers Association. I had worked very hard in my career. In the blink of an eye I had lost it all.

The same day I sat my parents down and explained I was going to prison. My mother tried really hard not to cry, but they were shattered. Over the next few days I told everyone I knew. They were all devastated, stunned, and everywhere I went I left people in tears. Hardest of all was telling my son. He was only seven and breaking it to him still haunts me.

But what dwarfed every other emotion were my feelings for the cyclist's family. I lived in a nightmare world of sorrow and regret. It took nearly a year for the case to come to court. Every morning and every night I thought about the consequences for the victim's family. Every moment of every day, I longed for forgiveness. At every corner I had to ask myself: if I hadn't had a drink could the accident have been avoided?

During that year I wrote a letter to the victim's wife, expressing my great remorse. It was the hardest letter I have ever had to write. When I received a reply accepting that it was just a terrible accident, that I was forgiven, I wept. I was overwhelmed by her compassion.

But living with such grief and torment prompted me to ask myself whether my own life should continue. Many times throughout the year the easiest option seemed to be suicide. Had I been younger, less experienced in life, I doubt whether I could have coped, but I was able to do so through the incredible support of my girlfriend, family and friends, all of whom knew that my actions on that dreadful night were totally out of character. More importantly, I have survived thanks to support from the victim's wife, who has humbled me with her forgiveness, and who, knowing of my previous character, spoke on my behalf at my sentencing trial. Without her forgiveness I would not be here today.

As the day of my trial drew closer it seemed the media was preoccupied with reports about prison. Like most people, my attitude was that prison is a holiday camp – I believed the reports I read in the newspapers. It was not until the day of my sentencing trial, my first day in prison, that I realised that newspapers only tell one side of the story . . .

1

Court 13, The Old Bailey

FRIDAY 6 OCTOBER 1995; 4.30 P.M.

'Will the defendant please rise.'

I stood up on trembling legs and looked towards Mr Justice Hooper. It was almost a year since the day of the accident, a year I had spent on bail, living and working in a community that sometimes seemed to forget the trouble I was in. It had been an enormous strain trying to carry on as normal, knowing that things would never be normal again.

Throughout the past year I knew I was going to prison. I knew I *should* go to prison, I was guilty and that had been my plea. I longed for the punishment to begin, so that it might bring some relief. But I had dreaded the ordeal of having to face my day in court. For weeks I had tried to prepare myself. For endless hours, alone in my flat, I had tried meditation and self-hypnosis to help me survive the ordeal.

The judge started his summing-up. I locked my eyes onto the electric light on the wall above his head, and concentrated. I could hear the judge speaking, heard the words 'three years' imprisonment'. Then the gavel banged.

To my right, I could see the court usher beckoning to me. Showing no emotion I turned, picked up my overnight bag and walked towards the door. Within steps of the exit I glanced up at the public gallery and glimpsed my father's ashen face.

*

The holding cell beneath the Old Bailey law courts is a place few get to see. It's small — about the size of a standard family bedroom — dark, covered in dust, and smells of sweat and urine. This is where convicted prisoners wait after their court appearance, before being escorted to prison — a place where expressionless façades crumble as reality comes crashing down. There were eight of us in the cell and I immediately felt like a fish out of water. Unlike the others, for me it was an enormous relief that my punishment was finally to begin; and apart from one man, I was dressed conspicuously smartly. My companions' clothes looked creased and dirty, and I now realised several of the men had come straight from prison, where they had been on remand. I had come from home, through the leafy green countryside. My navy suit had been given to me when I represented Europe in the 1992 PGA Cup matches against the Americans. As I sat down on the wooden bench by the door, I loosened my tie, undid the top button of my shirt, and slouched against the wall, trying to adopt a similar pose to the others.

In the far corner of the cell a figure knelt on the filthy floor. 'Fifteen years, fifteen years,' he kept on murmuring, as tears streamed down his face. Seated next to him, the only other smartly dressed man wore an Armani suit and an open-necked shirt. A long scar ran across one cheek on his dark skinned face — he looked like the actor Al Pacino. His dark eyes studied his neighbour as if he were inspecting some insect. Mild interest — no sympathy.

I had no idea how long we would have to wait but as the minutes passed I couldn't help noticing, on the wall next to me, a scribbled 'Hall of Fame', topped by the IRA and including familiar names of other infamous killers.

After an hour we were joined by two other men, one small, the other tall, black, and sporting a Rastafarian hairstyle. Al Pacino knew him and raised his eyes in greeting. 'They dropped the murder charge; gotta go back for sentencing on a manslaughter,' he said, slumping down on the bench.

There were still a few spare places to sit, but the smaller man, with hands clenched tightly at his sides, paced back and forth across the room. A tramplike figure sitting next to me looked at him. 'How did you get on?' he asked.

'An eight and a four consec,' he snapped. 'Twelve years for a few fuckin' 'E's. Next time I'll show 'em what drugs is – bastards!' I'd never seen such a dangerous individual and I kept my gaze firmly on the ground.

The cell was now becoming crowded and oppressively hot, but only a few minutes later, an officer came in to announce that it was time to move. We were led away, single file, into the outside courtyard where we were met by the kind of vehicle I had so often seen on the news. Many times in the past I had wondered what these large white buses were like but never in my wildest dreams had I ever thought I would see the inside of one. They're known, in the trade, as 'sweat boxes', aptly named, as the compartment allotted to each of us was like an upright coffin. My space was almost custom-made: being only five foot seven inches tall, my small frame fitted neatly on to the rock-hard seat; but I could see the discomfort of the large black man in the casket next to mine. He was shuffling from one buttock to another, his shoulders barely contained within the sides; for him the sweat box must have been a nightmare. But, to be honest, my thoughts were elsewhere.

My father would be at home now, delivering the news to my friends and family. Fortunately they had been prepared and expected a prison sentence, but my main concern was for Ben, my son. Because of the nature of my work, I had been able to spend many hours with him in the beautiful surroundings of my Surrey golf course base, and we had developed a particularly close relationship. He meant more to me than anyone and I worried dreadfully about the effect my long absence would have on him. For the first time that day I felt a tear run down my cheek.

Locked inside the mobile fortress we were driven across town to Brixton prison. I felt as though I was going off to war.

*

It was late when we passed through the gates of the imposing Victorian prison and, rather than going through the administration process that night, we were paired off and led away to our cells. There was no choosing 'room mates' and I followed my partner, Al Pacino, up the three flights of iron staircase to the top landing.

Filth lay everywhere. I had expected the establishment to be run on military lines and I'm quite sure that no self-respecting sergeant would have let his barracks sink to such a squalid state. Old bits of food lay underfoot, dustbins were overflowing and the walls were covered in grime. I couldn't believe that with so much manpower available no cleaning seemed to have been done.

At the top of the stairs, a guard opened one of the heavy steel doors and, with a nod, motioned us to enter. I went in, but as Al followed, his arm was grabbed. 'Want to go "on the numbers"?' the officer asked. Al just looked at him, turned, and made his way into the cell. He must have caught my puzzled look as he moved towards me.

'Don't worry. I'm not a nonce,' he said. 'There's a few people that want to get me, that's all. I shot their boss, but no way I want protection.'

I didn't know what he meant by 'nonce' and 'numbers' and I wasn't about to ask, but, by the sound of it, Al was the first 'hit man' I'd met. I thought they were meant to be men who merged into the background, chameleon-like, the *last* person you'd think of. Al looked as though he'd been born for the job. It was while I was reflecting on the way my fellow inmate possibly earned a living that the officer reached in and pulled the heavy door back into place.

Over the months while I awaited trial, I had tried to picture what prison would be like, but never had I imagined that hearing a cell door slam shut could be so devastating. I stood transfixed, literally shocked by the sound and the dreadful feeling of finality it gave me. The last bolt slid into place and I realised my punishment had only just begun. I took a deep breath, turned my back on the solid steel door and surveyed my new home.

7

Apart from on television, this was the first prison cell I had seen. The once-white walls were now heavily stained a sick shade of yellow. Later on, I discovered that the colour comes from cups of tea, hurled at the wall in frustration, and thousands upon thousands of cigarettes. Large areas were scrawled with messages of pain and revenge, almost gouged out of the paint. On the far wall, well above head height, was a minute window, but it was so dirty that I couldn't see out of it. Underneath it, to one side, was a narrow bunk bed. Two folded sheets and a green blanket lay on top of the heavily stained mattresses. There was a toilet and a sink, though the latter looked as if it had never been cleaned: the plug hole was barely visible. The toilet wasn't much better. By the look and smell of it, flushing had not been on the agenda of the previous inmate. I tried breathing through my mouth, but still couldn't shut out the stench.

I consoled myself with the thought that I wouldn't have to endure this situation for long. At court my references had been impeccable, the pre-sentence report had recommended community service and the victim's wife had pleaded on my behalf for the most lenient sentence. Everyone had assured me that I would serve out my time in an open prison.

Al stowed his gear on the bottom bunk. 'I'll take this one,' he said. I climbed up to the top, sat on the mattress and looked down at the grey stone floor. I've always hated heights. The way my dreams had made me thrash about over the last few months I thought it odds on that I'd be taking a tumble – it seemed a long way to fall.

After 'bang up' (an apt expression after hearing the door slam), we had ten minutes before 'lights out', during which Al went to sit on the toilet. Out of politeness I pretended to read a message that had been scrawled on the wall, but I couldn't help noticing that, when he finished, he reached into the bowl and extracted a small cellophone packet. After drying the parcel, he opened it up, inspected the contents, and then placed what looked like three sparrow's eggs on our minute table. He looked up and caught me watching. 'Only good thing about going to court,' he said.

'What?' I asked, knowing he was unlikely to be a closet ornithologist.

'Crack cocaine. Want to buy some?' I shook my head and lay down facing the wall. I'd never used drugs and I hoped I never would, but I'd read stories where inmates had forced drugs on the innocent to make them users. I knew drugs were available in prisons but I hadn't expected to encounter them quite so quickly.

I closed my eyes and for the first time wondered if, physically, I would be able to survive my ordeal. I was very tired, the events of the day had taken their toll but it was no good trying to sleep. The noise that filled the jail was deafening. Men were shouting to each other from cell to cell. Others were screaming and hammering on their doors in sheer frustration. It reminded me of a film I'd once seen set in a Victorian lunatic asylum. I lay without moving and listened to the noise for what seemed like hours. I was playing possum, I suppose, but surprisingly I didn't even think very much. I was in shock.

Next day, Al had to go back to court and was collected before dawn. In total, I'd said about ten words to him. It was a case of ships passing in the night, but I'm damned sure he had more of a lasting effect on me than I did on him.

I spent all morning behind my door, which had been opened and left ajar, but no one came in to see me and I sat hiding in my cell, too scared to go out. At lunchtime the door suddenly swung open and my heart missed a beat, but it was only a guard who told me to pack my gear. Initially I thought I was being transferred to another prison but instead, it was to another cell. It was not a good move.

The man with whom I had to share was huge: about six foot four and massively overweight. I wasn't sure how to approach him, whether to shake hands or be completely dismissive, but I wanted to appear friendly. I did not want to make enemies. 'Hello,' I said, smiling. He looked me up and down, then revealed a set of yellow, tobacco-stained teeth with what could only be described as a leer.

'Hello, boyo,' he said slowly, in a thick Welsh accent. Had I not been terrified I might have laughed. I felt like a lamb led to the slaughter and realised that the dismissive approach would probably have been the best bet. Again I was stationed in the top bunk.

On the short journey to my new cell the officer had given me a blank sheet of paper and an envelope. Each new inmate, he explained, is allowed to write one letter, that the prison will pay to post. The officer also told me that I was allowed one 'reception' visit and that I should notify my prospective visitors in the letter. That afternoon I lay on my bed and wrote to my parents, but I didn't dare tell them what conditions were really like, or how frightened and depressed I felt.

Taffy (he assured me) was a poet, and late that evening he treated me to a rendition of his latest effort, 'Blood on the bones in Aberfan': a title I shan't forget easily. He read it with all the expression he could muster. 'I can sing it as well if you like,' he offered enthusiastically. There was little I could do to stop him.

I wasn't sure which was worse, his body odour or vocal talent, but both were dwarfed by the smell of his rotting feet as he prepared for bed.

I tried to erect some form of barrier with my pillow just in case Taffy wanted to 'play'; then, unable to shake off the feeling that my worst scenario might become reality, I remained awake all night, ready to protect myself from the madman of the valleys. At one point, for about five minutes, I froze with fear when the bed started shaking, accompanied by some heavy breathing. Later, when he began to toy with his lighter, flicking it on and off under my mattress, I was in a state of near panic. Taffy had just started a twelve-year sentence for arson.

I had to suffer him for three days, during which I showed virtually no interest in him. But he had obviously taken a shine to me. He confided in me that, when eventually released from prison, I should seek the sanctuary of his favourite haunt, the walkway underneath Waterloo Bridge. With much painstaking detail he demonstrated the most effective way to beg.

The next few days passed in a blur. I could not sleep. I was numb with fatigue, and only once was I allowed out of my cell for exercise, and then only for twenty minutes. Because it wasn't raining, we were permitted to walk outside round a small yard. I walked alone for much of the time but after a while I was joined by a man who introduced himself as Pete. A powerful little Irishman, he was serving ten years for attempted murder. After he had described his crime in meticulous detail, I mentally nicknamed him Pete the Machete. We only spoke for a few minutes. He was anxious to find out what happened to Al the hit man, but I could tell him nothing. That afternoon Taffy was moved, and I spent my fifth night in Brixton alone.

At first I couldn't believe my luck – a night without fear. However, when the steel door once again slammed shut, I was left in the dark with nothing to do but think. Cut off from the world and conscious that my punishment had begun, it was almost the first time since the accident that I felt I could look at the remnants of my life. In the darkness, the feeling that I had lost everything overwhelmed me. I had separated from my wife and just before the trial I had told my girlfriend Bronya that it would be better for her if she didn't wait for me, but I was missing her so much now. I ached with loneliness for my little son, but, I could not let him see me in this cesspit. I had lost my job, my flat and with it all my future. I was haunted by guilt at having taken away someone's life – that would never leave me. There was absolutely nothing to look forward to.

For six hours I sat at my small desk, bathed in moonlight, and tried to find a way that I might keep going. It was a desperate situation and everything pointed to the easiest solution: to end it all, there and then. In golfing terms, 'to retire'.

Ironically, it was that very expression that saved me. Years before, as a young golfer, I had retired several times from tournaments when not doing well and had come to realise that nothing is more humiliating. Thus in later years, when facing a resounding defeat on the course, I had disciplined myself to look neither back nor forward, but instead, to concentrate on the present and finish the round, focusing on one hole at a time. Often it still ended in defeat, but more than once I had survived.

It may seem ridiculous that such an unlikely comparison with my present predicament could have guided me in the right direction. I do not want to belittle my situation, but having been a professional for twenty years, I perceived my life very much through golfing eyes. When my mind finally related the problem to something I could understand, I saw how I might survive. I knew it was going to be difficult, that I wasn't really facing up to my problems, but if I lived for the present and worried neither about the past nor the future, perhaps somehow I could carry on.

At eight o'clock that same morning an officer came in to see me. 'Hodgkiss,' he said (no one in prison would ever get my name right). 'Pack your gear. You're moving. You're being transferred to another nick.'

'*Thank God*,' I thought. 'Where to?' I asked, expecting him to say Ford Open Prison.

'Wandsworth.'

I'd never heard of it. 'What's it like?'

He looked at me for several seconds, opened his mouth as if to say something, then turned and walked away.

I packed my few belongings into my small bag, sat on my bed and waited to be called. Somehow I had got through my longest night, and I approached my move with renewed purpose. I didn't care what Wandsworth was like, it had to be better than Brixton.

2

New Boy: Wandsworth

I had spent much of my twenty-year career travelling round Europe, staying in top hotels, so the word 'Reception' evoked images of large carpeted areas, comfy armchairs, mahogany desks and polite concierges. However, the reception area at HMP Wandsworth gave the word a new perspective: decaying rubbish, wooden benches, stone floors and brutal 'screws'. It was no cleaner than Brixton; if anything it was worse. Continuing the tradition of getting my name wrong, 'Hodgkinson 2478' was called out loudly by an officer and I followed him at a respectful distance along a scruffy, badly-lit corridor. We went down an iron staircase to the depths of the prison – the 'dungeon', I later found it was called, because it was below ground level. He left me outside my new cell as he reported to the landing officer, and sheepishly I opened the tiny peephole to look inside.

Three bodies lay on three beds. The light was off – it looked like night-time but it was midday. Three buckets stood on the floor and I realised there was no toilet or wash basin. I felt very, very weak and sick. Five minutes later the officer returned, opened the cell door and I went in. The door slammed shut, as I was locked in. Three faces turned towards me, three pairs of eyes drilled into me: the new boy.

'Give us a fag,' said one of them.

*

To my right was the only empty bed in the cell and, without having to move, I put down on the dirty, stained mattress the bag of prison issue clothing and bedlinen that I had been given in reception. Slowly I reached into my pocket and dug out my cigarettes. There was no need to walk across the room as only three paces separated me from the furthest bed and, with as much confidence as I could muster, conscious that my body language posed no threat, I held out the opened packet at arm's length.

'You might not like them,' I apologised. 'They're Silk Cut Ultra Low.'

One of the men – Mediterranean-looking, medium build, in his thirties – eyed them suspiciously. He looked lean and hungry – not one of Caesar's choices.

'Jesus Christ – fuckin' "civvies", ain't you got no burn?'

'What's burn?' I asked.

'Burn – tobacco, fuckin' 'ell, this your first time inside?'

''Fraid so,' I said, aware that I'd already been sussed. 'I've just come from Brixton – Pete the Machete told me it's as bad as it gets there, but I must say Wandsworth doesn't look too good.'

'It's the worst, Wanno's the fuckin' worst – always has been, always will be,' he spat out as he took one of the cigarettes.

'My name's John,' I ventured further.

'Guido,' he replied with a small nod.

I looked at him as he slipped the cigarette between his lips and flicked the lighter. He took a deep drag but with nothing there to bite into his lungs he withdrew the cigarette, snapped off the butt and tried again.

'Fuckin' fresh air, these,' he said, but this time smoke was blown out and he nodded in the direction of the other two men.

'Tommo,' he said, indicating the nearer. Then, flicking his eyes across to the furthest bed, 'Manolitto – ignorant fucker.'

I almost smiled – it sounded like a Red Indian name. I looked across at the inert figure but realised he bore no resemblance to an Indian brave – he lay tucked up tightly in a defensive ball. At least in this quarter there seemed no threat. I then looked across at Tommo. He was lying on his back, legs splayed, his bulk swamping the bed. He was a big man, definitely a snorer. His bald shaved head, inches from Guido's socked feet, was turned in my direction and on his neck, proudly displayed, was a tattoo – Chelsea FC.

I reached across and offered him the packet of 'civvies'. He took one.

'Who d'you support then?' he asked in a deep, throaty voice. My loyalty to Spurs nose-dived.

'The Blues,' I said. 'I'm a great fan of Glen Hoddle.'

'You don't look much like a fan.' I refrained from thanking him.

'Never got much chance to go – used to work on Saturdays.' He didn't comment and, appearing to have passed the interview, I moved across to the last bed and held forth my offering.

'Don't give 'im nuffin',' came Tommo's voice from over my shoulder.

Manolitto's eyes held mine for a second before he turned away to face the wall. One of Tommo's legs flashed out and smashed into his bed.

'Introduce yourself, you Spanish piece of shit,' Tommo said viciously. The body lay still. Without knowing, I had blundered into the front line and I wasn't ready for it. Slowly I made a tactical withdrawal back to my bed, my space.

'One day you're really gonna get it, Mano,' Tommo added.

I sat on my bed in awe of such hatred. Mano was obviously not flavour of the month and, whilst part of me was drawn to protecting the persecuted, I was relieved that the hate normally reserved for the new boy was being absorbed by the Spaniard – poor bastard.

'How long you doin'?' asked Guido, breaking the silence.

'Three years.'

'Fraud?'

'No, driving offence – drink-driving offence.'

'Fuck me – bit steep, innit? You kill someone?'

'Yes,' I said, shocked by the brutality of the question. It was something I was still struggling to face; I certainly couldn't talk about it. I sat down on my bed and fumbled around with my bag. It was too dark to unpack, but my actions were enough to halt the conversation. When Guido stopped peering at me I lay down on the bed and closed my eyes.

The morning had been hectic. Three of us had been moved out of Brixton, two to Wandsworth, one to Ford. The businessman who was going to Ford had breathed a sigh of relief when his paperwork was completed. It had needed all my sportsmanship to congratulate him on his good fortune.

Before my own transfer and another dose of the 'sweat box', I had been allowed to buy a phonecard out of the money I had brought with me to prison. The money, confiscated on arrival, is held on account, and every week you're allowed to spend a small amount. Two pounds my first week – just enough to buy one phonecard. I had warned everyone not to expect any calls for a few days. I had no idea what the situation was going to be regarding the phone, but that morning I was given the chance, and I called my father. He had received my letter containing news of the permitted 'reception' visit and had booked to see me in Brixton the following day – I had to let him know that I would no longer be there.

Fortunately an officer stood behind me while I was speaking, and it stopped me from becoming too emotional. Even so, I found it difficult to talk. I respected my parents enormously – they had given me so much support over the years. My mother had trained at the Royal Academy of Music and was a brilliant pianist, my father was an Oxford graduate, but when I announced, at seventeen, that I was going to give up my work in the bank and become a professional sportsman, they didn't bat an eyelid and actively encouraged me in my ambition. Throughout the last year, when I had felt in a no-man's-land, numbed by what I had done, they had shown an inner reserve of strength that had helped me considerably. They had given me the impression that they could cope with any situation, but during our short conversation I decided to gloss over Brixton's shortcomings and also tried to sound cheerful. After only a couple of minutes I was tapped on the shoulder by the officer. I explained I had to go. 'I just hope I feel a bit safer in Wandsworth, Dad.'

As I lay there reflecting on those words I was so thankful that he couldn't see me in my new surroundings.

The quiet that had fallen in the cell suddenly seemed far too morbid, and I turned to Guido. 'Mind if I put the light on?' I asked.

'Don't give a fuck what you do, but the switch's outside.' So it was the same system as at Brixton: during the day you could ask for the light to be put on, but at night the lights were switched out at ten o'clock.

'Don't you ask for it to be put on?' I asked, finding it strange they should wish to live in such gloom.

'What for? Banged up twenty-three hours a day. There's sod all else to do but sleep!' Tommo said.

'Don't you read?' I asked no one in particular.

'Tommo can't read and they've run out of comics in the library,' Guido said, propping himself up onto one elbow. I lit up a cigarette and pondered on the prospect of a sentence without reading. A sobering thought – no escapism.

'Not been in trouble before then?' Guido asked, looking across. I shook my head.

'Not like me then,' said Tommo. 'I've done a four, two threes, and a two. This one's nuffin' – a year, that's all, be out in three months.'

I wasn't sure what to say but it sounded an enormous amount of time spent in prison for someone who looked so young.

'How old are you, Tommo?' I asked tentatively.

'Thirty two, just gone.'

I did some mental calculations and realised that, with sentences totalling thirteen years, Tommo couldn't have spent much of his twenties in the outside world.

'Look 'ere,' he said, passing across a hand-painted card. 'Sandy, me daughter, sent me this for me birfday.'

17

It was a colourful little picture. 'How old is she?' I asked.

'Eight now. Only seen 'er twice though. Her mum let me see 'er the last time I was out, but I got nicked again after two months. Ain't seen 'er since.'

I was lost for words. I began thinking about Ben. He would be eight next year. The two of us, just about as close as a father and son can get.

'Yeah, well, I broke me fuckin' licence,' said Tommo, looking at me. 'But I've got another case pending – possession of a firearm. Bastard cossers set me up though. Me brief says I'll beat it with any luck. The search was illegal, see.'

'It'll be a "gate arrest" – they'll be waiting for you when you get out,' said Guido. My look in his direction prompted a further comment from Tommo.

'Guido knows it all. Got sixty previous, ain't you?' he said, turning to face 'the master'.

'Go on – show 'im yer previous, Guido.'

'Sixty?' I repeated, flabbergasted.

'Yeah,' he said with a grimace. 'Thirty-six I am now – done eleven years of bird.' He paused while he lit a roll-up cigarette. 'Last time I got out was Christmas Eve. Five fuckin' days later I was nicked again. No one should get released before Christmas, puts you under too much pressure. Anyway I've 'ad enough now – everyone's got their limit. Got to be real careful from now on.' He lay back on his bed, the conversation ended, and for a while the cell slipped into contemplative silence.

3

'Guv, I need a bucket'

It was nearly five o'clock in the afternoon before the lights came on and I was able to survey the cell in detail for the first time. With walls thick enough to deter even the most stiff-necked escapee and ceilings high enough to make the potential 'swinger' use his imagination, HMP Wandsworth made any form of escape an unlikely prospect.

The cells, designed in Victorian times, might well have been considered spacious, but a century later, housing four instead of two, they were cramped and oppressive. My seven-year-old son could have jumped, quite comfortably, from one bed to another without touching the stone floor. On the wall opposite the cell door, well above head height, two small windows allowed a worm's eye view of passing guards – or at least their feet, since we were below ground level. Heavily barred, these windows were left ajar, allowing at least some air to circulate and freshen the dank, sweaty-smelling 'biosphere'. With showers only permitted every two days (so Guido had informed me) and open-top buckets holding the 'slops', the smell was something only those from 'cardboard city' could initially stomach. It made me want to heave. I guessed that if I stood on tiptoe under the window I would just be able to grab breaths of fresh air.

It was, however, to the beds that my attention was drawn, and the fact that mine had still to be made. As I sat up I was reminded of the television advertisement – the one featuring the 'spring'-design bed enabling a person to sit without spilling the adjacent glass of wine. If that basis defined quality my bed was a cracker. 'Give' was not an expression one could use about the mesh of steel slats that sufficed as the base, and with one single inch of foam mattress as protection, only a Tibetan monk with a masochistic streak might have found it comfortable. Up until then my back had fortunately been used to better, and, as I draped my uniform prison green sheets and blanket over the metal monstrosity, my thoughts teasingly leapt to the Palace Hotel in Madrid, one of Europe's finest, where all the rooms have king-size beds.

Suddenly there was a noise of jangling keys outside and moments later the door swung open. 'Tea!' was shouted loudly by an unseen guard and immediately my three cellmates grabbed their plates and headed for the door. I followed suit, picking up the plastic knife and fork I had been given on entering the prison. But eating did not top my list of priorities – the lavatory did.

To my horror when I entered the corridor I found that the lavatories were closed. It wasn't long before I realised that when the door opened it allowed us out for one specific purpose, and only one. At teatime you collect your meal and return to the cell as quickly as possible – at teatime the lavatories are closed. There was an officer standing near me hurrying everyone along. With little option I went up to him.

'Excuse me, I'm new in today. I wasn't given a bucket. I need to go to the toilet. What do I do?' Succinct and to the point.

'Borrow someone's.' His lips moved but the rest of his features remained motionless. It seemed I wasn't a person with a problem: I was just a nuisance – an irritant – and he wasn't the slightest bit interested in me. There was no point in pleading. I stood in line behind the long counter and waited to collect my tea.

I'm not a fussy person. I had guessed that reports in the press suggesting that prison food bordered on *cordon bleu* were probably exaggerated, but nothing could have prepared me for the standard of food in Wandsworth. 'What is it?' I asked the inmate who stood serving behind the counter.

'Lasagne,' he replied, as he poured some onto my plate. The chef in Wandsworth obviously had a warped sense of humour.

Back in the cell I toyed with the measly bit of slush that could only be described as 'fat soup', but my mind was elsewhere and I knew I had to broach the subject.

'Look, Guido, I need to go to the toilet. I've asked for a bucket, but the bastard said I'll have to borrow one – can I borrow yours?'

He turned and looked me up and down as though assessing whether or not I was clean enough. 'OK,' he said, nodding. 'As long as you slop out for me in the morning.' He didn't really have much option. What else was I to do? I put my plate down and headed for the bucket.

I've always had a bit of a problem about peeing in front of people. I remember one particular night at the Albert Hall, when I had gone to hear my sister play violin in the Proms. At the interval, I had to go to the toilet. There were about fifty men waiting behind me and for love nor money I couldn't relax enough to go. I missed the beginning of the second half (poems by e.e. cummings) because I had to wait for the 'sit downs'. (A blessing in disguise when I heard the singing.) Standing up in front of my cellmates who were still silently eating, I tried to pee into the bucket. Total frustration. I wondered how long I'd be able to remain inactive without drawing attention to myself. I needed a distraction.

'If it's not a rude question, what are you in for, Guido?'

'Hoisting,' he said, pausing to shovel some slush into his mouth. 'Hoisting and possession of class A drugs.' (I could feel myself relaxing.)

'Got a right result with the judge. Before sentencing he asked to see my previous, a stack of it there was. Sixty convictions takes up loads of paper. Then he says, "Mr Gomez, it seems to me you've been in quite a bit of trouble before." Fuckin' understatement, that was. Then he goes on, "but prison doesn't seem to have done you

21

any good, I'll therefore sentence you to only two years with the understanding you undertake a drug rehab course." Guido paused to take another mouthful and I felt myself finally relax, my diversion having worked.

'He was a dozy old bastard,' Guido surmised. 'It was a right touch, thought I was looking at a five.'

He returned to finish his meal, but the conversation had been enough.

'Thanks,' I said, and put the bucket down at the end of his bed. 'I'll have to use it again tonight but I'll clean it in the morning.'

'Too right you will,' said Guido with a glint in his eye. 'You'll enjoy that.'

I turned to organise my possessions. From my bag I took out my 'new' prison-issue clothes, and laid them on my bed: a pair of jeans, two T-shirts, ominously, four pairs of secondhand socks and, worse, three pairs of secondhand underpants. I thought of the faded pair I was wearing – donned along with the jeans and sweatshirt after my strip search at reception, and blessed my girlfriend Bronya for insisting I undertake a course of Hepatitis B jabs.

Next to my clothes I put the other items which the prison had supplied: a bar of prison soap, some prison toothpaste, a towel, a large plastic cup, a toilet roll, and a small metal mirror, about six inches square with rounded corners (anti-suicide). All the toiletries that I had brought with me to prison had been confiscated. When the supplies of soap etc. ran out you had to ask for more, and I would come to realise that the officers responsible for handing out items used their power to cause maximum humiliation – it was wise to keep a few sheets of toilet paper in reserve, before asking for a new roll. The only items regularly handed out were disposable razors. Every Sunday morning an officer would come round and swap a used one for a new one. It would have to last a week and, if you happened to lose it, it would not be replaced when the officer returned.

I put my clothes away in the small cupboard next to my bed, on top of which I placed my most valuable possessions – the photos that I had been allowed to keep.

'Pictures of the wife?' Guido asked.

'No, I'm separated. My girlfriend and my son.'

'Let's have a look,' he said. I took them down and placed them in his outstretched hand.

'This your house then?' he asked, looking at the one of me and my son.

'Sort of. I don't live there any more – the ex does.'

'Where d'you live then?' he asked as he turned to the next picture.

'Guildford,' I replied.

'Fuckin' 'ell, I know Guildford. It's a great place,' he said, propping himself up on one elbow. 'You know B and Q on that new estate?'

I nodded.

'I've had bundles out of there mate, bundles,' he said, with real enthusiasm.

'Yeah,' joined in Tommo. 'I done loads of nickin' there as well. Got a bloody great big car park, hasn't it?'

'Straight down the A3, nice and close to the M25, perfect,' said Guido. 'Fuck me, I'd love to live in Guildford.'

I almost smiled. I had lived in Guildford for ten years, ever since I had sought a job offering more security than simply playing tournament golf. The West Surrey club had advertised for a head professional. I had taken the job. I became responsible for the golf shop and employed two assistants to help me, but the enthusiastic membership also encouraged me to play tournaments. I could not have found a place where I felt more at home. Now I had lost it all but I know that I had more enjoyment there in ten years than most people do in a lifetime and I couldn't help looking back with fondness rather than regret. I once read that the gods envy anyone who is too happy. In my previous situation at West Surrey I can understand that. However, I had made a decision not to dwell on the past.

'You've hoisted in Guildford then?' I said, returning to the conversation and guessing that 'hoisting' constituted some form of bulk shoplifting.

23

'Too right, out of that B and Q – drills, saws, bundles, mate. It's a right easy touch.'

'Drills?' I asked. 'But aren't you seen? I mean, a drill's pretty big.'

'No, dead easy. Just hide it under a big coat,' he explained.

'Bit suspicious during summer, isn't it – wearing a big coat?'

Guido looked at me, his eyes narrowing. 'You catch on quick,' he said. 'You don't use a coat in the summer, you have a spotter – bloke who causes a distraction. When no one's looking you grab the stuff, dive out and bosh, you're off. It's easy, even Mano can do it.'

I turned to the young Spaniard. 'You a hoister as well?' I asked.

'Yeah, but not like them, I just do it for kicks.'

'No you don't, you lying bastard!' lashed Tommo. 'You spend the dosh on that stupid car of yours so you look good – you're a fuckin' waster, Mano – not like Guido and me. We're doers, we've got serious previous to prove it.'

I had to bite my lip. It wouldn't need the brains of Kavanagh, QC, to pick holes in that philosophical argument.

'So how do you get rid of the stuff? That's always intrigued me,' I asked Guido.

'Why, want to do some nickin'?' asked Tommo.

'Course he fuckin' doesn't,' said Guido. 'Does he look like a fuckin' hoister?'

'No,' I said, in an attempt to clarify. 'I had some gear stolen once and wondered where people get rid of it.'

'What sort of gear?'

'Oh, just some golf clubs,' I said. But it was more than just a few. Twice in the space of a year the shop at West Surrey was ram-raided. The second time I had to spend several nights in the freezing cold protecting my stock while the shop front was rebuilt. The dust and filth were a nightmare, I was not compensated for my loss of earnings and my insurance premiums went through the roof.

I was seething. My rage had been exacerbated by reports in my newspaper showing that these *bloody* criminals, even if caught, would enjoy a 'salmon and champagne lifestyle' – a *menu* for God's sake, and all these bloody prisoners absconding from home leave. *Where had justice gone?!*

Prison was easy, my newspaper told me – it was a holiday camp. Fired up by reports such as these, I used to phone all TV polls to register my vote, make myself heard, and on those cold lonely nights, with gritted teeth I would imagine myself their judge and executioner. I'd wipe the smile off their faces: *Birch them – bang them up – make the bastards suffer.*

'Hey, listen up,' said Guido loudly, obviously realising my mind was elsewhere. 'Ping clubs mate, they're the ones you want. Break into a boot and find some Pings, it's one-and-a-half cash for certain. No problem flogging them down the pub. You play golf, do you?'

'Used to,' I said, unclenching my fists.

'Any good were you? I tried once – fuckin' useless.'

He jumped up from the bed, faced me and took a swipe at an imaginary ball. I knew he'd never make a golfer.

'So you can make a bit of cash hoisting?' I said, hoping to change the subject. I had no intention of revealing my past quite so quickly.

'Just a bit,' said Guido, now sitting down again. 'Grand a week, no problem – but you've got to if you're on the gear.'

'Is that drugs?' I asked.

'Fuckin' 'ell, don't know what you're doin' here. You should be in Ford, mate. "Smack", "brown", heroin – doesn't matter how much dosh you get, it's never enough. I know people who do five grand a week on "crack" and they're still gagging for more.'

'How, though? Surely your body can only absorb a certain amount?' Except for what I had seen on television, I knew little about drugs.

'Listen, I'm tellin' you the fuckin' truth, you know nothing. If you're cluckin' you'll do anything for a fix, *anything*. Wish I'd never seen the stuff.'

'Cluckin'?'

'Yeah, withdrawal symptoms.'

'Visit in two days though,' said Tommo. 'Hang in there mate, got a joey coming, we'll be sweet then.'

It took me a while to get used to the various expressions I heard in prison – a 'joey' is a parcel of drugs smuggled in on a visit. But rather than continually draw attention to my inexperience I decided not to ask too many questions. However, two things I did need to know – how to get on the telephone and how to book a visit.

'Ask a screw about the visit,' said Guido. 'But you have to book to use the phone in the morning. You better be out quick though, or all the times will go.'

My sanity depended on contact with the outside world, but I knew I would be up in time to book my call. In all my years as a tournament golfer never had I missed a teeing-off time through oversleeping. No matter where I was, or how late I'd been to bed, I always seemed to be up early. I was a natural early riser.

Exhausted from lack of sleep and my introduction to Wandsworth, when the lights went out at ten I fell blissfully asleep for the first time in days.

4

'Slopping Out'

I was right when I'd guessed Tommo was a snorer. Guido turned out to be a hybrid snorer and sniffer, and Manolitto whimpered.

My blissful sleep had not lasted. I had woken in the early hours, and then only slept fitfully. But I still awoke at six, mid-dream, and reality came flooding back. I lay staring at the ceiling, no radio for companionship, isolated from the outside world. I felt alone and depressed. It wasn't even twenty-four hours since I'd arrived in my new home, transferred from one hell-hole to another, and my calculations left me stunned: five hundred and thirty-five days to go. I backtracked through my mental calculations and found the concept of seventy-six weeks less distressing, eighteen months almost acceptable. I decided against getting a calendar.

As I lay waiting to get up I felt drained of energy. Only the prospect of setting in motion a telephone call to my son dragged me up. I rose, dressed and livened up in anticipation. When the door opened at seven-thirty I was out as fast as a greyhound from his trap.

No running on the landing was shouted at me from inches away as I passed an officer, and I slowed to a fast walk, but our cell was at the far end of the landing and by the time I reached the application officer there were already fifteen bodies in front of me.

'I need to book a telephone call, please,' I said to the shaven-headed officer when it was my turn. He stood and looked at me without saying a word. It must have been my puzzled look that prompted him to comment. 'I need to book a telephone call, *Guv*,' he said, emphasising the last word. I realised the pompous bastard wanted a title.

'I need to book a telephone call, Guv,' I repeated.

'Time?'

'Anytime after six, please, Guv.'

'No calls after four o'clock.'

'But . . .'

He cut me off before I could explain that my son might not be at home before four. 'Two times left: 3.40 or 3.50 – which do you want?'

'3.50, Guv,' I plumped for.

'Name and number?'

I pronounced and spelt my name out slowly so that he could write it down correctly, but the mess he made of it was a fair indication of his intelligence. No wonder we all have numbers, I thought.

'I also need to book a visit. I haven't had one yet and I need to know how to book one, Guv.'

'Is it due?' he asked.

'I don't know. I had a reception visit booked at Brixton but I don't know how to book one up here, Guv.'

'Ask the SO (Senior Officer) later,' he said. 'Now move along,' and I was dismissed. I had not been told any rules or regulations since arriving in prison and I had the distinct impression that the officer enjoyed making me feel uncomfortable. As I hurried back I decided that he'd probably been bullied at school. If he wasn't gay, as many of the officers in Wandsworth were reputed to be, I pitied his wife.

When I got back to the cell Guido's bucket was waiting for me. 'Do it properly, and scrub it out with the brush,' he said, as I picked it up at arm's length and disappeared out of the door. I suppose he had the right.

'Slopping Out'

In years to come there will be things that I shall doubtless forget about prison, but 'slopping out' won't be one of them. I walked along my side of the landing to the recess area which catered for forty-five of us, pushed open the saloon swing doors, and there it was – *Hell itself.*

With my first intake of breath the stench hit me and I almost gagged. In the far corner were two sit-down toilets, one with no door, the other with the door shut, but being only three feet of wood at hip height it offered little privacy. A queue of inmates holding toilet rolls waited as the two men, bent up with effort, tried to hurry. To my immediate right was the washing-up area for plates, cups and hands, a trough four foot by two foot, surrounded by a mass of bodies anxious to slosh water over the dirt. Three taps constantly blasting out freezing cold water ensured an overspill and in places the mess lay half an inch deep on the floor. To my immediate left were two dustbins for leftovers from the previous meal, but so important was it to get to the trough before the over-spill soaked trouser legs and feet that food was often slung onto the floor to add to the evil soup.

In the far corner, opposite the toilets, was the 'slopping out area' – two large porcelain sinks with huge plug-holes for the waste, and a tap that was either off or blasting out water with the force of a fireman's hose. I watched as the water splashed off the bottom of the buckets, sending spray everywhere. To my left, next to the dust-bins, were the urinals, blocked up and overflowing with deposited slop from the impatient, who couldn't wait for the waste sinks – the mess flowed freely.

I was so angry. I wanted to grab whoever was responsible for dragging this disgusting, inhuman practice into the 1990s by the scruff of the neck and throw them headlong into this filth. Forty-five inmates were expected to complete their tasks in ten minutes. Nice one. With gritted teeth and holding my breath for as long as possible I slopped out and returned to the cell, only to have to collect my toilet roll and wait my turn in the queue. It was some time before I calmed down.

*

Since I had arrived in prison the weather had been foul and nearly every day exercise had been cancelled. Now, for once, the sky was clear. At nine-thirty we were called out for exercise and I wandered out to the yard with Tommo and Guido. Manolitto elected to remain in the cell but there was no way I was going to forgo my second opportunity of fresh air in nearly two weeks.

No matter where you go in HMP Wandsworth, the internal structure of the prison means you have to pass through its geo-metrical centre, a circular hall which over the years has become a shrine to the regime. In the middle of the floor lies a marble circle embossed with a large brass star and any inmate who sets foot on this symbol of authority is in serious trouble. You pass round it anti-clockwise, in single file, without talking, hands out of pockets, shirt buttons done up to the neck, and scrutinised by gleeful officers who are ready to pounce and scream at any one who violates this ritual. Fortunately I'd been warned what to expect by Guido. It struck me that the only group of megalomaniacs who could have devised such an infantile tradition were second formers at my old boarding school. There were about fifty of us from 'A' wing heading out for exercise and the line moved slowly through the prison, but it wasn't too long before we reached the large iron door that led to the outside.

There are certain everyday expressions that through over-use lose much of their significance, and walking out into the yard I realised that 'fresh air' was one of them. I breathed it in as if it were an elixir, and it struck me how lucky I'd been to spend most of my life in the open. I gulped in the air and became heady with the 'fix' of oxygen. The yard was the size of three tennis courts back to back, surrounded on three sides by high fences with razor wire wrapped round the top. We had entered the yard from 'D' wing and as I stood surveying the scene I looked up at the building that blocked in the fourth side.

The wing looked as imposing as it was monstrous: like a huge three-decked man o' war, the small dark rectangular windows reminding me of the gun ports of the *Victory* in Portsmouth. It stretched away in the distance for a hundred yards or so in perfect symmetry, not a brick out of place. I knew our wing was identical, though our cell was effectively below the water line and hidden from view. It was a daunting place to live. Everything in the yard was grey and looked filthy, even the hundreds of tatty-looking pigeons that flew round or perched on the long wires that stretched from end to end. The wires were a protection against landing helicopters, the IRA having successfully broken out using that method a few years previously.

On the ground next to the wing building were paper parcels, and as we walked past them on our first circuit I turned to Guido: 'What's all this paper doing out here?'

'Shit parcels,' he replied.

'What the hell are they?' I asked, guessing but not wanting to believe.

'If you have a crap at night,' he explained, 'some cells throw it out the window. So don't fuckin' tread in one or you'll bring it in the cell.' I was shocked. I couldn't decide whether I was locked up with people who were naturally disgusting, or whether they were normal human beings who had been warped by the Wandsworth regime. I just couldn't believe we were allowed to walk about in such filth.

By now there must have been about two hundred inmates in the yard. About half joined the slow train moving continuously round, the other hundred or so sat on the ground at one end, forming two distinct groups: black and white. On each circuit we would pass within feet of a hundred pairs of staring eyes.

Occasionally a body would break rank from the train and bend to the ground. 'We call them "swoopers",' said Guido, who was looking decidedly pale. 'They're pickin' up fag butts'.

I watched as another 'swooper' fell on his prey amongst the pigeon crap, put the butt to his lips and lit up. I'd never smoked much, maybe five cigarettes a day, but I always discarded the cigarette after I'd smoked half. If I wasn't careful I was going to be followed round the exercise yard like a trawler followed by seagulls.

After a few more laps Guido's attention was caught by a small, bearded man, pretty much the same size as me, but older than most of the inmates – maybe mid-forties. His arms were folded across his chest as though he were cold. As we passed him on the far corner he told Guido that he'd be joining us next time round.

'Who's that?' I asked, knowing it might sound inquisitive but wanting to know whom I'd be mixing with.

'Just a mate I've done a bit of bird with. One of the best blaggers in London is Steve. Cossers are desperate to nick 'im, surveillance, the lot. All he's in for is a petty drugs charge; be out soon. One of the most respected guys in here, so watch your step.'

On the next circuit the small man moved smoothly into step with us and immediately nodded in my direction. 'He's sweet, our new cellmate – green but sweet,' said Guido.

'How do, the name's Steve,' said the bearded man, actually holding out his hand, my references from Guido apparently powerful.

'Hi, my name's John,' I said without expression. I'd never met an armed robber before and I thought the best bet would be to remain as forgettable as possible.

Steve turned back to Guido. 'Got any burn?' he asked.

'Got nuffin', but I'm cluckin' bad. Wanna do a card deal?'

'Fuckin' 'ell, you still on the gear?' said Steve.

'Yeah. 'Ad a boot yesterday mornin' and I'm starting to feel desperate. I need a joint bad.'

'We could do a deal with Floyd. Tommo, are you in?'

'Yeah,' grunted Tommo.

'What about your mate?' he said, looking at me.

I shook my head. 'Thanks for asking though,' I said. I knew they were talking about a drug deal and though I wasn't interested I appreciated being asked and included in the group. I thought of the young Spaniard back in the cell who was distancing himself from his potential allies. I'd learned the importance of getting on with people in my early days on the golf tour. I pitied the young man back in the cell, who probably felt the world was against him.

As we turned the far corner Guido flicked a nod towards a group of black men behind us and after a few moments we had company. 'Reespect, Guido,' said the dreadlocked black head.

'Card deal, Floyd, six for a quarter?'

The tall black man went into discussion with his partner and, after nodding agreement, turned back to Guido. 'Lunchtime, be last in the queue.'

'Sweet,' said Guido. The two black men peeled away and it seemed the deal was done.

Steve turned towards me. 'How long are you doin'?' he asked.

'Three years,' I said.

'He plays golf,' said Guido. 'Thought you'd like to know.'

'Fuckin' 'ell, I love golf,' said Steve. I couldn't believe it. 'You any good?' he went on.

'Not bad,' I said, trying to keep calm.

'What's your handicap?'

I had long since decided that my best chance of survival was to try to gain a powerful ally, and although I wanted to keep my past life quiet, it was now or never and I decided to trust my instincts. 'Well, actually, I didn't have one, I'm a professional – well . . . was.'

'Fuck off.'

'No, honestly, I was.'

For the next few minutes I was quizzed in depth about my golf and what I was doing in 'Wanno', and I was pleased that Guido didn't seem to notice that I had previously held back when the subject had been broached in the cell.

'Jesus, this ain't the place for you, mate,' Steve proclaimed. 'Look, I've gotta go now but we've gotta talk.' He turned towards Guido. 'Take care of him, I want a golf lesson,' and with that, he slid away.

'Seems a nice guy,' I said to my companions.

'Hard as nails is Steve. Plunged a couple of nonces in Parkhurst. Get on the wrong side of him and you're history. He knows everyone.'

Bloody hell, I thought, *better not give him a slice!*

★

On our way back to the cell I tried in vain to spot the SO to ask him about my visit but I couldn't see him and we were then 'banged up' till lunchtime.

'Tell me,' I asked Guido, who'd visibly livened up since the drug deal had been fixed, 'what does "plunged a couple of nonces" mean?'

'You don't know what a nonce is?'

'Not really.'

'A nonce is a sex offender, child molester, anything dodgy.'

'I thought they were kept separate, for their own protection,' I said.

'Yeah, well, they start off on the numbers – protection under rule 43 – where they're locked up on their own, but as time passes they get filtered into the system. When they're found out they're done.'

'How do the guys find out though?'

'Screws tell 'em, they hate "bacons" as much as us.'

'And then they're plunged?'

Guido lay down on his bed and kicked off his shoes. 'Plungin's a stabbin', but depends on what they've done. Sometimes it's a bucket of boilin' water with sugar in it thrown over their bollocks – rips all the skin off, fuckin' terrible that is. Saw it done to a geezer in Albany once, bloke died of a heart attack, good riddance though if you ask me.'

I tried to imagine the pain, the sight of another human being punished in such a way, even if he were a child molester or a rapist. It seemed that whatever punishment the courts handed out, it was nothing compared with that meted out by prison inmates. I wondered if during the next eighteen months I would see prison justice carried out.

5

Pete 'the Psycho'

Discovering information from officers in Wandsworth reminded me of when I was a kid picking up rocks on the beach to find crabs. All the rocks looked the same, but some hid jewels.

At lunchtime when the door opened I made a beeline for the landing office but, with the elusive SO still unavailable and my frustration levels climbing, I threw out the question to an officer no more senior than the one I'd asked in the morning. 'Guv, could you tell me how I go about booking a visit?' This time I hit the jackpot.

'Where've you come from?'

'Brixton, Guv.'

'Did you have a visit booked before transfer?'

'Yes, for today, Guv.'

'Your people can have the visit here tomorrow, if you can let them know.'

WOW! I couldn't believe it was so simple after the other officer had been so unhelpful. 'Thanks, Guv,' I said. 'One more thing. I still haven't got a bucket and I need one, Guv.'

'You'll have to ask someone else. Now move along.'

I came to learn that each officer only had one piece of information to impart. Their capacity to help seemed to be determined by their IQ. I marked this one down as the 'visits officer' and moved along to the back of the long dinner queue.

Every meal is an explosive situation in Wandsworth. 'Twisting' doesn't go on (not even Oliver would have the nerve to ask for more), and 'portion control' is meant to ensure equal distribution; but jealousy is rife among the starving and, as the queue moves along the counter, each inmate scrutinises the amount on the plates in front and behind, to make sure he's not losing out. Perhaps the fuse paper of the inmate in front of me had been lit earlier in the day, but the larger sausage handed out to the guy next to him started the countdown.

'Hey, mate, give us a bit of your sausage.'

'Fuck off.'

THREE . . .

'Don't tell me to fuck off, you lucky bastard.'

TWO . . .

The finger in the chest led to the main rockets firing.

ONE . . .

'Don't prod me, you wanker!'

ZERO: WE HAVE LIFT-OFF . . .

I'd never seen a fight before, not a violent one. A fist flashed out taking the guy with the over-large sausage in the neck; he stumbled. A left foot swung out and caught him on the knee, which neatly deflected the boot in the groin. He went down with his sausage like a ton of bricks, only to take a right foot in his chest. I just caught a glimpse as the boot lashed into his head.

The next moment pandemonium broke out. A whistle was blown and suddenly every officer in the place threw themselves into the mêlée, screaming *Behind your doors!* – a command leaving no room for misunderstanding, but I was so far away from my cell that I was in two minds what to do. A hand grabbed my arm and pulled me violently into the nearest cell. The door slammed shut and I turned to see Steve the blagger. 'When they say "Get behind the door," you gotta move quicker than that,' he said. 'You'll get bent up if you don't'.

'Thanks, Steve, I appreciate it,' I said, then moments later, 'What's "bent up" mean?'

Steve moved to the door and looked through the small peephole. 'Come 'ere,' he said, nodding towards the hole.

I moved to his side and squinting, with one eye closed, I had a full view of the fight scene on the landing. There must have been six officers outside, and initially all I could see was a wall of uniforms, but after a moment they separated, and I could see the inmate who had started the trouble. His right arm was bent up behind his back in an arm lock so extreme that to relieve the pain the man automatically bent forward. An officer had his neck in a hold and was twisting his head to one side at an impossible angle. Truncheons were in their hands but I couldn't see whether they'd been used. The man was then led away, screaming in pain. I couldn't see the other inmate, but he was no longer on the floor. I turned back to Steve. 'Looks painful,' I said.

'Fuckin' is,' he said. 'Probably get more painful, too, when they get him on the block.'

'What happened to the bloke on the floor?'

'Down the block, too, if he's well enough. They'll sort it out later but most of the time, guilty or innocent, a fight's a fight and he'll get blamed just as much.'

'All for a bit of sausage,' I said.

'Listen,' said Steve. 'Guys set off at the smallest thing. I knew a bloke in Long Lartin once who borrowed a quarter ounce of burn off a geezer. When he was asked to return it he told the bloke he'd borrowed it from that he hadn't got it. As he's talking the burn falls out of the cupboard. Guy comes back twenty minutes later, stabs him forty-eight times, dead as a dodo. Geezers are right on the edge in 'ere. You gotta recognise the signs.'

I nodded. I knew when to listen – this was advice from somebody who knew what he was talking about. We spoke for a few minutes and after a while the door opened and we were let out. There were no signs of the fight on the landing, everything was back to normal and not one inmate displayed any reaction. 'How often does that happen?' I asked.

'Every time the whistle blows,' said Steve. 'Once a day at least.'

Once again we joined the queue and eventually I collected my sausage and cabbage leaf. 'Thanks for the help again, Steve,' I said, as I made my way to leave.

'Catch you later,' he said, nodding, and then as an afterthought, 'Keep your head down. Don't want to see you get a battering.'

Back in the cell I managed two mouthfuls of my fat-soaked sausage and threw the remains in the bowl we used for rubbish. Guido managed half of his and even Tommo couldn't eat the revolting morsel.

Because of the fight the lunchtime drug deal had been postponed, and Guido was trying to work out whether it could be completed during 'association', when, for two hours, inmates were allowed to mix. It supposedly took place every two days, but more often than not it was cancelled because of staff shortages. Theoretically, we were meant to have association that afternoon.

Suddenly we heard keys rattling in the door and moments later it swung open. An officer came in and looked round. 'Esposito?' he asked.

'Guv?' answered the young Spaniard.

'Pack your gear; you're moving.'

We watched as Manolitto stuffed his possessions into a large transparent plastic bag. Within minutes he walked out of the cell. It all happened so quickly. No goodbyes, nothing. It seemed really strange to me, so cold and impersonal, almost like not shaking hands after a game of golf.

'Must've been worried you were goin' to batter 'im and asked for a transfer, Tommo. That's why the screw stayed – keep us off 'im.'

'Yeah, well, good riddance,' said Tommo.

'Where's he gone to?' I asked.

'Dunno. Another wing, maybe another nick. They never tell you.'

I wasn't exactly feeling at home, but to some extent I'd settled down, and to find a spare bed waiting to be filled I found disconcerting. Because there was no opportunity of airing frustration against the guards, someone had to take the brunt of pent-up anger. Manolitto had been persecuted by Tommo not because he was Spanish, young, or introverted, but because he presented the easiest target in the cell. Someone had to be the fall guy. Manolitto must have hoped that, as 'the new boy', I would take some of the flack, particularly as I looked fairly small and vulnerable. It must have been a disappointment to find that Tommo still regarded him as the one to suffer. I was left hoping that when the new man arrived I would be able to retain my position of third in the pecking-order.

At two o'clock the door opened for association and, on Guido's advice, I dived out with my towel and soap and headed for the communal showers on the other side of the landing.

I had listened to so much speculation about rape and buggery being the biggest pastime in prison that it was a case of head down, back to the wall, and escape as quickly as possible. Six of us crowded into the shower at the same time, and I can't remember ever washing so quickly. It was such a relief to remove the dirt from Brixton, the transfer and a day in Wandsworth. It was also a relief to emerge unscathed. My whole body tingled when I got out, not because of hot water (that had already run out) but because the prison-issue soap I had been given had peculiar bits in that made it like sand paper. But whether scraped or washed clean it felt great.

After towelling down, while trying to keep my clothes off a floor that was already under water, I dressed quickly and then headed out to the landing. My telephone call, booked for around four o'clock, was to take place during the two hours' association, so I had the phone card I'd acquired in Brixton with me. I dumped my towel and soap by the cell door, pinpointed the exact location of each of my allies (knowing that my loudest shout would alert them), and then, rather bravely, I wandered round to have a look. I tried to appear as casual as possible – as though I belonged. But no sooner had I taken three paces when a voice shouted out, 'Hey, you!' I looked around to see an officer glaring at me. 'Come here,' he said, pointing to a spot in front of him. I made my way across.

He put his face close up to mine, and I could smell his breath. 'Did I see you with your hands in your pocket?'

'Yes, Guv,' I said, not realising I had done something wrong.

'You know that's against the rules,' he said with a scowl.

'I thought it was only round the star, Guv.'

'Well, it's not. It's everywhere.' He then leaned right up close. 'If I ever see you with your hands in your pocket again – you'll end up down the block,' he warned with a sickening grin. I was then dismissed. I wandered off, knowing I had been lucky to survive, but until I knew the ropes, it was likely that, somewhere along the line, I would inadvertently break the rules again. The officers must have had fun playing this game. The odds of winning were stacked heavily in their favour.

With my hands now firmly stuck to my sides, I made my way to the end of the landing where a pool table was constantly in use, but the menacing figures holding the cues reminded me of a Charles Bronson film where one of the bad guys was given a severe beating, so I avoided getting too close. Right outside our cell was a table tennis table, but the light was so bad that it seemed playing was done mainly by feel, and most of the time was spent hunting for the ball. It really was *that* dark. The electric lights were weak and any natural light from the landing above (which, being above ground, had windows) was shut out by the large nets that were strung above us. These were there to catch anything thrown from the other landings, as the 'dungeon' was the dumping ground for lousy lunches and the occasional 'shit parcel'. It had also saved the lives of numerous officers who had been pitched over the side.

At the other end of the landing was a television and I made my way towards it. During association a video was shown, and the one that day was a violent American gangster film. It seemed an odd choice for some potentially volatile people, but I stayed to watch for a few minutes. There were probably thirty men tightly packed into the dark space underneath the landing stairs and most were standing as there were only half a dozen chairs. It was like entering a cave.

I've never been one for communal television watching. It's something I had to endure though, when I was the professional at my club. After 'captain–pro' matches on Saturday afternoons, I used to sit with the members in the luxurious clubhouse watching golf tournaments beamed live from Sky Sports. I had a very good relationship with the members, but I used to cringe at the incessant analysis, as every opinion under the sun (except the right one) was offered as to why Sandy Lyle had hit out of bounds, or why Langer had missed another putt. Watching television in Wandsworth was exactly the same, but when the bad guys took their first drubbing the ensuing comments came from men who knew what they were talking about.

'That's shit, he'd be dead by now. Look at him, he's still running around.'

'Yeah, and that bird, she's just plunged the geezer and not a drop of blood on her.'

'Can't plunge a guy like that, anyway.'

Whoever the director was, he took some fearful criticism, and I wondered how he would've handled the views of the 'experts'.

Time passed slowly but finally, after the umpteenth look at the cheap watch I had bought specially for prison, it was time for my call and I climbed the stairs to the telephone area. The six phones attached to the wall were within feet of the landing office and there was no privacy: all conversations were recorded and listened to. I walked up to the office to register. 'I've got a phone call booked for 3.50, Guv.'

'Show us your phonecard.'

I took out the green plastic card similar to those used on the outside and handed it to the officer. 'Where did you get this?' he said, glaring at me.

'I brought it with me from Brixton, Guv.'

'It's not signed on the back.' On the back of the card there was a small place for your signature but at Brixton, a similar category 'B' prison, you didn't need to sign the cards.

'I didn't know you had to, Guv. I mean at Brixton . . .'

'I don't give a fuck about Brixton. What's your name?'

'Hoskison, Guv.'

'If I ever catch you with an unsigned card again, Hodgkiss, I'll put you on report. Understand? You're lucky I'm going to let you make this call.'

When I took back my card I was trembling. I can't remember ever having to bite my tongue as I did then. How the hell was I to know you had to sign the card? It was as if information were deliberately withheld to cause maximum humiliation. I was directed to phone number six. I dialled the number. Pulse-rate up around a hundred and ten, I waited for an answer.

'Hello,' said my son. His little voice hit me with the force of a battering ram and I almost broke.

'Hi, Ben, how are you?' I said, trying to make my voice sound light and happy.

'Dad, how are you doing?' he cried out, sounding really excited. 'What's it like in jail?' I'd told my son I was going to prison six weeks before the trial. Even though Ben was living with his mother I saw him almost every day. He was following me on his bike one morning as I went for a run – one of the many things we did together. I stopped after a couple of miles and walked as I explained I wouldn't be around for some time. I can still remember his face as I told him, but I refused to make it a sad affair, and explained what a great time we'd have in the future. He took the news well. Even so, both my ex, Jane, and I kept a close watch for signs of any adverse reaction. A few days later on his way home from school he said, 'Mum, Tony doesn't believe me – Dad *is* going to jail, isn't he?' Jane didn't know whether to laugh or cry. His teacher claimed it was the best possible reaction, that Ben was bottling up nothing and accepting it well, probably because we had made the least fuss of the tragedy for his sake.

Hearing his happy bubbling voice on the phone raised my

spirits. We chatted for about four minutes, but I was constantly aware that my valuable card was running low and that I didn't have long. At that time of day the telephone ate the units with an insatiable appetite and much faster than a phone on the outside. Now my time for this call had run out. I promised Ben I would phone again the next day, and explained that if I didn't call, it wouldn't be because I didn't want to, but because I couldn't. Then I put the phone down. Only a few minutes was left before my time was up. I didn't have time to think, I simply dialled the next number.

After asking for Bronya's department at work and waiting impatiently while I was put through to the correct extension I was finally greeted with a shriek of delight. It's true I had told Bronya not to wait for me, but deep down I so hoped that she would. It was more an act of self-preservation than generosity. Throughout the previous year she had supported me more than I could have possibly hoped, and was one of the main reasons I had been able to survive, if not the main reason. The thought that she would be there at the end of my sentence was something that I just couldn't allow myself to hope for. But now my need to see her overrode any reservations, and I had included her on the reception visit slip I had sent my father. We spoke only a few words but there was really no need to talk at all. Her empathy simply flooded through.

'Time's up,' an officer blasted at me from inches away, shattering the moment with practised skill. A quick goodbye, and Bronya and I were separated. I turned back to the insanity of Wandsworth.

Emotionally I had been watered and fed. Undeniably the telephone calls were a lifeline. But they left me with an overwhelming feeling of sadness. If I felt so bad after a phone call, I wondered, how would I cope after my father's and Bronya's visit the next day?

Back in the cell Guido and Tommo were in a good mood and this helped to sweep away my feeling of melancholy. The card deal delayed at lunch had now been completed and Tommo had also 'ponced' some burn. They were discussing whether to light up a 'spliff' there and then, but their decision to wait until after 'bang up' proved to be the right one, for, moments later, the door swung open and our new cellmate entered. It was the first time I'd seen Guido anything but confident – I could almost hear the alarm bells. The new man seemed to ooze evil. He was extraordinarily thick-set, about five foot ten, and his mouth was constantly at work as though he'd eaten something and was trying to recapture the taste. I moved across and sat down next to Tommo on his bed.

'Where you from?' Guido asked the new man warily.

'Brixton,' he answered. 'Name's Pete,' he added, and turned round to unpack his things. (The officer had left the light on.)

'On the gear, are you?' Guido asked. A question prompted (I found out later) by the mouth movement – a sure sign of an addict.

'Yeah, just spent a month in the hospital unit suffering large amounts of "liquid cosh". Talk about cluckin'. Gotta stay here for tests now. Bastards want to send me back to Broadmoor.'

Broadmoor! My God!

'What are you in for?' Guido asked.

'Stabbed a copper,' he paused, then dropped the bombshell. 'With a needle.'

I glanced at Guido and saw him sign to Tommo.

'What happened?' Tommo enquired, pushing for the full story.

'I was jackin' up when the cosser bastards burst in. Stabbed one in the leg – told 'im I was HIV positive.'

I sensed Tommo tense and I shifted my position further onto the bed so that his body was directly between me and our bestial inter-loper.

'Are you?' asked Guido, who was now standing close to us at the end of his bed.

'Dunno. I wanted to get psychoed off. I hear voices, see. Told the judge I wanted to give all coppers Aids. Took a right beating in the cells that night; bastards kicked my ribs in.'

Guido had apparently heard enough and moved back into the depths of his territory. Tommo didn't seem to mind that I remained in his. We sat in silence for some time, reflecting on our new cell-mate.

It seemed an eternity until five o'clock, when the door opened for tea. As soon as Pete left the cell, the three of us huddled together.

'He's a fuckin' psycho,' Guido said. 'Gotta get rid of him.' He turned to Tommo for his verdict.

'He's a bad 'un. Gotta jog 'im on.'

They both turned to me and I realised they were asking my opinion. I was surprised and in a ridiculous way delighted that mine counted. 'Scares the living daylights out of me. He's terrifying, needs putting down,' I said, making it a unaminous verdict.

'Right, we won't be able to talk much tonight,' Guido said. 'John, first thing in the morning, get to the SO, and tell 'im how fuckin' dodgy Pete is, and that he's got to be moved. We'll back you up.'

'Why me?' I said, aghast.

''Cos the screws don't trust us and they'll already have sussed you as a straight goer. It's the only way, trust me. They'd never do what we asked'.

'Do it, John. It's the only way to get rid of 'im,' Tommo added. 'Just don't take no for an answer.'

With the other two showing so much concern I became even more nervous. 'All right,' I agreed. 'I'll do it if I can find him, but you guys had better watch over me tonight – don't let that nutter come anywhere near me.'

After tea, which consisted of two slices of dry bread and a piece of liver with so many veins running through it that it was impossible to cut with a plastic knife, a deep sense of foreboding settled on the cell. None of us relished the prospect of the forthcoming night. There was little talk; it was as if we were getting ready for battle. What made matters worse was the new man's weird behaviour as he sat on his bed, rocking from side to side, seemingly locked away in a secret world of his own.

Just before lights out, I glanced across sternly for a last look at my allies – then I lay back. When darkness invaded the cell, sheer physical fear made me nauseous.

6

My First Prison Visit

My survival instinct kept me on red alert throughout the night and I dozed fitfully, my resting pulse-rate sliding to only a fraction under eighty. Only once did my heart threaten to come bursting through my rib cage.

At three o'clock, the Broadmoor veteran clambered out of bed, used his bucket, and went on tour. A quick sortie into Tommo's territory raised the hairs on the back of my neck. Then he crossed onto my side of the cell and 'mission control' hit the panic button. His menacing bulk came to a halt two paces from me. He stood immobile, his dark shadowy figure looming over me. I experienced fear of a different order: not the fear of missing a putt or mortgage payment, this was gut-churning, sickening, physical fear and my heart-rate jumped into new territory. I lay very still, but underneath my pillow my hand gripped my plastic knife. Recently in Wandsworth one of the inmates had suffered an attack from his cellmate. At razor point he'd been pushed onto the bed and only saved from the intended rape by an officer who happened to look through the peephole and intervened. My imagination knew no boundaries and, if pushed, I was ready to spring into action. I could hear the monster's heavy breathing and, through half-closed eyes, I watched his body swaying back and forth. My neck and shoulder muscles were bunched with tension, ready to deliver a frenzied attack.

46

After an interminable pause, he turned and made his way back to his bed. As I tried to relax I felt enormous empathy for anyone who reacts when threatened. I would probably have been prosecuted for grievous bodily harm had I been pushed to defend myself using my knife. One is meant to use minimum force. The law, I decided, must have been made by someone who'd never been scared witless.

In the morning as soon as the door opened, I headed straight for the SO and explained our problem. I hoped for a positive answer.

'I thought we might have problems there,' he said, looking at me. 'I'll see what I can do.'

He must have seen the worry in my face, but even so, he didn't appear to be concerned. I wandered back to the cell with little optimism. Guido and Tommo were waiting for me, Pete was slopping out.

'Well?' they asked in unison.

'I'm not sure. I gave it my best shot. We'll just have to wait and see. Some bloody lookouts you were, though, the guy was on the prowl at three.'

'I know. I was awake. I was just shitting myself, that's all,' Guido said. 'Don't worry, I would have helped if he'd done anything. Fuckin' scary though, isn't he?' he added, grinning.

Breakfast was swallowed in silence, no one felt like talking. The reality of our predicament was sinking in – perhaps there might be another night ahead with the madman. But as we finished, the door opened and three officers came in – in fact the most brutal of the regime who permanently roamed the 'dungeon' keeping 'the scum' in order.

'Pack your gear, Naylor, you're moving down the landing – your cellmates don't like you.'

Pete looked round, the comment needless, the reaction immediate. 'What d'you mean they don't fuckin' like me?' he growled menacingly, his eyes passing from Tommo to Guido and

47

landing on me. I couldn't afford to look guilty, I just tried to look puzzled.

'You'll be better off somewhere else, mate,' Guido said, trying to break the tension.

Pete grunted, clearly seething that he'd been 'fitted up', but with the officers watching he could only pack his gear. Five minutes later he was gone.

'What bastards!' I said, when the door slammed shut. There had been no need to mention that we had instigated the move and, perhaps naively, it was only then that I realised that these officers couldn't be trusted.

'Better keep out of his way for a while,' Guido said.

Outside the rain hammered down, and it was obvious that exercise would be cancelled. Although I felt tired, I was also tense and needed to do something energetic to relieve the stress. For ten years, five times a week, I'd run four miles, but during my year awaiting trial I had stepped up the routine, knowing that I would need to be fit to cope with the pressure. Over the last few months I had doubled my weekly mileage but since entering prison I'd been totally inactive and my body yearned for exercise.

'Look, guys,' I said, 'I'm going to do some jogging on the spot. Okay?'

Tommo smirked. 'Joggin' in 'ere?' he said. 'Are you sure?'

I sat on my bed, took off my clothes and, wearing only prison boxer shorts and training shoes, I limbered up. I started off, conscious of the two watching.

'He's a fuckin' nutter,' said Tommo. 'Should be 'im who's goin' to Broadmoor.'

I thought back to where I used to do my jogging – a stark contrast to my present surroundings. I tried to lose myself in effort as I looked at the grey wall that faced me. Drops of sweat splattered onto the floor as I started to build up speed and out of the corner of my eye I could see Guido, lying motionless, as if mesmerised by my pounding feet. It took me about ten minutes of heavy-duty work to reach that blissful point where through sheer physical exertion the body, for once, transcends the power of the mind and all thought is blocked.

An hour later my feet were in such pain that I couldn't carry on so I came to a halt. I looked at my two cellmates. 'Thanks,' I said. They shrugged acceptance.

No matter how hard or inconvenient it might be, I was determined to keep my exercise going in prison. In the 'dungeon' I was surrounded by gaunt, unhealthy-looking men, their flaccid muscles reflecting their lack of spirit. Exercise had been an important part of my life and I clung on to my fitness. It represented much more than just an economical heart-rate – it gave me access to temporary oblivion.

Unfortunately, whilst the exercise was brilliant, the aftermath was not. I stripped naked, put my bowl of cold water next to my bed and washed down. With my visit coming up, I wanted to be as presentable as possible, but with no shower available a damn good wash was the only option.

Half an hour later, the door opened and an officer came in to announce that the library would be open for ten minutes. I desperately needed something to read so I headed up to the second landing with Guido following.

Each wing in Wandsworth has its own library. It sounds good but since it consisted of two cells knocked into one, it was rather on the small side, in fact very much so. Only allowing ten inmates into the library at one time was not a security measure: there was simply no more space.

All the reading material available for over two hundred inmates was crammed into four bookcases. One section contained a large assortment of comics and magazines, every one of which Guido assured me he had read. Opposite, on the far wall beneath the window, were the foreign language and easy-to-read books. I browsed through a couple of these and was astonished at the simplicity of content, which reminded me of the 'Janet and John' books I had read years ago when I was learning to read. I couldn't help but smile and think of Bronya. Ever since I had met her she had been trying to persuade me to read something other than a Dick Francis or a Terry Pratchett. Finding me looking at *Nerve* in gigantic print would have made her throw back her head in exasperation.

Eventually I selected a very grubby version of Jeffrey Archer's *Kane and Abel* from the main fiction section. I chose it because it was the thickest book there, plenty of pages being my main priority, as our next visit to the library was a whole week away. Guido, armed with a *Judge Dredd* comic (which he'd read once before), followed me onto the landing.

'Why don't you try a good book?' I suggested.

'Nah. Never read a book, they take too long if you ask me.'

Well, you're not going anywhere, I thought. It seemed there was little enthusiasm to do *anything* in Wandsworth. Just a load of apathetic bodies idly waiting to get back on the street.

By the time we returned to the 'dungeon' we had a new cellmate. The turnover and shifting of inmates was incredible. Our new man had been moved from the other end of the landing. He explained that he'd fallen out with his other cellmates. Not another nutter, I thought. But no, Tony McCloud was just an eccentric Scotsman, and a very fit-looking Scot at that, who was tanned (sure sign of only recent imprisonment), about forty, and who obviously knew the game.

'Got any burn?' he asked in his thick Scottish accent, beating Guido to the draw.

'Got nuffin',' said Tommo, who was lying on his bed staring at the ceiling.

'Canteen tomorrow, thank fuck,' observed Guido.

Canteen day is about the most important event in prison life. Each week, inmates are allowed to spend their wages if they have a job, for instance cleaning (an average of £6), and, if they have any, up to £10 of private cash. With that money they have to buy phonecards, at £2 each, all toiletries (I'd been told not to rely on prison soap and toothpaste, all too often the stores run out) and, if there's anything left, tobacco or food, depending on their priorities. With such a small amount to spend it is inevitable that two or three days before canteen day, provisions run out and 'burn' becomes a much sought-after commodity on the black market. Guido and Tommo tried to overcome the problem by keeping their cigarette butts in a tin. When they ran out of fresh 'burn', the next stage would be to unravel the old butts and rescue any tobacco that was left. After that was used, like all the other inmates desperate for a smoke, the only course available was to borrow. Wandsworth was definitely a 'sellers' market' and several inmates specialised in making a 'quick buck'. The universal 'deal' in Wandsworth was 'borrow one, pay back two' and if you were willing to pay the price a deal was always available.

For many the temptation was too great to miss. They would borrow, knowing full well that they would be unable to pay back the following week. Over the months it became clear that canteen day was also when punishment for missing a payment was meted out for all to see. Every new prison inmate should be warned about the dangers of borrowing.

Canteen day was not going to be much of an event for me, as it takes an eternity for private cash to be transferred from one prison to another, and I'd already been told that all I would have to spend was £2.50. I could have borrowed some items but I knew it was the road to ruin. I was simply going to have to be more than frugal for quite some time.

Tony, our new cellmate, turned out to be an invader of space. He walked round the cell taking the unusual step of shaking hands, but then, rather than withdrawing he stayed close, within the 'personal zone', and I found him somewhat unnerving.

'*Kane and Abel*?' he said, his eyebrows rising with interest as he noticed the book on my bed.

'Yes, a good long read.'

'Good ending, when the two guys . . .'

'Shut up, Tony,' I interrupted, before he gave the game away, but Guido, grinning, decided to push for more.

'Go on, Tony, when the two guys what?'

'Don't say a word, Tony,' I said, between clenched teeth.

Guido tried to get the answer from the Scot but my warning was apparently enough, and nothing more was said, though I knew Guido was unlikely to give up completely. It was too good a game. Fortunately the door opened and it was time for lunch. I was becoming accustomed to sitting on my bed, eating off a precariously balanced plate, and normally I would have tried to eat what was on offer. However, with my visit not far away I was feeling that familiar sensation of butterflies that I experienced before a golf tournament, so I missed out lunch and lay quietly on my bed reading and waiting for my first prison visit.

At three o'clock the door opened and I was on my way: through the prison, round the central brass star (where again I marvelled at the enormous pleasure it afforded the gleeful guards, lying in wait for a new inmate to castigate), and on to the reception wing. By the time we reached the entrance to the visit-area my pulse was racing.

'Hodgkinson,' shouted the officer who had escorted me, and then left me standing alone at the gate. I was wound up tense with anticipation and uncertainty. My thoughts drifted back to 1991, when I had qualified to play in the British Open at Royal Birkdale. As I stood on the first tee waiting for the tournament to start, I was so nervous. At the time I was suffering from a dreadful bout of 'yips' on the greens. Members from my club had driven up from Surrey especially to support me. Television cameras covered the whole event and every score was to be published in the paper. I had considered withdrawing, afraid that I would achieve a dreadful score which would be tantamount to professional suicide. In those circumstances, perhaps more than any other, I had disciplined myself to deal with one hole at a time. Somehow I managed to make the cut, play on the last two days and pick up the biggest cheque of my career to date. I thought I would never experience tension like it, but I was very nearly sick waiting to be called through to my visit in Wandsworth.

Eventually, a rather dirty-looking guard, smelling strongly of whisky, let me through and led me to a small room.

'Got anything you shouldn't have?' he snapped.

Not knowing what I was allowed, it seemed a ridiculous question to me. I had nothing to declare and passed on to the next section.

'Hands above head,' he ordered, and I duly obeyed. It was only a rub-down search, one of many that inmates are randomly subjected to, but the involuntary reflex still appeared as he frisked my crotch. The other officer present stepped forward and held out a revoltingly soiled harness, which was slipped over my head and fastened behind my back. It was worn to stop inmates escaping by swapping places with visitors, but it made me feel exceptionally degraded – which may well have been its secret objective. I felt like a carthorse and was glad my son Ben wasn't coming to see me.

Given the nod, I walked through to the visits room, where I was led to an empty table. It was a small room, considering over seven hundred inmates used it, and I realised why the visits in Wandsworth were so short – twenty minutes every two weeks. Guards sat on raised platforms near each table and cameras attached to the ceiling were positioned to home in on any irregular transactions.

While I waited, watching the entrance door, I thought of Tommo who was expecting to pick up a drugs parcel, and wondered how on earth the transfer could be carried out with such tight security. Above the door was a notice that stated visitors found with drugs were liable to prosecution. The penalty would be six months in prison.

After a long wait, a door opened and Bronya and my father walked in. At first they couldn't see me and for some seconds I watched them impassively as I tried to adjust to the rush of affection that swept through me. Then they spotted me. From across the room I saw them smile and as they walked towards me I felt my bottom lip start to tremble. They must have known that I was choked with emotion because they didn't expect me to speak for a few moments, and it was all I needed to pull myself together and put on a smile.

I had tried really hard to make myself presentable but, without any mirrors in the prison, except for the small one we were issued with, I had no true impression of how I was looking. I could see, though, that they were shocked by my appearance. I'd never been very big but during the last two weeks I must have lost over a stone. 'How are you?' asked my father, showing immense concern as he sat down opposite me at the small table.

'I'm fine, Dad – really,' I forced out.

'But you're so thin – you've got to make sure you eat properly.'

'It's only because my clothes are big, Dad, don't worry,' I said, but it was as though somebody else was speaking. I yearned for a reassuring hug but only minimal physical contact was allowed.

The visits room had a snack bar selling refreshments – tea, coffee, fizzy drinks, crisps, that sort of thing – a chance for the inmates to OD on Mars Bars. My father offered to fetch the tea and buy me a few special treats, leaving Bronya and me alone.

We sat opposite each other at the table and at first I found it very difficult to talk. She was staring at me and I could see how worried she looked. 'I really am all right,' I said, trying to reassure her. But she'd seen me through the worst year of my life and could now read me like a book.

'No, you're not,' she said, a tear running down her cheek.

'Did you have to wait long?' I asked. She knew I would not be able to cope with pity – I was trying to keep my emotions on hold, so that I wouldn't break down. Reluctantly she let the conversation drift off in another direction.

'You know how I can't cope with queues,' she said bravely. 'Well, Wandsworth could give tips to Disney World. They make you do it in stages.'

She described how they'd played the waiting game: standing out in the cold on the prison steps – and waiting; checking in at the visitors' centre – and waiting; being escorted through to the waiting-room, and waiting to be searched. Then the long wait before finally being called.

I reached across to hold her hand. 'You're freezing,' we both said simultaneously. I explained why I was cold. Being in one of the last cells on the block meant that not only was the food cold by the time it reached us – so was the heating pipe.

'Can't you complain?'

'No.'

'We've got to get you out of here,' she said.

I couldn't manage more than one Mars Bar, but later I regretted not stuffing myself whilst I had the opportunity. My father told me about the marvellous support I was getting from friends and former colleagues, and how everyone was quite sure that it would be only a matter of a couple of weeks before I was sent to serve out my sentence at Ford Open Prison.

Both my father and Bronya had been busy writing to official bodies, trying to ascertain prison procedures. Both had been fobbed off by Wandsworth. 'The prison does not enter into conversation with either friends or family of the prisoner,' they had been told. The bad news was that after continually pestering my probation officer with phone calls, Bronya had finally been told that it would be unlikely for me to reach 'D' category status until I had served at least six months. Until then I would be a 'C' category prisoner – someone who could not be trusted.

And then, in no time at all, an officer came over to us. 'Finish your visit,' he said. New to the situation and anxious not to put a foot wrong, the three of us stood up straight away and said our goodbyes. With Bronya and my father watching I fought to maintain some dignity as I was led away.

Back in the cell I lay on my bed and considered the age-old question: is it better to experience elation and excitement, that will invariably be followed by depression, or to go through life taking no risks? Their visit had been brilliant, but the knowledge that it would be two weeks before the next was intensely depressing. Some prisoners preferred never to have visits: they were simply too painful. But for me the pleasure far outweighed the pain. If a phone call was the equivalent of being watered and fed, Bronya's and my father's visit amounted to an emotional banquet.

7

'Chasing the Dragon'

An hour after I had returned from my visit, Tommo came back to the cell smiling like a cat who'd stolen the cream. The parcel of drugs he'd been expecting had obviously been delivered.

'You got it!' exclaimed Guido, who had been sweating profusely in anticipation.

'Yeah. Had to swallow it though – the screws were watching too closely.'

'You'll have to puke it up. I've gotta have it,' said Guido.

'I can't,' said Tommo. 'Never been able to.'

Guido leapt up. 'No' was not an option. 'Listen,' he said, going over to the corner where his water jug lay. 'We'll fill this up with salt – you drink it – you'll bring it up all right.'

'I hate that,' Tommo said, but Guido was not to be deterred. He poured salt into the jug and stirred it. He handed the jug of brine to Tommo.

'Go on, mate, drink it quick.'

Guido's need for a 'fix' dominated the situation and, with admirable bravery, Tommo took the jug and started drinking. Water poured down his chin, soaking his shirt, but he managed to gulp down the whole pint. As soon as he'd finished he began to gag. I watched, cringing – if anyone was going to throw up it was me.

Guido held his slop bucket in front of Tommo's face and I heard the liquid slosh down onto the bottom.

'Fuck it,' said Guido. 'It hasn't come out. You'll have to try again.' He came across to me. 'Borrow your water, John?' he asked, but it wasn't really a question. Before I could answer he picked up the new water jug I had been given with a slop bucket and poured in more salt.

'Go on, my son,' urged Guido, as Tommo manfully downed a further pint of brine. The salt, I learned, had been collected over a long period and was saved for just such emergencies. This time, as the contents of Tommo's stomach were spewed out, Guido yelled in delight. 'There it is! There it is!' he shouted, and reached into the mess to extract the small cellophane packet. It was a sight that I shall never forget.

The drugs, Tommo informed me, had been collected in the usual way, and I couldn't believe it was so easy. The visitor surreptitiously drops the 'joey' into a cup of tea, which is then drunk by the inmate. The penalty for an inmate who is caught is a mere few days added to his sentence. I would have thought six months in prison for the visitor might have acted as an adequate deterrent, but apparently not. A threat only becomes a deterrent if there's a danger of being caught and, months later, I realised that detection under the current security regime is very rare indeed.

Tea came and went and I could feel the excitement mounting in the cell. Tommo had bought two items with a small amount of the 'smack' he'd received – some 'burn', and two batteries for his radio, which a few moments later came to life. It suddenly dawned on me that I hadn't read a newspaper or heard any news reports since I'd been in prison. It was like being on another planet.

After tea we were just settling when an officer delivered the mail we were waiting for. Over a hundred people wrote to me during my first weeks in prison, and every word of support gave me strength and helped stave off that crushing feeling of total isolation.

Every day, letters from Bronya, my parents and my closest friends urged me to keep cheerful and I doubt I would have survived without their encouragement. Many letters included the writers' phone numbers, and said that if I needed to talk, I must ring. But that, of course, was impossible. I tried to answer by return, on prison notepaper mainly, but also on some that I had borrowed from Guido. To most, I sent brief greetings, but when I wrote to my son I made up stories. He loved tales about thunder and lightning, storms, castles, dungeons and evil wizards. I didn't have to look far for inspiration.

Writing to Bronya enabled me to escape the squalor by mentally transporting myself to her side. Pages I wrote, pages I received. One day she sent a letter that had been dabbed with perfume. It was the best treat I had been given for months, and from then on, it became a regular thing. Often I would go to sleep with an envelope lying on my pillow. You have no idea how comforting it was. Receiving letters and writing home was a crucial pastime for me, and I felt sorry for Tommo who was unable to read or write.

While I wasn't exactly warming to Tommo, I no longer found him intimidating and, that night, when he offered the prison paper he couldn't use, I wondered for the first time about his background.

'Where are you from, Tommo?' I asked.

'Chelsea. Around that area,' he said, taking a deep drag on his fag.

'Is that where you went to school?'

'Never went to school really. My Dad taught me everything I know.'

The story emerged bit by bit, but by the sound of it Tommo's full-time education finished when his father went away for his second term of imprisonment for drug-dealing and grievous bodily harm. When I was learning how to hold a cricket bat, Tommo was learning how to roll a 'joint'.

An hour later I finished my letter-writing and took more notice of the preparations taking place in the cell. 'What are you doing?' I asked. I had already gleaned that it was heroin that Tommo had smuggled in, but I had no idea what they were doing and my question seemed to excite Guido.

'Can't get needles in here, so we "chase the dragon".'

'What's that?' I asked, intrigued but apprehensive. On current form, simply being present in the cell while heroin was taken might be enough to implicate me. I was worried that my prison sentence would start off with a conviction. Guido was involved in a delicate operation and it was several moments before he answered.

'We need foil, see,' he said, straightening up. 'That's what we've just done.'

I suddenly realised why Guido had been so delighted to find an empty packet of Benson and Hedges cigarettes at teatime. For two hours it had been submerged in a jug of boiling water, collected from the urn at teatime, and the outer covering had peeled away from the soggy box. Guido was left with a perfect layer of golden foil, and, after carefully drying it between his bed sheets, he moved on to the next stage.

From his toilet roll he tore off several sheets which he rolled tightly into long tapers. 'Need them for a light,' he said, in answer to my quizzical look. 'That's why they only let us have matches. They think they can stop us 'booting up' by banning Kit Kats (because of the foil) and lighters (hence the taper). They've got no chance.' His lips parted in a malevolent grin.

I lay back and tried to get into *Kane and Abel* but couldn't concentrate, so instead I listened to Tommo's radio that was playing in the background. Close proximity to drug addicts was new territory for me. It was scary being in a cell with people who were visibly changing, but at the same time I was fascinated, wondering what would happen next. By now apparently everything had been prepared and all we had to do was wait.

Tommo had missed out on tea. Apparently he wasn't feeling like it after Guido had made him throw up. Suddenly, he announced he was 'starving' and suggested it was time to open the tin of tuna that Guido had been given earlier in the day. 'A favour for a favour,' Guido had said when I congratulated him on his present.

'Want something to eat, you two?' he asked Tony and me. Some things you turn down in Wandsworth but half-decent food isn't one of them. We both nodded vigorously. The only task before eating was to extract the tuna from the tin. Unfortunately there was no tin-opener, but I was shortly to learn there are ways round such trivial problems.

Guido was obviously the opening expert and from the top of his cupboard he took down the small metal mirror that each inmate is supplied with. About six inches square, with rounded corners, it looked far from suitable. Putting the tin on the floor, Guido set about his task. Gripping the mirror he lifted up his arms and drove down one of the rounded edges into the top of the tin. I could tell by the noise alone that nothing had happened. He repeated this action like a robot until, at last, the battered top gave up resistance and the mirror crashed through. Oil splattered everywhere.

After he had levered back the edges, making a small gap through which he drained the remaining oil into his slop bucket, Guido began to prise out the meat with his fork. Bit by bit the thin slithers fell into his pudding bowl until the tin was empty. Guido had had the foresight somehow to smuggle in a few extra slices of bread at tea, and minutes later I was tucking into half a round of tuna sandwich.

It was a pretty professional job. By the standards of the outside world it was a long way from good, but in prison it was exceptional. Rather like fish and chips tasting better when eaten from newspaper, a stale tunafish sandwich is five-star food in Wandsworth.

'We'll buy more tins tomorrow in canteen,' Guido said. 'Want to buy with us, John?' It was a kind offer but with only £2.50 to spend I could hardly participate in group buying, and I explained as much. The reaction surprised me.

'You gotta wise up, mate. That's why we fuckin' asked you cos we know you'll be short. You won't survive in here unless you accept help when it's offered.'

I remembered how when I had played the golf tour I had lost several opportunities of sponsorship through not wanting to appear pushy when the subject was broached, and I now realised it was time to learn the lesson. 'That's kind of you,' I said. 'I'd appreciate that,' and I did, too.

The drug orgy was to begin just before lights out after the last check had been made. Until then, it seemed, Guido was happy to talk.

'You going back to golf when you get out of here?' he asked.

'Not sure if I can.'

'Well, if you want to do a bit of work you'd be great at the tweedle.'

'Cor, wouldn't he arf!' said Tommo.

'What's "the tweedle"?' I asked.

'Next league up from hoisting, that's what it is. You buy something cheap like a ring from Woolworth's, go to a jeweller's and ask to see a tray with something similar on it. Then your partner comes in, makes a distraction, and you swap the crap for a bit of pucker "tom".'

'What's "tom"?'

'Tom foolery, jewellery. See, we can't do it cause we stick out a mile. Posh geezer like you, well – you've got it made. You can make big bucks at the tweedle.'

It was the first time I'd been asked to do something so obviously illegal, but not wanting to appear critical, I nodded at Guido as though I'd consider the proposal.

'You can make good money nickin' cars now, though,' said Tony, demonstrating his career was more diverse than just one-dimensional hoisting.

'I thought that was meant to be harder now, with all the security in cars,' I commented.

'No chance,' said Tommo. 'I can break into any car and drive off within seconds.'

'How d'you do it?' I asked. I had always been fascinated. When I was the professional at West Surrey it was a regular occurrence to find someone had locked their keys in the car. We used to try to get in with coat hangers and all sorts but we were never able to. However, the men from the AA, incredibly, would have the doors open within seconds. If I paid attention to these lessons perhaps it would give me another string to my bow!

'Depends how much time you've got, but all you need is a piece of scaffold piping about a foot long and a spark plug,' said Tony, who then proceeded to give me a detailed lecture on how to get into a top-of-the-range car, start the engine, overcome the steering lock and drive away.

I had to laugh. I was reminded of discussions between professional golfers as to the best way to swing a club. All three of my cellmates tried to convince me that their way was the quickest, but in the end each method was ridiculously simple. Tony had one or two techniques that Tommo hadn't come across before, and Tommo was particularly attentive at one point, and obviously eager to put this information to practical use. In the same way that I used to be eager to try out a new golf theory, I could see Tommo champing at the bit. At least while inside, they were able to update their skills. A short stretch could be treated as a useful refresher course.

'Which is the hardest sort of car to break into?' I asked.

'Ford Cosworth, cos it's got a second steering-lock mechanism inside the steering column. Bit of string and a coat hanger takes care of it but it takes a bit of time, see. Best avoid them,' Tony said.

After my lesson I felt confident that, if ever I were stranded and my life depended on it, I would never be short of transport.

At ten o'clock, as soon as the last check had been completed by the officer, Guido moved across to sit on Tommo's bed, blocking the view of anyone who looked through the peephole. Tony, who had become more and more rabid-looking as the night progressed, sat on the edge of his bed. I could almost see his tongue hanging out. Tommo reached across to his table and turned the radio up, then Guido lit the first slow-burning taper and 'the dragon' flared.

The heroin had been placed onto the foil over the lighted taper, which heated the rocks until they melted. Using the empty tube of a biro the toxic fumes were then sucked up, deep into the lungs. I couldn't tear my eyes away but all the time I was panicking that an officer would walk in. I watched as the heroin bubbled and skitted across the foil, the pipe chasing the fumes (hence 'chasing the dragon'). A sweet, sugary smell filled the cell and I wondered if I might be affected by the fumes myself.

The voices of both men sounded dreadful, grating, as though the fumes had torn their throats to shreds, but their eyes stared longingly at the foil as each took his turn to 'fix'. It surprised me how short a time it took, and after only a few minutes it seemed they'd had their fill, but there were still 'bones to be licked'.

'Want a bit?' Tommo asked me, noticing I was watching, but the impression I had formed of Guido was further confused by his vehement response.

'No, he fuckin' doesn't! And don't ever tempt 'im Tommo – give it to Tony.' I was grateful to Guido for acknowledging my innocence, but at the time had no idea how rare that quality is in prison. Without anyone questioning Guido's decision, the last vestiges of the 'dragon' were thrown in the direction of Tony, who sucked its dying breath into his lungs.

When I was about ten, my father talked to me about the evils of drugs. We were in the car at the time and his warning had such an impact on me that I can still picture the building we were driving past – the Royal Surrey Eye Hospital. By all accounts, both Tommo's upbringing and his father's attitude were diametrically opposed to mine. That night I was thankful that the warning I had received had proved sufficient, and that I had been able to watch the proceedings without feeling tempted to participate.

With little else to do, once the drugs had been taken and my cellmates were tripping out in a world of their own, I slipped into bed and tried to relax. Because I was experiencing so much so quickly, living 'for the moment' was proving easier than I thought. As I was reflecting on what I had just witnessed, my defensive wall was abruptly torn down. Suddenly my mind was ripped away from the present and, without warning, flung back to the past. Tommo's radio was still on and Elton John was singing a song I knew so well:

> It's four o'clock in the morning, dammit,
> Listen to me good,
> I'm sleeping with myself tonight,
> Saved in time, thank God my music's still alive.

As the music carried through the dark I quietly mouthed the words of the song. Like everyone, I have my special songs: 'Someone Saved my Life Tonight' was the first song I ever learned on the guitar. I had been caught unawares and for a fleeting moment I tasted a forgotten security. It wouldn't happen again if I could help it.

When the song finished I tiptoed across to Tommo's bed and switched the radio off.

Back in bed I tried to sleep and was on the threshold of blissful oblivion when suddenly Guido stirred.

'What's that noise?' he asked, in a rather sluggish voice. I was surprised he could even speak. I listened carefully but couldn't hear anything. It occurred to me that he might be imagining things, but he was insistent. As he was the only one who had heard the noise, it had to be coming from his corner, and we turned our senses in that direction. After watching for several seconds I saw something scuttle across the floor, moving fast towards Tommo's bed.

'Cockroaches!' shouted Tony. 'Fuckin' cockroaches!'

Knowing what to look for, I was able to make out a number of small black shapes, but a match suddenly flared and lit up the cell. It was like a scene from a horror film. A seething black mass swarmed round the slop bucket, and the disgusting sight sent a shiver down my spine. Startled by the sudden light, several of the black shapes darted towards my bed, too fast for the shoe I hurled in their direction, and disappeared beneath me.

'What the fuck shall we do?' said Tony, but until the smell of tuna was gone there was little we could do. The 'dungeon' was always susceptible to the odd bug, Guido informed us languidly, but since the mobile food counter had been permanently positioned near our cell the problem had become worse, and I could see it was going to be a regular occurrence if we opted for extra food.

'I'll have to borrow your bucket tonight, Tommo,' Guido said. The thought of having to get up to have a pee to find you're treading through a mass of cockroaches made me squirm. We had no option but to try to sleep, but I couldn't help thinking of the army beneath me, and dreaded that, at any moment, one of them would start to clamber up my leg. I fidgeted around, my skin crawled for ages, and I couldn't get comfortable. Eventually I closed my eyes and attempted to meditate . . . 'Relax and breathe' . . . 'Relax and breathe' – to the exclusion of everything.

8

The Ultimate Test of Tolerance

I awoke on Friday morning to the sound of rain hammering against the window. Only really keen members would be playing golf at West Surrey today, I thought. I had slept badly. In my imagination, cockroaches continued to crawl onto my bed but only a couple of times had I leant over to see if they were still around. With the morning light illuminating the cell I sat up and glanced at the floor, but there were no visible signs that a marauding mass had been on the scrounge hours before.

I looked across at the rest of my fourball. Both Guido and Tommo were still out for the count; Tony had his back towards me. I checked the time, and lay for a couple of minutes, wondering what my son would be doing at school that day, and thinking about Bronya; then I clambered out of bed. Intrigued as to the state of Guido's bucket I crossed the space separating our beds. At the bottom of the brown bucket two dark shapes lay motionless. Cockroaches, I thought, were alleged to be so durable that they could live in lands devastated by a nuclear blast, but they'd met their match in Guido's slops.

When the door opened ten minutes later, I was still the only one up and I went out to stand in the queue to hand in my unsealed letters and book my daily call. It was pretty quiet on the landing, but I came to realise that in prison, this was typical of Fridays and weekends. Since Thursdays were the main drug delivery days, it was a case of the morning after the night before. I wandered back to the cell, completed the usual chores and waited for breakfast. I was ravenous but by the look of my cellmates, it seemed the only thing likely to be on their menu was 'cold turkey'.

Breakfast was a sombre affair. Lousy food is edible when there's someone to have a laugh about it with, but the others were still asleep so I sat in silence, chewing on the lumpy pig-meal porridge, made with water, and felt a longing for home comforts. My companions were still sleeping two hours later, when the door opened and 'canteen' was called. I didn't know whether to wake the others up. Fortunately, as I dug out my identity card, Tony stirred and I left him to do it.

I went out onto the landing, made my way up to the second floor where a gate was open, and joined the small queue which led round to the canteen door. With only £2.50 to spend for the week, it didn't take me long to decide what I needed. One £2 phonecard, a packet of Rizlas, a Mars Bar and eight penny chews. I used to buy more from the tuck shop at boarding school.

Buying phonecards was the major purchase of all inmates and I didn't realise how much profit the prison service made out of our phone calls until much later in my sentence. Not that I blame them; it just seemed a case of false economy. The likelihood of an inmate reoffending increases the longer they are out of contact with home. It would seem only sensible to encourage communication. But using the phones in prison is prohibitively expensive, and many inmates whose homes are far away simply can't afford it.

I saw an advertisement on television asking how much people estimated a twenty-minute call from Dartford to Heathrow would cost at the weekend. The answer was fifteen pence. Fantastic value. At the weekend in prison a local call lasting twenty minutes ate a whole £2 card. During the week, phoning before six would give you about six minutes for your £2. The prison service may well enjoy a substantial profit from the phones, but set against the cost of housing individual inmates at over £25,000 a year, they'd be better off encouraging inmates to 'phone home'.

As I went back to my cell with my purchases I passed Guido and the boys on the stairs. There were no greetings: they looked ghastly. I saw plenty of 'clucking' inside and it always looked horrendous, like the worst possible hangover. I wondered whether the 'hair of the dog' theory would be put into practice later in the day.

Unfortunately it was still raining and once again our period of exercise in the fresh air was cancelled. Instead, our one weekend association period was brought forward and, as 'kit change' was due, I grabbed my dirty clothes and dashed along to where the officer instructed me to wait. I was, characteristically, first in the queue. I don't know whether it's a good thing or not, but I've always been like it: waiting at airport terminals, practice grounds, in cinema queues – and now prison. I wondered where I'd picked up the habit. Certainly I'd never known my parents to be late for anything, and my son Ben was already showing similar traits. When he was four, I was collecting him from playgroup when his teacher saw me in the playground. 'We're a little concerned,' she said. 'He always has to be first.'

Well, don't look at me, I thought. *Wanting to be first, needing to win – no way.* I'd done too much fruitless struggling in my time to wish it on my son. But perhaps I wasn't giving enough credit to a young child's powers of observation. I hoped that an overactive competitive instinct would be the worst trait I would pass on to my son. I thought of Tommo's father and his drug abuse and violence, and couldn't help but feel sympathy for my cellmate.

After a wait of several minutes the solid steel door swung open and I entered the cell which constituted the laundry room. The smell of clean clothes was immediate. Even though I tried to keep myself clean, my clothes were impregnated with the smells of prison: stale smoke, stale food, the recess area – there was plenty of contaminated material around. Unfortunately we were only allowed clean clothes once a week. 'One for one' was the enforced policy: whatever you deposited you could take away. Two officers perched high on top of the large pile of laundry presided like fifth-form bullies and watched, smirking, as I stripped off. I was made to put all my dirty kit in the correct baskets and only then allowed to put on clean pants (the cleanest I could find, that is), socks and jeans – I now required a 28-inch waist, I'd lost so much weight. Picking up clean sheets I left the room and made way for the next inmate to enter the domain of the pocket dictators.

With association having only just started and the landing relatively quiet, I noticed the showers were empty. Hot water would last for about five minutes. After that, if you wanted a shower you would have to stand in the freezing cold room and be blasted with icy water. Many of the inmates elected not to do that – they were called 'soap dodgers'. I quickly dumped my clean bedclothes in the cell, grabbed my wash kit and dived in. Being first in the shower queue was a definite bonus.

When I returned to the cell Tommo was just coming out. Since I had finished my chores, I elected to spend the two hours of association behind doors. Guido was lying on his bed looking rather pale. 'How do you feel?' I asked.

'Crap.'

'Want a cigarette? I've got a few left.'

'Yeah, so 'ave we now. Thought you were going to buy with us.'

'Well, you were asleep and I only had £2.50. I needed a phonecard, which left me with nothing.'

'Fuckin''ell, when we tell you it's sweet, it's sweet. You're too nice, mate, you gotta learn to use people more. You had fifty pence left after your phonecard; we could have put that towards another tin of tuna.' He sat up on his bed and pulled his knees tight to his chest.

'Chuck us a fag, then.' I lobbed the packet across. 'And don't always say "yes", sometimes you gotta say "no", even if you've got enough. You'll have blokes coming onto to you all the time if you don't. Bet that's how you got in 'ere.'

His words tore through me, and my mind raced back over the months to the night of the accident. I knew that Guido was right. It had been weakness on my part that had led me to go over the alcohol limit. I had broken an ingrained discipline, cultivated over twenty years of travelling to golf tournaments, because I had been too worried what others might think of me. I thought my professional reputation as a teacher was at stake and stayed to argue a point. It was no one's fault but my own. They didn't know I was ill and hadn't eaten for three days. *If only I'd said 'no'.*

There was a lull in the conversation. Guido lit a cigarette, and I looked around at the surroundings and contemplated the hell that saying 'yes' once too often had created.

'When do you get out?' I asked him.

'Not long now, another seven weeks, nuffin'.'

'Will you go back to hoisting?'

'Got to, really; there's fuck all else I can do, my mum won't have me back, got no digs and all me mates are "smack heads". I'll get back on the gear, see, and I'll have to do more nickin'.'

'What about help from here, probation, that sort of thing?'

'Probation?! Do me a favour! I haven't seen them all the time I've been 'ere, ain't seen no one.'

'What about the rehab course you were meant to do?'

'Never got started'.

'But surely you don't want to come back in here?'

'Course I don't! I'll just have to be careful. I won't get a job, no one'll have an ex-con, and I can't kick the habit.'

It was my own fault for believing the media. I expected there to be educational facilities: it would only be my problem if I didn't come out with a degree. I'd expected rehabilitation, education, probation, and believed that anyone who reoffended would only have themselves to blame – but clearly this was not so. Anyone serving a sentence of less than four years is given their release date the day they enter prison; thus there is no incentive to behave well. If your sentence is less than four, you serve half. Only if the sentence is *over* four years is an inmate exposed to the parole system whereby theoretically he can earn early release by showing that he's addressed his offending behaviour.

For the vast majority of 'under fours', helping to cure the fundamental cause of their crimes is ignored. Without help it was almost certain that Guido would reoffend and I couldn't help feeling that it was irresponsible to let him go without making any effort to prepare him for life after release. He needed help and he had received none whatsoever.

'I'll get out with my £46 discharge grant and stay with friends,' explained Guido. *From the proverbial frying pan into the fire*, I thought.

'Most guys go back to hoisting but get caught after a few months cos they take more risks – they've gotta, see. After a few months "outside" they get back on the "smack", big time, and need the extra money. When they get back inside their habit's controlled again – sort of like a health clinic, the nick is.'

I looked at Guido and tried to understand the nightmare of his lifestyle. It appeared to be a vicious circle. I couldn't help but feel disgust for a system that so publicly condemns drug-related crime, yet does little to cure it. I was no expert, but it seemed to me that there could be a wing specifically for prisoners convicted of drug-related crimes, that they could have closed visits, where it would be impossible to make deliveries, and that there should be mandatory drug courses. With the possibility of substantial increases in sentence for anyone breaking the rules, and the incentive of shortened sentences for those who abide by them, surely such measures would help to address this growing problem. Of course, the prison officers responsible for bringing in twelve per cent of all drugs would be liable to immediate imprisonment. But my ideas weren't new.

'Everyone in here knows that, has done for ages. Ask any "smack head" and they'll tell you, but these bastards don't give a toss if you come back or not. At least "inside probation" used to give us a chance – now we don't even have that. The politicians don't want to know about spending on rehab. Hundred and thirty prisons, there are, only three with drug units. We're just banged up for a year, then kicked out on the street. It really pisses me off when the likes of fuckin' Howard criticises us when he does fuck all to help – bastard!'

I sat in silence for a few minutes, absorbing the torrent. 'Look, I'm not bragging and I don't want to interfere, but I'm pretty good at writing letters. Why not let me write to the council on your behalf and try to get some form of help when you leave?'

'What sort of help?'

'So you don't reoffend. I don't know but there must be something,' I said positively. He looked up from thumbing through *Judge Dredd*.

'There's a housing association I tried once, not for a house or anything flash, but a drug-free hostel away from my manor, but I got no answer.'

'Let me try again,' I said, looking at him. After a moment he gave me a small nod. 'Got the address?' I asked, determined not to let the idea sink without trace.

'Can't it wait?'

'No. It won't take you long to find it. Where is it? In your box?' I said, moving towards his bed to provoke a reaction.

'All right, all right, I'll get it.'

A few moments later I stood with the address in my hand. I mapped out a letter for Guido, asking for help: '. . . I was desperate to leave the area where I was too easily led . . . I wanted to break my habit and needed help to put me on the right road . . .' The letter was suitably pleading, and I was just about to read it to Guido when we heard a whistle blow.

Somewhere outside a fight had broken out, and both of us leapt up to the peephole to see what was happening, but it was at the other end of the landing. Half an hour later Tony returned, looking sick. 'Tommo's been done,' he said. 'Down at kit change, that bloke Pete, the psycho, was there, took a swing at Tommo.'

'Fuck it,' said Guido.

'Is he hurt?' I asked.

'There was a general bundle. Had part of his ear bit off,' said Tony. 'Screws threw us all behind the doors and piled in, bent them up and took 'em down the block.'

'Hope Tommo got in a couple of digs too,' said Guido. 'Didn't just lose an ear.'

'Reckon he must've bust someone's nose, there was blood everywhere.'

With any prisoner on drugs possibly HIV positive, Tommo must've been a worried man. 'Think he'll be all right?' I asked.

'Don't know,' said Guido. 'Won't be coming back 'ere, though.'

Even though Tommo wasn't the most magnetic of personalities, he'd been fair to me, and I felt sorry for him. It might have been any one of us out there. If the guards hadn't told Pete that we had asked for him to be moved, the fight wouldn't have happened.

'We'll get some other bastard in 'ere now,' Guido said. Once again the expectations of another body coming in unsettled me. No consistency. Incredible frustration. Wandsworth was proving to be the ultimate test of tolerance.

9

The Raid

Four days after Tommo was taken to the block, an officer came in, collected his possessions and, when pressed, explained Tommo was off to the Scrubs.

'Don't forget his photos,' Guido said, getting up to prise the most personal of Tommo's effects off the wall. 'And tell 'im to keep in touch,' he added, as he handed over the photos, although since Tommo was unable to write, it was a token gesture. After his fight with Pete we knew Tommo wouldn't be coming back, but now, at least, we knew he was well enough to travel.

Just four days had passed since my arrival in Wandsworth, but they seemed like four weeks. The grinding routine distorted time and I felt more and more as if I had been dumped in the 'dungeon' and left to rot. Every day I phoned little Ben, or my parents, or Bronya; these calls were my only contact with reality. There was no news of a transfer, and conversations focused on how to push the system into action.

I had now spent two weeks 'inside', and not one official had spoken to me regarding my future. Not one prison rule had been explained, and I had no idea of my entitlements. It seemed information was deliberately held back. During exercise I had gleaned from Steve the blagger and Guido an accurate picture of what *should* be happening: induction on arrival (for an explanation of the system); sentence planning (what goals you should try to achieve during the sentence); assessing risk level (what risk level you are); and, finally, reallocation to a new jail. Rather like the early days of my golf swing: great in theory – lousy in practice.

Pushed into action through frustration, one morning I asked an officer: 'Guv, I've been here for over a week now; when do I go on induction?'

'You don't from here, not on this wing,' he answered mechanically.

'But Guv, I thought everyone goes on induction.'

'How long you doing?' he asked, looking at me for the first time.

'Three years, Guv.'

'Three years!' he exclaimed. 'You shouldn't be on this wing. This is for short-term sentences, short sharp shock stuff, under one year only.'

'Well, how come I'm here then, Guv?' I said, my frustration growing rather than abating.

'Must be the overcrowding.'

'But how do I know what's meant to happen to me, sentence planning and all that?' I asked. 'My family needs to know,' I said, hoping forlornly that an appeal on their behalf might make him more sympathetic.

'Just have to wait, won't you? Now move along.'

I was herded back to my cell. I wanted to scream, to shout for someone to help me, but the cell door slammed shut – like clamping the lid on a pressure cooker. Unfortunately Guido was in a baiting mood, and after he had repeatedly goaded Tony into revealing the end of *Kane and Abel*, the Scot finally succumbed. I hadn't finished the book, and this provocation was enough to push me over the limit. I leapt up from where I was trying to relax and smashed both fists down on top of my cupboard, which shattered. I neither felt nor noticed the ugly gash that a nail had opened on the underside of my hand until red drops appeared on the floor.

'So you have got a temper then,' Guido said, with an inanely stupid grin. 'Better not let the screws see that cupboard. They'll nick you.'

I rarely lost my temper. My first golf coach Jack Busson had seen to that. One day I had been struggling with my game on the practice ground and out of sheer frustration I threw my club down. Unknown to me, Jack was watching. For the next month I was obliged to sweep the shop, wash windows and clean members' shoes. Never again did I vent my spleen on the course. But when I had a shop of my own, if I needed to shake my assistants into action, a quick burst always got results. In prison, though, I quickly learned that no matter what the provocation, outbursts have to be held in check. My tantrum had not impressed anyone.

'Come at me with a blade and I'll be worried, but unless you're prepared to back it up don't lose yer rag,' Guido said, looking at me. 'Little guy like you'll get eaten alive.' It was a useful and timely lesson, because the next day Jimmy Baker moved into our cell. Guido summed him up as 'low life', and he was to push me to the edge.

Sacked from his kitchen job for accepting bribes, Jimmy had been sent down from the second landing to the 'dungeon', which compounded my suspicion that I was in the punishment zone. Grey, thin, hollow eyed and permanently sweating, Jimmy turned out to be a heroin addict of gargantuan appetite, and a dealer to boot. Every time the door opened, some snake would come slithering in looking for a deal. In hushed tones Jimmy would explain: 'There'll be nothing till Friday – be sweet after the visit.'

On Thursday, the day after his arrival, Jimmy was suffering badly from the effects of heroin withdrawal – he was clucking, and obviously needed a 'fix'. I watched with revulsion as he sweated and puked his way through the day. His hands trembled when he rolled a cigarette, his nose ran continuously, and he only occasionally wiped it clean with his sleeve. The odour his body gave off would have deterred even the bravest of predators. Not once did he even attempt to wash.

Throughout the night he can hardly have slept a wink – every time I woke up he was smoking. I wasn't sure what was worse:

being subjected to the sight of him during the day, or listening to him coughing and snorting his way through the night. In the morning, he looked like the grim reaper.

Jimmy had a visit booked that day; I still had a week to wait. I longed to see Bronya and recapture the elation I'd felt at her visit the week before. I felt empty and dehumanised – I needed to see her to recharge my emotions; however, with visits two weeks apart, Friday alternated between being the best day of the week and the worst. Today was definitely one of the very worst, and I struggled through my depression until Jimmy returned in the late afternoon.

Hardly had the door slammed before he retched up his delivery and set about 'booting up'. He sat on his bed and made no attempt to conceal what he was doing. I watched him go through the same ritual that I had witnessed in this cell a few days before, his rabid mood reflecting his total dependence on heroin. Just before teatime he staggered over to my bed carrying what was left of the parcel.

'Goin' to stash this under your mattress,' he said to me. 'They won't look there. You're too much of a straight goer.'

'No way, Jimmy,' I said. 'Keep them with you; don't come near here.' The line was drawn, my bed was a no-go area – 'enter at your peril'.

For a moment he stared at me, intimidatingly, hoping I would fold, but for once I found it easy to say 'no'.

'Wanker!' he said, and proceeded to hide it under his own bed.

The problem with my allies was that, with heroin around, they were hoping for the odd 'bone' to be thrown, so I was on my own. The whole atmosphere in the cell had changed. There was little banter, in fact hardly anyone spoke. After tea, during which Jimmy had obviously 'sorted' one or two clients, we settled down for the evening.

It was about six o'clock when someone from the second landing stuck his head out of the window above and shouted down, 'Hey, Jimmy, you bastard – you owe me. You're short.'

Jimmy went to the window, his co-ordination looked shot but somehow he managed to push it open. 'That you, Izzy?' he called up, to which he received a string of expletives. 'Can't be short: I've given out four eighths. Got nothing left.'

Even the salivating dogs, Guido and Tony, were annoyed by his obvious stupidity. The path where the officers walked was only yards away.

'Fuck's sake, Jimmy, shut up' Guido warned. But with the carefree attitude that 'smack' promotes, Jimmy continued to announce his profession to the world. When he finished he sat down, got out his parcel, cut it into two pieces with a blade from a broken disposable razor and wrapped them individually in cellophane. One piece he hid in a crack of the window, the other went into his pocket. When he'd finished he turned to Guido.

'Don't tell me to shut up again or you won't get any of this,' he said, slapping his pocket. I could see Guido holding himself in check. The problem with heroin addicts is that they are volatile: a basic fist fight could easily turn into a horrific stabbing.

There are no words strong enough to express how much I hated Jimmy Baker. Looking back, the officers must have been watching him, just waiting for something like this to happen. At seven o'clock, without the customary warning of jangling keys, the door flew open and the three most feared guards on the wing came charging in.

'Against the wall! Against the wall!' they screamed. For a split second there was pandemonium, but in that time I saw Jimmy's hand whip into his pocket, pull out the small parcel and swallow it.

'Against the wall!' one of them screamed in my direction, and I quickly moved over to the door where part of the wall was exposed. 'This is a cell spin. Anything you shouldn't have, tell us now!' shouted the shaven-headed officer, who regularly boasted of his two periods of suspension for brutality.

No one said a word as the three officers hovered with truncheons drawn. 'Take them away,' said one to another officer waiting outside. The three guards remained in the cell while we were led out to the landing and lined up against the wall.

'Hands out of pockets, no talking, eyes to the front!' yelled the officer as he watched us like a hawk. My mind went into overdrive – I was in real trouble. I knew where the drugs were, I knew who had shouted out of the window, and I knew they were going to ask me.

It was several minutes before the door opened and Guido was manhandled into the cell. I stood on the landing trying to listen to what was going on but could hear nothing from behind the closed door. Eventually it opened again, and Guido was led away by two officers. It was Tony's turn next.

I stood with my back pressed hard against the wall, I was in a terrible predicament. I was used to sorting out problems on my own – professional golf can be a lonely existence – but for once I desperately needed someone in there batting with me. After several minutes Tony came out and was taken away. Whether the order was random or by design Jimmy was called next, and I was left on the landing to fret alone. I hoped beyond hope that Jimmy would confess, but eventually he came out and I was called. I was really terrified.

'Right, strip off'.

I took my clothes off.

'Bend over, legs apart.' I complied, feeling little humiliation. I had no respect for these men.

'Wider,' said one of them, and I felt a truncheon bite into the inside of my knees.

'Right, who's the drug dealer?'

My mind was working in a peculiar way. It felt as though I was part of some dubious 'B' movie. 'Sorry, Guv, I don't know.'

'Don't fucking know?!' he shouted in my face.

'Guv, I'm a professional sportsman. I don't know anything about drugs.'

'Don't be so fucking naive,' he spat out between clenched teeth – I could feel the venom. 'Who called out of the window?'

'Guv, I've been asleep all afternoon.'

The whole episode reminded me of *Midnight Express*, but that film took place in Turkey – *not London*. My options weren't great:

'nicked' for aiding and abetting in drug-dealing, or 'grassing', only to face a future on the numbers. I gritted my teeth and doggedly stuck to the 'I know nothing' strategy. It must have been frustrating for them. They obviously hoped I would crack and nail Jimmy. My stubbornness amazed even me, considering the threats being bandied about. Eventually, the officers let me go, realising I'd learned about prison justice – the fear of being labelled a 'grass' is worse than anything they could throw at me. I was literally almost sick with relief.

Minutes later we were all back in the cell. Nothing untoward had been discovered, but the atmosphere was far from celebratory. Apart from the resentment we felt towards Jimmy, the cell had effectively been sabotaged during the search. Beds had been overturned, mattresses split open, and the sheets lay in a pile on the dirty stone floor. Every picture had been ripped off the wall, even the photos had been taken down – it looked as though the place had been blitzed.

Jimmy, however, was quite unconcerned at the devastation, and went to the window to retrieve the parcel he'd carefully tucked into a hidden crack. He then proceeded to pull down his trousers and pants, and to hide the parcel under his foreskin. After witnessing such a revolting act, it was difficult to think of him as human.

Half an hour later, when the cell had been more or less put to rights, the door flew open, and 'Against the wall!' came blasting at us, as the second wave of the search started. The routine was repeated, and again we stood outside as Guido was led in and interrogated. After a few minutes the cell door opened and he came out, escorted by an officer who led him upstairs. It was Jimmy's turn next and after a short time I heard him cry out in pain. I can't say I was sorry. When Jimmy was finally led away I expected Tony to be next in, but moments later both of us were released and allowed back into the cell. They had found what they were looking for. We didn't say a word as we surveyed the scene – the cell had been turned upside-down for a second time, and it left us speechless.

I sat on my upturned bed, rolled myself a cigarette, thankful that the whole sorry escapade was over, but my feeling of relief turned to horror when, an hour later, the door opened and in stepped Jimmy. He looked pleased with himself – *bastard*.

'They asked me what the lump was. Told them it was an abscess,' he explained, smiling – *smiling!* 'Made me pull my foreskin back, but that's illegal, see. I've told them that the search was illegal. Have to go to an outside court now, not some stupid fuckin' adjudication in 'ere. Have a good boot tonight, now,' he said.

'What's happened to Guido?' asked Tony.

'Got nicked for unsigned phonecards. Probably let him off if he grasses me up.'

It was a petty charge and Jimmy was probably right, they would want him as a witness, but I knew Guido wouldn't say a word, preferring to suffer the 'nicking'. It was a shame: I wanted Jimmy to get caught.

He sat down on the edge of his bed, picked up his bucket and, with practised ease, retched up the contents of his stomach, including the parcel of heroin he had swallowed. He picked it out and dried it. I shouldn't have said anything but I was so annoyed. 'You're crazy, Jimmy. Guido would still be here if you hadn't been so stupid and shouted out of the window. Boot up again and I'm asking to be moved in the morning.'

'Do that and I'll fuckin' plunge you,' he said, and I realised I was almost in too far. Had it not been for the *Kane and Abel* incident, I may well have been tempted into a show of anger, to front him out by saying something stupid like 'Try it,' but he probably would have done, and so I kept my mouth shut.

That night was the most frightening of my life. When the lights went out Jimmy began an orgy of drug-taking. He rolled a taper about five foot long, and stuck it to the ceiling with some old porridge he'd scraped out of the rubbish box. It hung down above his bed like a stalactite. After preparing the foil and heroin, he lit the taper, which burned at a ferocious rate even though tightly rolled. The whole cell glowed red in the light of the flames. The grotesque shadow of his bent-over body, as he manically sucked in the fumes, was etched on the wall and looked like the devil at play. It was a scene from hell.

Again and again he inhaled the fumes of the 'dragon' and it was hard to believe how much punishment he gave his emaciated body. I've never been so fearful for my own safety. As the night progressed he became more volatile, screaming occasional obscenities at the guards – and at us. I could see Tony lying in bed watching, as though confused, longing for the 'bone' to be tossed in his direction but wary of asking the maniac. I lay rigid with fear, unable to sleep, and watched as the whole parcel was used up. It must have taken two hours. I wondered how many men had been led to evil ways by mixing with slime like Jimmy Baker.

That night seemed endless. Sleep was impossible, and I could not disengage my mind from the terror of my incarceration with this loathsome, drug-crazed being.

10

Goodbye to Hell

The morning after the drugs raid, bleary-eyed and mentally wrecked, I got up early to clean the cell. I certainly didn't want an officer barging in and seeing all the mess. Jimmy had crashed out in a heap on his bed and Tony was asleep, but the charred remains of foil and tapers covered the floor. I set about sweeping up. When the door finally opened I went straight to the SO and told him that I *had* to change cells. He looked at me closely and didn't argue. Nevertheless, it was a whole week before I was moved to a single cell on the second landing.

During that time, hostilities between Jimmy and me stayed on 'red alert', but because he was suffering so badly he seemed incapable of anything physical beyond survival – just. Even so, the threat was ever-present beneath the surface. Guido never reappeared after being led away. To secure some form of ally, when Steve the blagger asked about the raid I told him I was scared stiff of Jimmy, and asked him for advice. That afternoon, during association, the problem was resolved, and Jimmy received a 'hands off' warning. I had no idea what form it took, but when we were banged up for tea his face seemed whiter than normal and he would not look me in the eye.

'Jesus, what did you say to him?' I asked Steve, the next day.

'Never you mind, but you owe me a lesson.'

The game of golf had proved useful to me on many occasions: it was a great door-opener; but the privilege of being associated with the game had never before served me so well. From then until I was transferred, I took every opportunity I could to talk to Steve about the golf circuit and explain the basics of the swing. He was intelligent and caught on quickly. He was also confident, and thought nothing of stopping during exercise to take practice swings in front of two hundred inmates as he got me to explain the lessons. It was a small price to pay for protection.

I didn't generally mind talking about the golf circuit. I was able to do so without evoking too many painful memories, although on one occasion I simply couldn't go on. Steve had wanted to know about the golf tour abroad and I was relating an experience that I had had as a young professional. I was playing in the Swiss Open and in the third round I happened to play with the American Lanny Wadkins, a world class player and the imported star of the week. We were surrounded by 6,000 spectators. It was the first time I had played with such a famous player and in front of such a large gallery, but although nervous and slightly shaky, I started off with five consecutive birdies. I shall never forget my feeling of pride and the ecstatic applause of the fans as I moved to five under par. After the round I took the cable-car at the back of our hotel to the summit of the Sierre mountain. I stood at the top surrounded by the Alps and looked down to the valley below, where the course was bathed in sunshine. It was the most magnificent sight I have ever seen. No one came to disturb me. All sense of time was lost as I soaked into my soul the incredible sensation of absolute freedom. When my mind recaptured the passion of that private moment, amidst the fear and squalor of the exercise yard in Wandsworth, I could feel my lip start to tremble and my eyes fill with tears.

'I'll try all this when I get out – it had better work,' said Steve, changing the subject when he realised I was struggling.

Over the next few weeks I relied heavily on Steve. It seemed such a contradiction that he was a wanted man, yet he was someone whom I could trust. Throughout my golfing career, I had met literally hundreds of people, from bank managers and celebrities to the struggling self-employed. Steve seemed no different from any of them. I never saw him take advantage of anyone, he protected the persecuted and in his everyday dealings he was an honest individual. I wondered how such a fundamentally sound man could end up in so much trouble. One day during association I decided to ask him.

'My mum got involved with another bloke, pimp he was – she was on the game, see. He used to beat her up something rotten. Eventually she kicked him out. She couldn't take it any more, but he kept coming back and threatening her. One day she was scared witless and phoned the coppers – bastards did nothing. Nearly fourteen I was. He came round, found us in the kitchen and I watched him slash her face and break her arm in two places. She was screaming something terrible and I thought he was going to kill her, so I grabbed a knife and stabbed him. There was blood everywhere; it was horrible.'

Steve went on to explain he was taken to a young offenders' boot camp. It was there he met and began to hang out with the wrong crowd, who encouraged him into a life of drugs and crime. 'That was it, really, came out fitter and stronger – could outrun anyone, but I couldn't get a job. So I did loads of nicking. Ended up doing banks.'

The circumstances that had led Steve into a life of crime were those I was to hear of over and over again during my eighteen months inside. Such a first offence invariably resulted in a prison sentence, during which 'first timers' mixed with habitual criminals who victimise those who try to abide by the rules. And with drugs so readily available, and everyone telling you that 'bird is easy if you're doped up', it is hardly surprising that many young offenders become addicted to drugs.

There were first-time offenders in Wandsworth serving short sentences, some as little as a month, for crimes such as petty insurance fraud or non-payment of fines. Of course they needed to be punished, but after a month in Wandsworth some were walking out as heroin addicts, and potentially much more of a threat to society. Stirring the least bad with the worst was no solution. I wondered why there were no prisons devoted to first-time offenders who are determined to return to a normal life. At least in such establishments they could be protected, and given opportunities, particularly with regards to future employment.

Had Steve been sent somewhere like that in the first place, perhaps he would have turned out differently. After his release I suppose it was inevitable that one day Steve would get caught and, six months later, I learned that he had been arrested during an armed robbery on a south London bank. With a guaranteed prison sentence of fifteen years, his life was all but over.

During my last few weeks in Wandsworth I became increasingly frustrated when I saw young, innocent-looking men led down to the 'dungeon' or mixing with dealers like Jimmy Baker. If I could spot it, so could the officers, and on several occasions during exercise I wanted to go up to them and say: 'Look, *look*, protect that man.'

But they simply wouldn't have listened. Realising that I could do nothing to help, I became more and more of a loner, content to spend my time locked away, rather than in such rotten company.

Up until then, most of my time in Wandsworth had been focused on survival, but suddenly being shut away from danger gave me an opportunity to think more. Often I found my mind slipping back to the past where it would linger dangerously in the dark recesses of guilt and remorse. But I still found it difficult to confront what I had done on the night of the accident and the consequences for all concerned.

To stop myself from tumbling into an abyss of depression I would rely on heavy exercise, and so claw myself back from the edge. Sometimes in the darkness of the early hours I would find myself running on the spot, desperately pounding out the miles in search of a safer place. Over the weeks my feet became battered and bruised but the physical pain was nothing compared to that of the mental torture of reflection. Increasingly I came to rely on physical discipline as a form of escapism.

With the frustration of not knowing how long I would have to remain in Wandsworth, I decided it would be a helpful mental exercise to start keeping a diary of anything interesting that took place – although being locked up on my own for such long periods meant that not a great deal happened. Occasionally I would leap up when I heard a whistle blown by a guard, signifying a fight, but apart from mealtimes and exercise (when it wasn't raining), it was a lonely existence. When I look back and read some of the entries I realise what a bad state I was in.

One great bonus was that Bronya had sent me a small mono radio which I left permanently on, for company as much as anything. There seemed to be a preponderance of programmes on crime and punishment, nearly all of which informed me what an easy touch prison had become. At least it used to make me smile.

My days focused more and more on the early evening when I would be able to phone Bronya and Ben. The calls were my lifeline, and I never failed to book one. On one particular day, however, shortly after I had moved into my single cell, I felt so intensely isolated, so panic-stricken, that only the thought of my next call sustained me. I was first out in the morning and booked it for 3.50. Locked away behind my door I thought about nothing else all day. At 3.45 I got out my phonecard and waited to be let out. At 4.00 I was still waiting. They had 'forgotten' – and it was by no means the first time.

In sheer frustration I kicked at my cell door. 'I've got a phone call booked, Guv,' I shouted. I heard footsteps outside. 'What time was it booked for?' he asked. '3.50, Guv,' I shouted back.

'Bad luck, you've missed it then, haven't you?'

I still have the scar where I punched the door.

Unfortunately there was no way I could afford my phonecards as well as extra food, but deciding that my mental health was more important I went without additional nourishment and limited myself to two cigarettes a day. Consequently my weight dropped to 9st 3lb, my skin started flaking and, for the first time since I was a teenager, my face became covered in spots. I didn't think I was looking too bad until, on a visit, Bronya burst into tears when she saw me. My mother and father, too, were worried about me, and anxious to know what was happening about a possible transfer. But it was impossible to find out anything.

Over the weeks I had used every ploy to try and discover what was in store for me, but the system was designed to discourage all such attempts. To start off any procedure, you had first to fill out an application form: I had filled out many. On the first, I requested to see a Senior Officer. I handed the completed form to the officer who books the telephone calls in the morning, and who has complete authority over the destination of the request. He asked me why I wanted to see the SO and I explained that it was to do with my reallocation to a new prison. He then told me that had nothing to do with the SO, and that I should ask to see the allocation officer.

The next day I filled in a form asking to see the allocation officer, but when I handed it in, the officer asked me why I wanted to see him. I explained. He asked me if I had been assessed as a security risk. I had no idea and asked how I could find out. Evidently I had to see the officer who assesses risk.

On another form the next day, I asked to see the risk assessment officer, but the officer told me that I wouldn't be risk-assessed until my 'record' was sent to the prison. I pointed out that I had no previous record. That threw him. He suggested I contact my solicitor and have that fact brought to light.

It took me a further three days and many valuable phone units to get through to my solicitor. He told me that the prison had already been notified that I had no previous convictions. Once again I asked to see the risk assessment officer but I was told he was busy, and that it was pointless putting in the request. Finally, one morning, I put in one last form asking to see the Senior Officer because of 'personal problems'. I was at the end of my tether. The officer, however, would not pass on the form until I had told him what I wanted to discuss with the SO. I explained that my family were desperately worried that they had heard nothing about a possible move. I needed to reassure them that it would not be long. He informed me that that was not the SO's problem, and that I should put in a form to see the allocation officer. And so it went on, and on, and on . . .

I knew that my friends on the outside were shocked at the conditions under which I was being kept, and were trying to get me moved to a more suitable prison. Letters had been sent to the relevant authorities; one even found its way to the Home Secretary Michael Howard. My solicitor had come to see me and had expressed disbelief at my situation. But there was no word from anyone within the prison.

One day, six weeks after I entered Wandsworth, I found out about the board of visitors, a group of people responsible for looking into complaints from inmates. Deciding I could do no further damage, I subtly played off one SO against another and got them to agree to let me put my case forward.

Not one piece of information had been passed on to me regarding my future in prison: there had been no induction programme, no sentence planning, not even the book supposedly handed to inmates, explaining their rights. Incredibly, my father had a copy of it. He once said to me on the phone, 'But it says on page 27 . . .'

'What book are you talking about, Dad?' I said, intensely frustrated.

'The book you're given when you enter prison.'

I had heard a rumour that such a book existed, but in Wandsworth I was more likely to chance upon the Dead Sea Scrolls.

The board eventually met, heard my case and agreed I shouldn't be on 'A' wing, that I should definitely have had an induction programme and that my risk assessment should have been carried out. But I wasn't the exception, I was one of many. The following day a young officer came into my cell to do my sentence plan. He looked incompetent, and from the questions he asked I thought he was.

'Anywhere that will give me an opportunity to learn a new trade, just in case I can't return to golf, and somewhere where I can keep myself relatively fit, Guv.'

'But you've got eight "O" levels.'

'Yes, but I need a trade, Guv, something I can be self-employed in.' I knew there was little chance of anyone gaining employment if they had a criminal record, but he seemed to think learning a new trade was a complete waste of time, and that every jail had a gym.

He then assessed my risk level. He opened a book, looked down the columns and announced that because I was serving a three-year sentence I would not be considered a low-risk prisoner for at least six months. By that time, I thought, I might well be a raving junkie. I considered telling him that my barrister had told the judge my character references were the best he'd ever seen, and that I'd never committed a crime before. But I could see the young officer was just going by the book and the system could not cope with anything else.

The next day he came back. 'End of the week you're moving to Coldingley,' he said.

'Where's that?' I asked.

'Woking,' he said, slamming the door.

Before leaving, I said goodbye to Steve, who was due out any day, and asked him whether he had heard of Coldingley. 'Used to be a "B" cat, good nick then, but it's gone downhill since. Bit dodgy now, so keep yer head down.'

It wasn't what I wanted to hear, but Woking is a rural town in Surrey not more than ten miles from Guildford, and although Steve obviously thought it slightly 'dodgy', I couldn't imagine a Surrey prison to be all *that* bad. It had to be better than Wandsworth.

By this time Guido had been released. I knew it was unlikely to be his last time inside and hoped for his sake that he had been able to find somewhere to live, away from the temptations near his home. I had sent the letter I wrote for him, but have no idea whether he received a reply.

Tommo was now in the Scrubs and Steve would shortly be trying out his new golf swing. After waiting three weeks, Jimmy Baker was eventually taken to an outside court where he was prosecuted, and seven days were added onto his sentence (it should have been seven years). He was also transferred to the Scrubs. Only Tony the Scot remained in our old cell.

I had now been in prison for forty-six days and forty-six nights – no time at all, really. But in that time I had learned how to 'hoist', how to steal cars, where to buy drugs and how to take them. I had several times been in considerable danger – yet somehow I had survived. Now I was being transferred to a prison where the inmates had proved themselves to be more trustworthy, so that less tight security was required. It was somewhere I would feel safer. And so, with a sigh of relief, I picked up my bag, walked out of my solitary cell and headed towards the centre of the prison for the last time.

I have always been a great believer in discipline. My favourite master at school, Mr Tomlinson who taught maths, had had a fearful reputation. He had enforced some odd rules (how could combed hair and clean shoes make us better at maths, we would ask), but even though he was a strict disciplinarian, he was fair. The rules in Wandsworth were not the problem. They were all understandable. It was the way they were enforced that led to the extreme bitterness felt by all inmates. I made my final circuit round the 'altar' and watched the faces of the smirking 'screws', and I realised that it would make no difference to redesign the prison unless they removed the 'star', that potent symbol of a needlessly brutal regime.

As I stood in the reception area waiting to be transferred, the steel doors to the outside opened and a new batch of inmates arrived. There were about ten of them, some big, some small, but it was the last one in the line, a youngster, who turned to me.

'What's it like?' he asked.

11

My New Home:
Coldingley

The morning I left Wandsworth – 21 November 1995 – was cold and damp, and the drive to HMP Coldingley in Woking was no joyful ride into the country. Slight though I was, I still found the narrow confines of the sweat box intensely claustrophobic. It must have been nightmarish for the other nine inmates being transferred with me.

A small window, black from the outside, allowed me a view of the countryside as we sped down the A3 and I was filled with longing when we passed the turn-off for Guildford, knowing that Bronya was at home no more than two miles away. It was strange seeing the outside world again: the trees were leafless now, reminding me that the cycle of life continued whilst I was caught in a time capsule.

The whole journey was bizarre: such a familiar route, yet the instinctive feeling that I was going home was so far removed from reality. I was suffering from 'conditioned response' and was relieved when our journey came to an end, the large electric doors at Coldingley rising like a huge portcullis, inviting us in. At the sight of the high fences topped with razor wire all thoughts of a less secure environment evaporated. I thought back to the last conversation I had had with an officer in Wandsworth.

'Got a bad reputation, Coldingley, one of the worst "C" cat

nicks in the country. But you'll get stuck here if you're not careful. Best get on while you can and try to get a transfer from there.' Closet-compassion from a Wandsworth 'screw' – heady stuff. Mind you, with over six hundred of them in Wandsworth there *had* to be one or two sympathetic ones.

In the courtyard outside reception, we were left to wait in the sweat box for over an hour before anyone came to see us and, from the outset, it was obvious the regime was more lax. During that hour I had more than enough time to study the structure of the prison buildings. Built in the early 1960s it looked more like a comprehensive school than a jail, and the ugly architecture would have raised Prince Charles's hackles.

Eventually we were uncaged, and the usual processing of inmates took place in reception – a strip search, followed by a 'mugshot' photo session. I automatically adopted the facial expression I had used during years of prizegiving photos and, later, I found I was about the only inmate who didn't look like a mass murderer. Finally, we were issued with Coldingley clothes – jeans, sweatshirt and standard prison underwear – all of which were secondhand. I was, however, amazed to find that at Coldingley, in common with all other 'C' cat jails, we were allowed to wear our own casual clothes. I couldn't see the point in asking for much to be sent in: a pair of extra jeans and a T-shirt would do me, but my own underpants would be a bonus.

After being counted, inspected, and checked by the doctor rather in the manner of a herd of cattle, we were labelled 'clean' and led away to 'C' wing.

The accommodation quarters comprised four wings, each housing seventy inmates. 'C' wing was the induction wing for new arrivals, and had originally been designed for 'B' category security: I learned that officers used to be permanently stationed on each of its three landings. But since the prison had become a 'C' cat, the officers had disappeared to an office on the ground floor, leaving each landing unsupervised. Unless there was an emergency, the officers never wandered the landings, and this had led to a com-

plete absence of cleanliness and order. The landings were filthy:
stale, mouldy food littered the floor, dustbins overflowed, and the
windows were so dirty that almost no light filtered through. It
made me think of a building that mutants might inhabit, years after
a city had been 'nuked'.

On arrival I'd been delighted to receive a key to my cell, but
when I was led to my new home on the second landing and left to
unpack, I found that there was no keyhole on the inside of the
door: when you were 'at home', it remained open. Being locked
up in my impregnable fortress in Wandsworth had had its advan-
tages, and I immediately felt ill at ease. I was to live on this dark,
stinking landing with twenty-three other inmates – but with no
supervision. In Wandsworth you couldn't move without being
scrutinised. At Coldingley there was more privacy, but it quickly
became obvious that this had its dangers.

'Got any burn?' came a ridiculously low voice, and I turned
round to see a huge black guy filling my doorway.

Wow! I felt cornered, nowhere to run, no officers to hear my
screams. My panic had been activated by the doctor who had given
us a brief lecture on our arrival.

'If you want condoms, they're free at the medical centre.'

Well, no one was going to take me for a ride!

'Sorry, mate – got nuffin'' I said, putting on my best East End
accent, wishing I had a convincing scar – and hoping he'd seen
the film where the little guy is brilliant at Kung Fu. He lost interest and drifted off, and I realised that until we were locked up at
night I would be exposed to all predators. For the next ten
minutes defence became my top priority and I set about fortify-
ing my cave.

I quickly worked out a method to block the door with my bed.
I pulled a wooden hanger apart: with a nail at each end it looked
perfectly innocent until wielded. I removed the batteries from my
radio and lined them up on the window sill like '303' bullets so I
could hurl them at intruders. It was the best I could do. My most
effective line of defence, though, would be through using my ability

to get on with people and finding some suitable thugs to protect me.

It was half-past four when I finished 'digging my trench' and, with half an hour before tea, I laid out and checked my personal possessions. By now I knew that virtually nothing could be sent into a prison from the outside. Everything had to be bought on the premises but as I spent nearly every penny on phonecards I had virtually no possessions. I had even gone back to using prison soap which, I had decided, was the cause of my dry skin. The one apparent bonus of my new cell was the power socket on the wall, that enabled me to use my radio without batteries.

There was neither loo nor basin in the cell, but by the side of the power socket there were instructions for unlocking the door at night in order to use the toilet. If I pushed the marked button I would be put on a waiting list, eventually allowing the door to be electronically opened from downstairs. I would be allowed six minutes, after which I would have to be back at the cell, where I would have to press in a coded number to re-lock the door. Unfortunately, since the queuing time tended to be so unpredictable most of us would still have to use the bucket.

At five o'clock, armed with my plastic plate, knife and fork, I crept through the dark corridors and found my way down to the canteen where I had my first look at my cohabitants. At first I thought I had the wrong room – music was blaring out – but after seeing an inmate pass me with his plastic plate I entered.

'Yeah, welcome to the Bronx,' said the grimacing inmate behind the counter. He wasn't kidding. At Coldingley over seventy per cent of the inmates were black and, for the first time in my life, I was part of a minority group. It didn't matter to me (we were all in the same situation), but it surprised me.

I was reminded of a book I had read, *Bonfire of the Vanities*, and, as I sat down to eat on my own, in the far corner of the room, I could sense the openly displayed hostility towards 'whitey'. At a table two along from me, there was a group of about eight black guys. They were all wearing the same clothes, almost like a uniform

– huge baggy jeans, a string vest and each had a bandana wrapped round his head displaying the American flag. They looked like a gang from New York, not a group of inmates from a south London prison. On the table was a ghetto blaster, playing at full volume. I couldn't believe it was allowed. It seemed a complete reversal of the sadistic discipline I had encountered in Wandsworth.

By 'bang up' that night (at eight-thirty) I had made two important discoveries. On each wing at the bottom of the stairs were two phones which you could use without having to book (assuming you had a phonecard). Unfortunately, with over seventy inmates sharing two phones, there was a permanent queue and often I had to wait well over an hour. However, to be able to phone home, any time outside working hours, was a luxury, and the best aspect of Coldingley.

My other discovery proved to be the bane of the prison. Whilst I was delighted that the cells contained a power socket, that night I was subjected to an unexpected source of torture. In Wandsworth only small radios had been allowed but many of the inmates at Coldingley had come from less strict dispersal prisons and had brought their huge ghetto blasters with them. The noise was excruciating. In the cell to the right of mine, a young northern kid played Heavy Metal – Anthrax – at full tilt. To the left of me, the dreadlocked Rasta boomed out 'rave', and opposite, a member of the Bronx clan whom I had seen in the dining-room blasted 'jungle' music to every corner of the landing.

The thin walls dividing the cells shut out none of the volume and, even when my radio was turned up full, I couldn't hear it. For me, the biggest joke on the wing was the food-spattered notice at the bottom of the stairs: 'Anyone playing music too loud after midnight will be put on report.' That first night I only managed to sleep after the walls stopped shaking – at two o'clock.

The next day heralded (at last) my first experience of induction, where the prison system was explained. First of all we were shown round the prison. The gym fascinated me most. It was minute and it resembled an old, decrepit village hall, with the ever-present badminton court surrounded by weight-lifting areas. The floor-boards had gaping holes in them and, high above, the windows were either cracked or broken. I knew quite a bit about gyms – there were good ones and bad ones, but this one was a serious health hazard. A week later I was to read in the 1994 *Prisoners Handbook* that it was regarded as the worst in a British prison. I had to smile. In my sentence planning all I'd asked for was education and a gym. If this was the gym, I wondered what the education department consisted of.

Eventually we were taken to an office at the bottom of 'C' wing, where our instructor assumed we had all been through induction before. I hadn't, and said so.

'"A" wing,' he said, astounded when I told him where I'd spent the last couple of months. 'You shouldn't have been there. They *must* be overcrowded.' The only bonus I derived from hearing it again was that I shot to the top of the order of merit regarding 'street cred'. All the other inmates who had come from Wandsworth were from other wings, not 'Vietnam', as my old home was referred to. From the looks cast at me by several inmates, I was being reassessed. I sat back, tried to look like an SAS veteran and gradually learned about the system.

When you travel from court you are sent to a dispersal prison, of which Wandsworth is one. Nearly all dispersal prisons are designed to 'B' category security. The job of the prison is to assess the risk of an inmate's being violent and the likelihood of his trying to escape. This depends on police reports, previous convictions and character references, but the system fails at the first hurdle. Officers are too busy to fill in crucial forms and often don't read up on the previous character of an inmate – which is disastrous for anyone who wants to turn over a new leaf and use their time in prison con-structively. There is also no flexibility.

Once a prisoner is given a risk rating from 'A' to 'D', he enters a system of progression. After the dispersal prison nearly all are transferred at some point to a 'C' category jail. Thus, because of the nature of the system, many of the most dangerous prisoners, initially assessed as 'A', eventually reach a 'C'-risk jail (even though the process might take twenty years).

At Coldingley there were thirty 'lifers' who had progressed through each step and now found themselves in a lower-risk prison. Murderers, bank robbers, drug dealers, we had the lot at Coldingley, all mixed in together to make the most marvellous cocktail. At Wandsworth most of the inmates I had come into contact with were serving short sentences but some of the men at Coldingley were serving twenty-five years. This was indeed the 'major' tour and 'seniors' circuit!

Coldingley was an industrial prison with three main workshops – the laundry, metal shop and sign shop. Everyone was expected to work and, over the next few days, we had to prove our academic competence while we were assessed for work. To stay in the prison you had to be able to read and write (important with regard to safety in the workshops). It would have made sense to find that out before letting anyone come into the prison, but I came to realise that the paperwork from Wandsworth was so ineptly dealt with that no one could trust it. From our group we lost two because they could hardly spell their own names.

Having seen the gym, my revised expectations of the education department were spot on. Because of savage budget cuts, only twenty out of two hundred and eighty were on courses, and no trades were taught. At the time, GCSE English was about the most advanced lesson you could take. We were at Coldingley to work, and any ambitions I harboured of finding some kind of training for an uncertain future evaporated.

The only positive aspect of induction was that I met Ahmed. Also from Wandsworth, he was serving a sentence for 'grievous bodily harm', although when he told me his story, I couldn't believe he was in for so long, or that he had even received a sentence. He told me he'd been playing in a cricket match and was driving home with his brother when a van pulled up next to them at traffic lights. Ahmed's children were in the back, and when the van cut them up Ahmed let it go, didn't react. When this happened a second time, and his car was actually hit, he followed the van to get its number. It stopped and two men got out with spades. Foolishly, Ahmed's brother got out and was immediately set upon by the men. Ahmed reached into the back for his practice cricket bat (I loved that bit – no way would he use his match bat) and proceeded to become involved in the fracas. Ahmed was sure the attack was racially motivated, but he was pretty handy with the square cut and although his little finger was almost severed by a swiping spade, he scored a couple of boundaries. It was Ahmed who was prosecuted. The two men who had caused the trouble had previously been in prison for assault and burglary, but these facts couldn't be brought out in court. But what was insinuated to the jury in a devastating closing speech by the prosecuting council was that Ahmed was a very religious man. *A fundamentalist, even.* Ahmed got twenty-one months. In all the time I spent in prison Ahmed was the only person I met who had suffered what seemed to me gross injustice. A qualified engineer, Ahmed's professional background and intelligence made him an obvious choice for the metal shop. I, on the other hand, had asked for anything but that. The day before work started, at what was rather like a graduation ceremony, the 'qualified' instructor read out where we had been allocated: Ahmed to the laundry – I to the metal shop! After three days of being told about the prison by an extremely depressed-looking officer, it was nothing more than we expected.

Alone in my cell, that night I tried to summon some enthusiasm, but I felt terribly dejected. I was as apprehensive about my safety here as I had been in Wandsworth, if not more so. I missed Ben and Bronya, I was desperate to call home but I had no phonecards, my private cash not having been transferred by Wandsworth. My expectations that I could use the rest of my time constructively seemed to have come to nothing. And I had still only served fifty-three days of my sentence. Time and loneliness stretched endlessly before me.

At the entrance to every prison there is a notice that greets you:

'All prisoners will be treated with humanity and will be given every opportunity to rehabilitate themselves so that on release they may be successfully integrated back into society.' Suddenly I realised that it was a lie.

12

Never-Ending Noise

At Coldingley I tried to remain active, to live for the present, as I had vowed. My life revolved around work, keeping fit and my communication with the outside world in the form of letter writing and phone calls to those closest to me.

Work in the metal shop turned out to be far from hard, but the very fact that I was out of my cell all day tired the nine-stone skeletal frame I brought to Woking. Running on the spot in Wandsworth had been fine, as far as it went, but twenty-three hours a day locked in my cell, with little else to do but lie on my bed, had left me in an enfeebled state.

Every evening I went to the gym. Though at first I could only manage a pathetic amount of cardio-vascular work, I gradually built up to a point where I felt more like my old self and could complete the circuit I had devised with the help of the gym staff. They were brilliant, and had been from the first time I had wandered in to train. I can't remember ever having encountered such an intimidating atmosphere. The gym was packed with men, mostly black, who would have made the Incredible Hulk look small. They screamed with the effort of heaving impossible weights off the floor only to release their loads with earth-shaking reverberations. There was also a punch bag in one corner which was constantly in use. The heavyweights slugged it back and forward, driving their punches home with grunts of exertion, sweat pouring off them onto the floor. It was unbelievably noisy. I crept round the gym into the far corner and tried to look as insignificant as possible, but I was immediately noticed by one of the officers. He strode up to me with his shoulders swaying back and forth. He was a very powerful-looking man – he needed to be. 'New in, are you?' he asked.

'Yes, Guv,' I said, backing away slightly. He studied me for a moment.

'First time inside, is it?'

'Yes, Guv.'

'Well, you can cut that 'Guv' bollocks out for starters. My name's Pete; what's yours?'

Amidst all the anger and hostility on display in the gym, it seemed that here was an exception, and I felt my bottom lip start to quiver. 'Hoskison, Guv.'

'Your first name, I mean.'

'John,' I said quietly. I never thought one word would bring me to tears.

'Listen to me,' he said sternly, moving his body between me and the rest of the gym. 'There's a lot of bullying goes on in here. You've got to be tough, understand?' I nodded, licking up the tear. 'Any problems, you come to see me, right?'

I nodded again.

'Okay,' he said gently. I managed to regain my self-control. 'We'd better start working on that pathetic body of yours, then,' he said.

Apart from the confidence I gained from those first caring words spoken to me by anyone in authority, my mental and physical rejuvenation was considerably boosted by the improved diet at Coldingley, an industrial prison where the workforce had to have stamina. Because I was eating as much as I could at meal times, especially the fruit on offer, my weight started to increase and the awful state of my skin, which had been flaking and spotty in Wandsworth, began to improve.

Bronya immediately noticed the difference when she was finally allowed a visit. 'God, you look better', she said as she sat down at one of the thirty tables that made up the visit-area. 'Still far too thin but at least not at death's door.'

'The food's much better here,' I said, pleased that I looked more attractive than the last time but unaware that the governor was planning a massive reduction to the food budget.

The visit allowance at Coldingley was three two-hour sessions a month, a marvellous improvement on Wandsworth, but through a mix-up in the paperwork it was not until two weeks after I arrived that Bronya saw me in Coldingley. In that time we had both wallowed in the luxury of regular telephone calls, one in the morning at seven-thirty and one at night. Psychologically they were invaluable to both of us.

Every morning I also phoned my son, and I was thrilled to hear that he was doing well at school and coping without me. I hadn't let him visit me in Wandsworth. It would have been too emotional, probably for both of us, at a time I was trying my hardest to avoid emotional situations. Now, for the first time, I dared to look forward to seeing him again, but I had to know what the visiting procedure was like before I could risk exposing him to the prison 'experience'.

Bronya beamed a smile at me across the table. Throughout my life I had been very lucky; I had travelled abroad to the most marvellous places, all the while earning an income from a job that gave me enormous satisfaction. But when Bronya smiled so warmly at me, it dawned on me that all pleasures are relative. At that moment no one could have been happier than I.

'Tell me about work, then,' she said enthusiastically.

Her fascination with the workshops at Coldingley had been fuelled by a report carried out by the prison inspectors, that had appeared in the local press. A lack of control over inmates, home-made 'brewing kits', drugs, fighting and low morale featured prominently in the article, but I had not discussed the news over the phone as our conversations were still recorded.

'You wouldn't believe what goes on in here,' I said. 'The problem is, there are no officers in the workshops – just "civvies" overseeing the operation, and they're all scared stiff of the black guys.'

'But there must be someone in there with authority. What if there's a fight?'

'No one fights, not in the workshops. They're too doped up. First thing they do in the morning is smoke a joint.'

At that moment the small hatch that gave access to the canteen opened and, to be first in the queue (a woman after my own heart), Bronya leapt up to buy some tea. While she was away I thought back to my first day in the metal shop.

It was on the Monday after our induction period that I had first donned a huge pair of industrial dungarees that swamped me, steel-capped boots, two sizes too big, and shuffled to work. Twice on the way my flapping garment caught on door handles, bringing me to an abrupt halt, and I thought it ironic that after a two-day lecture on health and safety, I had been provided with lethal clothing.

About sixty inmates worked in the metal shop, which was about the size of four tennis courts, back to back. The area was divided into three sections. I was to work in the part full of prehistoric punch-and-press machines which bent and folded sheets of metal into drawers for filing cabinets. These in turn were passed onto the welding section and then finished off in the paint spray area. The absence of officers made me a bit jittery as the only apparent authority was a manager, a grey-haired, grey man called Tom.

The job the managers did, as far as prestige was concerned, was somewhat akin to that of a professional golfer working at a back-water nine-hole golf course with a drainage problem and rebellious members. It was the end of the line – and it showed. At any rate Tom's capacity to motivate a less than enthusiastic workforce must surely have evaporated and, after only a cursory explanation, he left me at my huge pressing machine; his passing comment, delivered in his grey monotone voice, was 'Just do the best you can'.

I was fascinated, though, by the thought of being in charge of something so huge, powerful and loud – my God, it was loud!

Although not my first choice of jobs, I decided that if I had to do it, at least I could try to do it well. It took me five minutes to learn the job, ten minutes to invent a more efficient method of handling the metal for maximum output, and fifteen minutes before I received a verbal warning.

'Hey, you,' came the deep West Indian voice. 'You workin' too hard.'

My mind was brought back to the present as Bronya returned with tea and chocolate.

'You know, I was warned off in the first hour of being in the metal shop for working too hard,' I said to her, as I took a sip of prison tea.

'Who by?' she asked.

'The black guys – they run the place. In fact they run the whole prison. All the officers are scared stiff of them; they daren't lift a finger because they're too quick off the draw at crying discrimination. They've got the place well and truly "tucked up".'

'What about the report that's come out? Surely that will make a difference?'

'I hope so. You've no idea how boring it is in there, but Tom was hauled in by the governor a couple of days ago, so things might change. He was talking about making me an inspector.'

'An inspector?' she exclaimed. 'Of what?'

'Of the work. It's disgraceful what gets put out. At the end of my first week we produced 2,000 pieces, 1,800 of which had to be scrapped because they'd been badly cut or pressed. The guys cut one wrong, and because they're not checked, the whole batch is out. My job will be to see the first one's correct.'

'But surely the inmates won't like that,' she said in a worried voice.

'No, they won't mind. We get paid by our rate of production. Last week we only got £6 for our forty hours. Not even the black guys liked that. Production won't go through the roof, but we might be able to get a few more right. Tom said he'd give me all the technical drawings so I can check the work as it's done.'

'But you're useless at things like that, you're a bodger. Attention to detail – you?' she said, aghast. I suppose she had seen one or two rather disastrous attempts of mine at DIY.

Bronya had bought four Snickers bars from the canteen and, not having tasted chocolate for a month, I steamed in. Relief wasn't the only thing I overdosed on that day.

'What about friends?' she asked.

'Got two, Bill and Ahmed. Bill's a burglar, he's spent a lot of time in prison, and Ahmed's a really good bloke, in for GBH.'

'Oh, they sound really nice,' she said sarcastically.

I explained how I'd come from Wandsworth with Ahmed but had only got to know him when we had passed through induction. I also explained how I'd stumbled across Bill.

It was during my first day in the metal shop. After I had received my verbal warning for working too hard, I decided to go 'on tour' for an environmental investigation. With all the huge machines, a welding area and a powerful compression paint spray, the noise should have been overwhelming, but all I could hear was the squeaking leather of my new boots. The eerie silence made me feel I was wandering through a ghost town.

I made my way to the far end of the shop floor, near the paint spray area which seemed as busy as my section, the inmates adopting the same working stance, feet up and smoking. It really would have made the most marvellous picture in one of the tabloids. When I reached the far corner I came across Tom (who looked as if he was hiding), and at first I was worried he would have a go at me for not working, but he greeted me with a weak smile. 'They've had a word, have they?' he said, and I realised how deep the decay went.

Huge stacks of metal stood against the far wall of the building, but as I made my way along I came across a partially hidden door. With the adventurous attitude that boredom fosters I turned the handle and pushed.

'Fuck's sake, shut that door!' came an angry voice. Without realising what I had stumbled across, I entered and closed the door behind me. Inside was a man I recognised from my wing. He was bent over a big plastic dustbin and out of a large jar he was pouring what looked like sugar.

'Hello,' I said. In reply I received a Neanderthal grunt.

I had decided to retreat when the man glanced up. 'Well?' he said impatiently.

'Sorry,' I said, holding my hands up. 'I'm going. I just wondered what you were doing, that's all.'

'Making hooch. What does it fuckin' look like?'

'I don't know – never seen it made before.'

He stopped pouring and straightened to his full height. About six foot five, grey haired with a particularly ruddy complexion, he looked as though he'd downed a few gallons in his time. I thought him about sixty and, weeks later, was stunned to find out he was only forty-five. Hooch was apparently no long life elixir!

'New in, are you?' he asked, his eyes assessing me.

'Came in from Wandsworth. Started work today.'

'Wanno, eh? Don't get many posh people there – bet it shook you up a bit,' he said, chuckling. 'What you in for?'

I told him – he passed no comment.

'Name's Bill,' he said, holding out his hand which I shook.

'John,' I said.

'Well, John, this is how I earn my phonecards. Barrel of hooch every two weeks, flog it on the wings. This is my office see, no one comes in here, not even Tom – got it?' he said sternly, to which I solemnly nodded. His face relaxed as he realised I took his threat seriously.

I looked at the dustbin. 'Tell me how you make it' I asked, fascinated.

'Dead easy – warm water,' he said, kicking the boiling pipes against which the dustbin rested, 'and loads of fruit and sugar. The rotting fruit ferments, producing yeast, the yeast turns the sugar to alcohol. Tastes shit, rots your guts, but sure numbs the brain – want some?'

Out of curiosity I took my one and only sip of the evil brew. It tasted revolting but was obviously as lethal as the fluid that once spilled out of the lawnmower onto the eighteenth green at my golf club, killing the grass overnight. It would have made a great weed-killer.

Just by the way Bill talked I could tell he was more intelligent than the average prisoner. After watching him put the finishing touches to the brew, we wandered out for coffee.

'Fifteen years I've done now – been everywhere. I'm a burglar by trade, see – doing a three at the moment.' He wasn't joking when he said he'd been everywhere – Parkhurst during the riots, Wormwood Scrubs, every wing in Wandsworth, in fact every prison I'd heard of. Over the next months I found he knew every infamous criminal.

'All changed now though,' he said, while we sat down and sipped coffee at one of the deserted machines. 'Just a tolerance test with all these "sooties". In the old days we'd have just thrown them off the fuckin' landings, but now they run the gaffs. Screws can't do anything – they'd get Bernie Grant up 'ere quicker than I could pick your pocket, and all that fuckin' music drives everyone round the bend.'

The music would in fact almost drive me to breaking-point in prison, but at the time of Bronya's visit I was only beginning to feel the effects of that incessant barrage of noise. When she asked what life in Coldingley was like, her last question before we parted, I replied, 'It's hard, but I can cope.' I had no idea of the depths I would sink into the following week.

It was my third weekend at Coldingley but for the first time the weather was foul and, with the library closed as it always was during the weekends, and no staff to open the gym, there was nowhere to escape to. Earlier in the week, at two o'clock in the morning, I had lost my rag at the noise from the cell below and had called out of the window. I knew I shouldn't have lost my temper – after all, I'd seen the results. In Brixton, on my landing, there had been a man who'd been found guilty of throwing a petrol bomb at some black guys after days and days of incessant pounding, and he'd got twenty-two years for murder. But I couldn't help it.

'Turn that bloody racket down,' I screamed, to which I received an immediate and ominous reply.

'You're gonna get it, whitey.'

For the next few days I lived in fear, but Ahmed and Bill kept an eye on me and I spent my free time holed up in my fort until the coast was clear. Even then, as I went round I took 007-type precautions, but I had learned my lesson, so complaining wasn't an option. On Bronya's advice I reported the noise to the wing office but I didn't dare pinpoint the source. The officers weren't interested and opted for the 'ostrich method'.

That Saturday I woke up at eight o'clock, shattered from the night before, and opened my cell door, only to be greeted with Dread on his first 'joint', followed five minutes later by music at full blast. With nowhere to go, I sat for four hours – till lunch – assaulted by the din. It was the mindblowing mix of three different types of music at the highest possible volume that distinguished it from anything I had encountered before. The afternoon was just as bad, and I could only escape for two hours, when I elected to get drenched outside rather than be battered by yet more noise.

At the weekends on the induction wing we were all locked up for the night at five-thirty. For eight and a half hours that evening I lay crushed by the noise, unable to read, write or think, and by the time Sunday came I was verging on a breakdown. For three weeks I had put up with the interminable racket – I could tolerate it no longer. After another unbearable, deafening morning, I went down to phone Bronya, as a last resort.

'Hello,' she said.

'Hi,' was all I could manage.

'John?' she said, knowing something was drastically wrong.

'I . . . can't . . . talk', I stammered, every syllable bringing me nearer to tears. I spent the next thirty seconds in silence, fighting for control. 'It's the noise,' I eventually got out, and after another struggle, 'I'll phone later.'

It was a cry for help – nothing in Wandsworth was comparable to this – and I staggered back to my cell. All the time I had been in prison I had managed to suppress and control my feelings of hopelessness, claustrophobia, self-doubt, loneliness, frustration, but now the unremitting noise had finally defeated me. It became a symbol of all these things.

Within fifteen minutes I had an officer at my door checking to see whether I was OK. He had to shout to be heard and I couldn't believe he didn't have the nerve to go in and shut the music off. It showed who ran the prison.

I learned that Bronya had phoned the prison and demanded, *absolutely demanded*, that something was done. She wouldn't accept 'no', I was told, and, like a hellcat, had managed to alarm the prison into action. Single-handedly taking on an apathetic regime, she had saved me from the abyss. I owed her my sanity. Within an hour of her calling I was moved to another cell, near Bill, on a quieter landing.

It probably sounds over-dramatic – after all, many people have noisy neighbours, but this was different. It was wall-shaking volume, from all sides, hour after hour, with nowhere to run, just an eight foot by eight foot cell for refuge.

Over the next year, I saw many horrific incidents that arose solely because of the intolerable noise-level. Everyone I knew suffered in some way. Even Bill, experienced as he was, had trouble. One night, a month later, on another wing, a black guy refused to turn down his music – it was two o'clock in the morning. After using the electric unlock to get out of his cell, Bill went to the emergency button on the landing and pressed it. An officer came up to see what the problem was and, after Bill explained, said he could do nothing.

This was too much for Bill. He slammed his fist into the landing door to try to get to the officer. The glass door had a wire mesh woven into it, which, as Bill's fist crashed through, tore his arm to ribbons, cutting tendons and arteries, and tearing lumps of flesh clean off. The surgeon said that he had been very lucky not to lose the use of his fingers. Bill only had to wear a plaster cast for six weeks, but the scars, both physical and mental, lasted far longer.

During my year and a half in prison I never once complained about being 'inside'. I had committed a crime and accepted that I had to pay. But when anyone inside is subjected to extremes of selfish, antisocial behaviour, the authorities should surely act with appropriate firmness. To pamper to the whims of a group, just for an easy life, is simply encouraging such unacceptable behaviour. For the sake of all concerned it should not be tolerated.

If there was one change I could make to a prison like Coldingley that would lead to more inmates being successfully rehabilitated, it would be to ban ghetto blasters and make all prisoners wear prison clothes. Why? For an inmate to break old habits he needs to change his lifestyle. To allow so much of his old personality 'inside', in the form of music and clothes, just encourages the 'gang' ethos and the battle is half lost. Change the face, change the music.

The Sunday night I moved to my new cell I lay back on my bed and in the luxury of a (relatively) quieter environment, I mentally thanked Bronya. I switched on my radio. It was virtually the first time I had been able to hear it since arriving in the prison.

13

A Trip to the Downs

A week after being moved to a quieter landing I received a set of earplugs through the post. Bronya's inspirational gift turned out to be invaluable. Whilst not cutting out all the noise, they blunted the attack; and every night since, my ears have been stuffed with foam. If anyone who reads this is unfortunate enough to be packing an overnight bag to take to court, make sure you take a set – you'll need them.

Being able to sleep at night proved half the battle. Instead of emerging like the living dead, I now leapt downstairs to make my calls home and was washed, shaved and nourished before the wing had come to life. With energy levels restored, life was looking up. But the improvement was more wide-ranging.

The adverse report on the prison had galvanised the authorities into literally cleaning up their act. The litter and waste thrown from the cell windows, which lay on the ground surrounding the wings like a covering of snow, was cleared. Officers roamed the landings more frequently, making sure that cleaners *cleaned*.

There was also a change at work. After a severe reprimand, Tom made an attempt to discipline the workforce. The 'Bronx' was dismantled, Bill's distillery plant closed and, just before Christmas, a fortnight after I had been on the verge of mental breakdown, I began to get to grips with my role as inspector. I was not solely responsible for the increase in wages to £10.50, but the proportion of scrapped work decreased.

I was expecting to move off the induction wing by January, to another, with less 'bang up' and more freedom. Life would still be far from pleasant – but it was nonetheless better. I was thrown into turmoil, however, when on 18 December I was offered a transfer to another prison in early January – HMP Downview near Banstead in Surrey, a supposedly drug-free establishment. Normally I would have sought advice from the probation officers stationed within the prison, who were there to answer questions on life inside and out – how to prepare for release, how to avoid reoffending – but they had been the first victims of the budget cuts and had been shown the door. Each inmate had therefore to rely on outside probation officers, who visited only rarely. The only alternative was communication by post. I was lucky: I could write letters, and the probation officer allocated to me was conscientious; but many weren't so fortunate.

It was Sod's Law that the first time I needed advice in Coldingley my probation officer was away and would not return until it was too late. There were three questions about Downview that I needed answers to. Could I phone home regularly? Could I learn a new trade? Was there a gym? I asked the officers on my wing but all they could offer was, 'It's supposed to be drug-free'. Rather ominously, I once heard it referred to as 'Brownview' (brown being a nickname for heroin).

Janet, head of the minuscule education department, doubted that anywhere would now have much education, but couldn't help with the other questions. Finally, I tried a 'governor's application', but in the same way that I had employed assistants to protect me from dissatisfied customers in the golf shop, so the SO protected the governor. 'You'll have to make your own mind up,' was his reply.

I spoke to Bronya who, typically, phoned Downview to ask questions, but she was given no information and remained uncertain as to what I should do. Her priority was my safety, and a drug-free prison sounded better, but mine was communication with home and this I would sacrifice for nothing. I took a gamble and decided to go – after all, *I* was drug-free. I said as much to the SO when he called me into his office to sign the acceptance form. By my name was a box that had been ticked, signifying I was to be transferred on a 'sale or return' basis, just like a box of dodgy golf equipment. I used to love the concept of 'sale or return' when I stocked the shop at West Surrey, but when it referred to me personally, I wasn't so convinced.

Rushing around, trying to decide on my course of action, had fully occupied my mind for several days and in no time Christmas was upon us and the festive season began. Christmas trees, holly, decorations, a whole assortment of bonuses for prisoners and a huge turkey dinner . . . *in my dreams*. I became so irritated by the exaggerated radio reports about the privileges inside prison that eventually, I had to turn it off.

That year, Christmas 'inside' started with the carol service – that's if you could get in. When the governor and his family, and the officers and their wives, and the managers and their staff were all seated, the inmates were left to battle it out for the last few pews. It was wonderful to witness such Christmas spirit!

Before Christmas Day itself I tried to spend as much time as possible in my cell – the landings had become too dangerous. Only a skeleton staff remains in the prison during Christmas week, which means there's no 'canteen'. To overcome that problem, inmates are paid one week's wages in advance, so that they can buy enough supplies to last. For two days there were more drug deals going on than the whole of the previous month. Add that to the hooch available and you really had some rocket fuel.

One inmate was sick right from the third landing as far as the telephone queue. The mess was still there on Christmas Eve when I made my way downstairs, and crossed to the visit hall. Yes . . . I had to take a deep breath. It was Christmas Eve, and my son had come to visit.

Unlike Wandsworth the visitors are already at a table when you walk in, and the atmosphere is much more relaxed. Give them their due, even the officers were smiling.

I had finally seen Ben on a Sunday morning, only two weeks previously – an emotional, joyful occasion. Now the excitement of seeing him again was incredible. He was at the table with my parents and my wife Jane. Even though the hall was packed and there were lots of distractions, they told me that Ben refused to take his eyes off the door that I would be walking through. He was in the GET SET position, and when I appeared he came hurtling at me with arms pumping. I caught him in full flight, and the hug he gave me cricked my neck.

For two hours he sat on my knee, talking a hundred words a minute. The energy he had was awesome, his enthusiasm bubbling over. I thought of the hours I had worried about him and the hours I would continue to do so, but he seemed to have overcome the hurdle of the first few months. He was doing well at school, he had his mates and, most important, he had got used to me not being there.

My parents and friends had shown tremendous support towards Ben, but ultimately it was his mother who was responsible for his wellbeing. Jane was guiding him through the minefield and, by all accounts, was doing a superb job. Sometimes people split up, that's just the way it is, but Jane and I have remained friends, and I will always owe her a debt of gratitude for the way she handled the situation. I would have sacrificed anything for Ben's happiness. Seeing him that day was the best possible Christmas gift.

My parents were marvellous during the visit. I know they wanted to ask in depth how I was and whether I felt safe, but in front of Ben these were questions best left unasked. I could see my mother watching me closely, and I realised that the concern I felt towards Ben, she in turn felt towards me. We kept our emotions under wraps and were all happy and smiling, but when it was time to go my mother came towards me with a look that I had known since I was a little boy. She put her arms round me and gave me a hug. The front I had so carefully maintained throughout the visit instantly crumbled and I collapsed against her. For the first time since entering prison, I felt totally safe. 'Keep going,' she whispered, giving me a squeeze. 'I'm so proud of the way you're coping.' There's encouragement, and there's *encouragement* . . . but then there's your mother's encouragement.

Twenty-four hours later, on Christmas Day, the dining-hall was closed for building repairs and, as my cell looked decidedly more decorative than the others (over eighty cards stuck to the walls with toothpaste – the universal glue in prison), Ahmed and Bill joined me for lunch. We were united, I think, by an instinctive feeling that no one should be alone at that time – but no one spoke much; our thoughts were elsewhere.

Two slices of turkey roll and some Christmas pudding constituted our feast, and when the last lump of custard had been swallowed, we were all quite pleased to see Christmas come to an end. Now all we had to do was wait for the workshops to open before life could return to normal – but it was a long wait.

There were now few 'supplies' left in the jail. The drugs had been consumed in a wild orgy, with no thought to the future, and everywhere you went men were racked with pain, and would do *anything* for a 'fix'. The price of the drugs that were still for sale had escalated so much that if you had anything at all of value in your cell it was likely to be stolen. It was a grim place to live and, after being holed up in my newly fortified 'keep', I was only too pleased when we returned to work. All Coldingley had in common with the outside world, during this festive season, was huge quantities of 'cold turkey'.

With just over a week to go before my move to Downview, an incident took place that reinforced my decision to be transferred. In mid-December three heroin addicts had come onto the wing. Gaunt, hollow eyed and shifty, their every move was dictated by their need for a 'fix'. There was hardly an inmate on the wing they had not tried to 'ponce' off.

On the night in question, I had waited in the telephone queue for over an hour when my turn came. Suddenly George, one of the trio, burst from out of the television lounge and, as I walked to the booth, he barged in front of me and grabbed the receiver. With the eyes of the queue on me I had to say something: to do nothing would have invited future persecution – the weak were the first in line to be bullied.

'George, I've been waiting an hour. There's a queue, you know,' I said, politely. Whether he had not heard, or simply chose to ignore me, he showed absolutely no reaction. He had his back towards me when I said it again. In one movement he turned and swung his fist. I just managed to move my head in time to avoid the full force of the blow, but his knuckles still caught the side of my face. Gaunt as he was, George was a pretty big man and I was spun back across the stair railings, his body between me and the safety of the surveillance cameras. As I recovered and instinctively went to move past, I must have moved too quickly. He misinterpreted this as a threat, and turned again to attack. I stared straight back into his vicious eyes. I had to front it out. I didn't want to fight – I'd lose; but with so many witnesses I knew that to back away from such injustice would mean never using the telephone again ('Oh, you can push in front of him, he'll do nothing').

For a few seconds he dithered. Slowly but *very* determinedly I made my way towards the phone. I held my right fist poised threateningly. He lowered his eyes. 'Fuck it,' he said, backing away before turning and storming off.

The point had been made: I had established my right to use the phone; but realising, after a few moments, that I was too badly shaken to speak, I put the receiver back into place. Keeping my head high I turned, walked slowly past the onlookers and headed for the refuge of my cell.

'You did the right thing,' remarked Tony, the 'lifer'. 'Better clean your face,' he added quietly as I passed him on my way upstairs. Moments later I felt the blood trickle down my cheek.

George had been desperate and it was only two days later, unable to pay his debts, that he went 'on the numbers' for protection, and disappeared down the block. The drug dealers were seething: he'd really stitched them up, and it was no wonder he had to go into hiding. Even though I was due for transfer, I was glad to see the back of him.

The night before I was to leave, I was throwing my possessions into a transit bag when Ahmed came into my cell. 'Hoski, Downview have offered me a place as well – I'm moving next week. Let me know if it's OK, will you?'

Over the weeks Ahmed and I had grown quite close. Most evenings we would meet up in the library and talk about sport, books we had read and, I suppose, life in general. He was like an oasis in the desert. To hear that my one real friend would be joining me at Downview was great news.

'That's brilliant,' I said, smiling, not minding in the least I was to act as the guinea pig. 'I'll write and let you know,' I promised.

The next day, I said goodbye to Bill, repeated my promise to Ahmed and was escorted to reception. There were two inmates to be transferred that day, and I was just wondering who my travelling companion would be when the door opened and the prisoner was brought in. I couldn't believe my eyes – it was George. Had the prison known I had a grudge against him they would never have sent us to the same jail. The whole point of 'ghosting' someone from the block (transferring him without anyone knowing why) is to introduce them to the new prison with as little fuss as possible. The prison had miscalculated that George meant nothing to me.

At first his lack of reaction made me wonder whether he'd made the connection, and I sat contemplating the situation until my 'escort' arrived and my wrists were handcuffed to the two officers responsible for me. With little flesh on my arms, the heavy 'bracelets' bit into the bone, and every time the burly guards yanked me around an excruciating pain shot up my arm.

I couldn't see the point of such tight security. There had been plenty of opportunity for me to escape during my year on bail, and since my prison experience had started it was obvious I wasn't violent. I didn't give a damn about being chained up, but to me the handcuffs symbolised the inflexibility of the prison service – a clear indication we were all being tossed onto the same rubbish tip.

When the paperwork was completed George was led to the waiting van (no sweat box this time). Hauled along by the guards, I followed. We were just passing the SPO (Senior Prison Officer) when he grabbed George by the arm.

'Last chance, Edwards. Blow this and it's back to Wandsworth for good.'

Little did the PO know that George's future lay in my hands. If I arrived at Downview and let slip to the inmates that George had been 'on the numbers' for running up debts, letters would be sent to Coldingley and the network of dealers would organise revenge. I had heard of knife attacks and horrific beatings following inmates through five jails – the racket demanded retribution and George would make a good example. If I wanted revenge, the opportunity had fallen into my lap.

The journey passed without incident, but with no view of the outside, it seemed endless. Wedged between two over-large officers I became very hot, and it was a relief when the van eventually stopped and the door opened to let in some fresh air. I sat behind George throughout the journey and now, for the first time since leaving Coldingley, I saw his face. As I went to get out he caught my eye. 'Will you grass me up?' he whispered. I looked at him, but before I could answer I was tugged away.

My first impressions of Downview, judging from the reception area, were favourable, and I felt I had definitely made the right decision. New carpets covered the floors, the walls had been freshly painted and electric lights shone brilliantly – it was clinically clean. But as we started to make our way through the prison, that cleanliness faded. By the time we had reached the induction wing it had all but gone.

My new cell was located on the ground floor at the far end of the landing, but with no heat and a cold wind whipping off nearby Banstead Downs the cell was literally freezing. It proved to be one of the coldest days of the year but, even so, it was a bit dispiriting to find ice on the inside of the window.

I tipped all my clothes onto my bed and threw on two extra shirts, a sweat top and another pair of tracksuit bottoms to keep in at least some of my body heat. Then, feeling adequately dressed, I went out to investigate my new home.

As I wandered down the landing, I saw a cell door slightly ajar. Inside I could see a young man sitting on his bed. I knocked and walked into the smelly pit. After introducing myself to the emaciated figure, clearly a 'soap dodger', I asked about the telephone and gym.

'Don't know, mate. Don't use either.'

I peered into several more cells on my brief sortie and asked the same question of anyone I could find, but it wasn't long before I understood what Downview was. I had thought that 'drug-free' meant a place for non-users, not a last resort for addicts, and I found myself surrounded by inmates who'd hit rock bottom – like a zone inhabited by zombies. The addicts may well have blown all outside connections and not have needed to use the telephone; may well have channelled all their energy into survival, rather than exercise – but that was not for me. Phone calls home were my lifeline and the eventual revelation that we were limited to five minutes a day, at booked times, and with those times clashing with gym hour, made it worse than Coldingley. Within twenty-four hours I realised my transfer had been a dreadful mistake. The next day I summoned every ounce of courage and went to see the Senior Officer.

'Guv, I did everything I could to find out about the regime here. I told everyone how important phoning home is to me, but nobody told me you have to book calls here just like Wandsworth. I also need to train – I'm a professional sportsman and I need to remain fit. Gym hour clashes with the phone times.' He studied me as I rambled on but suddenly he became impatient.

'It's the fucking cutbacks,' he said, slamming his fist onto the table, clearly annoyed about the lack of information available to any inmate since inside probation had been disbanded. He paused for a moment while he recovered composure. Fortunately, however, he was sympathetic. 'So you're telling me you want to go back?'

'It's not that I don't like it here, it's just that it's not for me,' I explained, feeling that my grievance might be taken as a personal criticism. 'But yes, I'd like to go back.'

With a speed born of irritation he grabbed the phone, picked up the receiver and dialled the number for Coldingley.

'You're lucky – they consider you a model prisoner and they'll have you back,' he said, as he replaced the receiver a few minutes later. 'Another inmate wants to come here. You're going to swap with him in two days – man named Ahmed.'

My heart missed a beat. I had completely forgotten about my friend. *God no!* I thought. We would pass like ships, I would be leaving as he arrived, and he would hate it here. Having four children, he used the phone even more than I did. I walked out of the office and back to my cell in turmoil. I could go back to Coldingley and not tell Ahmed – a pretty poor show of friendship. Or I could tell him and risk having to remain at Downview. As I contemplated what to do there was a knock on my cell door and an inmate entered. A drug dealer (ironic, I thought, in a drug-free prison) had come to 'interview' me, investigate the new boys from Coldingley, assess our credit ratings.

'Know much about the other guy?' he asked.

I could have nailed George there and then, part of me wanted to, but as I contemplated feeding him to the wolves, I suddenly realised that in the past I would never have thought of such a terrible thing. *This wasn't a game, this was real life.* I had been on the point of condemning another prisoner to a severe beating. After only three months inside, I was almost ready to adopt the code of violence. It shocked me.

'Don't know much about him, mate,' I said, taking a large step back towards civilisation.

Later that day I thought of George, sitting alone in his cell, no doubt wondering whether he was in trouble or not. I decided to let him know he was in the clear.

'I was asked about you earlier,' I said to him as I entered his cell. 'Told the guy I didn't really know you – didn't mention the numbers.'

I didn't expect thanks, nor did I get any. He looked pretty sick, and I thought he was probably 'clucking'. I was one of only ten per cent of inmates who didn't fail a urine test on entering Downview.

'Why don't you make an effort, George? Try to come off the gear.'

'Going to,' he said. 'Lend us two phonecards till tomorrow.'

He looked a sorry sight as I left him. I couldn't believe he was still prepared to go into debt. 'Downview' seemed a more appropriate description of his outlook on life than the scenic view over Banstead.

Having made one correct decision, the next one was relatively easy. I went straight to the SO and came clean about Ahmed. The man appreciated my dilemma, phoned Coldingley, and, after a long discussion in which Ahmed was consulted, he put the phone down and looked at me. 'Your friend has decided to stay there,' he said. 'But you're lucky. Someone else wants to come here – you're still going back.'

I felt as though I had holed a bunker shot to stave off a double bogey.

So six days after I had arrived at Downview I was transferred back to Coldingley. It was one of the coldest days of the year, −8 degrees centigrade in the wind, and it was snowing. The previous two nights I had worn four sets of clothes to bed, but knowing I was going to a warm prison, transported in a car while wedged between two officers, I wore only jeans and a T-shirt.

The journey clearly wasn't going to be very pleasant. One of the officers I was handcuffed to smelled as if he'd had a good drink the night before. He was seriously overweight, and I didn't like him from the outset. 'You should put some weight on, laddie,' he said in a thick Scottish accent, as he kept playfully pulling on the chain and sending more shooting pains up my arm.

We had driven about two miles and were just off Banstead High Street when we were in an accident with a van. It smashed into us with a sickening scrunch of metal, wrecking our vehicle. Silence followed as we all took stock; no one was injured and we emerged and walked to the side of the road. Within seconds a freezing wind tore right through me. Sleet lashed my face and, with only a T-shirt for protection, I stood shivering while the driver of our car argued with the van driver. While they were busy the Scot radioed for help, but there were no cars available at the prison and we had to wait for a taxi.

I'll never forget the next twenty minutes. People gathered around the spectacle of the wrecked car and the uniformed guards, but with the hands of my escorts stuffed deep in their pockets, the cuffs on my wrists were also clearly visible. I had suffered some dreadful humiliation in my time, such as when I shot the worst score of my life in front of a large crowd and television cameras. At the time it felt like the end of the world. But it was nothing compared to those excruciating minutes. I'll forget the numbing cold and the way the sleet stung my face; I'll probably forget how painful my wrists became. But one thing's certain: as the crowd stood and stared, I'll never forget their looks.

By the time the taxi eventually arrived, the two officers were worried they might be suffering from whiplash. I was informed that I was also probably suffering from it, so we all had to return to Downview for a check-up. But I was fortunate in escaping injury.

It's difficult to say anything positive about my experience at Downview. Maybe I didn't try it for long enough. It has a good reputation for helping addicts, but it wasn't right for me. People thought I was crazy to go back to Coldingley, which had such a bad reputation, but they hadn't appreciated how important phone calls were to me. As I was driven through Coldingley's gates I was certain that going back was the right thing to do.

14

Swinging on the Inside

A t Coldingley I returned to the status quo. I found myself on
the same landing, and in the same cell that I had first inhabited, but 'Dread' had moved and my next-door neighbour
was a 'lifer'. Tommy Foster was in his sixties and serving a 'twenty
stretch' for murder. He had a penchant for loud rock. His needle
had stuck somewhere in the mid-eighties when Rossi and the gang
opened at 'Live Aid', but his sacred uniform of faded denims,
waistcoat and long grey hair was not appreciated by the Rastas.
They looked on him as some sort of prehistoric oddball – but I
liked Tommy: he was easy to get on with.

At first I tried to hold a conversation with him, but I soon realised his hearing was as bad as his worn-out tapes, and we soon
slipped into communicating by signs – thumbs up and a smile when
'Caroline' drowned the jungle beat.

Our friendship grew to the extent of swapping milk and sugar
and, one night, even extended to a sandwich. About midnight,
knowing I was hungry, he knocked on my locked cell door and
asked if I wanted something to eat. I then heard the sound of
someone jumping up and down outside the cell, and soon a plastic
bag was slithering under my door. It contained a brown bread pic-
calilli sandwich, which, after his twelve stone had flattened it, was
about two foot wide, but it was a kind gesture and one I appreciated,

even though he was drunk at the time. He had already spent two years in Coldingley, and so was hardly a 'new boy', but in my short absence 'C' wing had taken on the responsibility of housing prisoners with behavioural problems. The two boxes of 'hooch' found in his cell on 'D' wing (the alcohol- and drug-free wing) meant that the 'brewmaster extraordinaire' was serving a two-month sabbatical.

It seemed a strange policy to expose new inmates (of which I was considered one) so quickly to the 'bad boys' of Coldingley but I had never been one to question the ref's decision. Whilst disappointed not to find myself on a better wing, as I had already completed one stint of induction, I knuckled down for two months in 'survival mode', although this time only on yellow alert.

In all prisons 'lifers' command respect from fellow inmates, and even though Tommy was regarded as 'odd', his time inside affecting him more than most, our friendship elevated me to a position of being almost untouchable and I felt far less vulnerable. In return for the sandwich I lent him my own mix, my Coldingley desert island disc, favourite tunes to be locked up with, that Bronya had sent me in for Christmas along with a Sony Walkman: 'Bleeding Heart' by Hendrix, Clapton's 'Further on up the Road', and the last, 'Free Bird', hardly the sentiments of a 'lifer', but as the anthem of the seventies, he loved it. With imaginary guitars tuned up, we blasted out the solos with a passion and I became a permanent member of the band.

My friendship with Tommy also gave me access to an unusual and normally exclusive club, that of the other 'lifers' in Coldingley, of which there were about twenty. Suspicious men and hard to get to know, but this was understandable, since they had spent up to twenty years experiencing every conceivable horror. Apart from Ahmed and Bill (of whom I now saw little as they had been moved to a wing on the other side of the prison), during the following months, I gravitated towards the 'lifers', preferring the company of men who had survived the hardest of times – the Ryder Cup squad rather than a county team.

During my first couple of months back in Coldingley, no longer having all my attention focused on survival, I couldn't help but think about my future. I started to panic. Every week I saw prisoners released onto the street with nothing to show for their time inside except a £46 discharge grant, and regularly news came through that, within days, they had been rearrested and were back behind bars. I still had over a year to serve, but not knowing whether I would be able to return to golf I had to make alternative plans, try to use my remaining time constructively. With hardly any opportunities available in Coldingley, I enrolled on a correspondence course with the London School of Journalists. My parents paid the £350 fee.

Fortunately they accepted handwritten work, but I had an electric typewriter at home and I applied for permission to have it sent in. My request was turned down. It was hard to understand why, particularly as I had shown that I was squeaky clean, but it was one of many reasonable requests that were being denied and in a move to ease the growing unrest the governor held a meeting to explain prison policy.

The governor was fairly new to Coldingley himself, and although he'd taken on a pretty dodgy environment it seemed in many respects that his hands were tied. His speech was neither long nor complicated and fell somewhere between admission and guilt, a hands-up, 'don't look at me' speech, pointing out that in future there would be few positive ventures inside. He was doing the best he could but the Home Office had directed that no further decisions were to be taken that could in any way embarrass the prison service, or, more importantly, the government. Effectively that meant no decisions.

The prison hierarchy may well have become paralysed but new, tough proposals introduced by the knee-jerking Home Office drew new battle-lines and simply made the prisoners dig themselves in.

Urine tests to help control drugs made the problem worse immediately. Up until January most drug users in prison were dope smokers. However, the residue of cannabis remains in the body for up to a month, whilst heroin is only detectable for three days. Almost overnight, drug users changed from dope to heroin in an attempt to avoid detection, a situation that created an epidemic of addicts and the worst sort of criminal – those reliant on hard drugs. The irony was that the tests had no effect on the number of drug users and, by September, the failure rate was so dreadful (76 per cent) that non-users, including myself, were tested to make the figures more acceptable.

The proposed plans for the treatment of repeat offenders, the 'three strikes and you're out' policy, also had a strange effect. Suddenly education *was* available in Coldingley. Pockets of inmates sprang up, swapping techniques and *modi operandi* so that they couldn't be nailed for the same crime. Armed robbers looked at the more subtle approaches of embezzlement and fraud; blackmailers became keen to investigate that one big hit on the banks. In fact, one particular evening I was privy to some role-playing. I had just returned to the wing after a session in the gym when I passed a group of three inmates having a chat. I knew them pretty well as they were from my section of the wing – two blackmailers and an armed robber. It was Terry, the armed robber, who spoke to me.

'Got a moment, Hoski?'

'What for?' I asked, suspiciously.

'Just gotta show these guys something,' he said, and went on to explain all he wanted me to do was stand behind a pretend till in a make-believe jeweller's and serve a customer, Jim (one of the blackmailers). I was intrigued and I had time to waste, so I went to the far end of the landing and took up my position.

'Afternoon, sir, how can I help you?' I said to Jim, who stood before me. After a brief conversation he nervously glanced round, reached behind his back and rather clumsily produced a sawn-off broom handle. Suddenly he was all over me.

'On the floor, on the floor!' he screamed, his face contorted with anger, the sawn-off pressed to my throat, pinning me against the back wall. Even though I was acting a part, my heart-rate rocketed.

'No, no, no, no, no!' cried Terry. 'For Christ's sake, you're not

Starsky and Hutch, the guy would've shit himself – panicked – you've gotta be much more casual.'

It was now teacher's turn and this time Terry entered my shop. 'Afternoon, sir, how can I help you?'

Terry glanced round nonchalantly, made a few casual remarks, then with lightning speed reached behind his back, swung the sawn-off under my nose and in the most menacing voice I've ever heard, hissed 'Do as I say or I'll blow your fuckin' head off.'

There was no question of my doing anything else, his whole manner exuded practised professionalism, and I wondered how many victims had felt the same dreadful terror. He smiled. 'Got it?' he asked the other two. As I wandered back to my cell, I crossed armed robbery off my list of alternative careers.

No adequate reason was ever offered as to why I was denied my electric typewriter, but as a fun exercise, in case I could use the skill in future, I decided to learn to touch-type. Bronya sent me an old instruction book and from a large piece of paper I cut out a key-board and stuck it to my desk with toothpaste. I practised every night but it was rather like trying to improve at golf without clubs, and although I persevered for some time 'the quick brown fox' never really took off.

Continuing in the metal shop was a waste of time. I was hardly going to get a job as an engineer, so when Pete the gym instructor offered me the opportunity of enrolling for an eight-week gym course I leapt at the chance. If successful, I would gain a qualification, the 'community sports leader award', recognised nationally by leisure centres and about the only worthwhile piece of paper I could take out of Coldingley. On 26 February I turned up for my first day in the gym.

That old familiar feeling of being the smallest hit me as soon as I walked through the door. Nine black and two white inmates made up the rest of the class, and their bulging biceps were almost on a par with their egos. The gym was not well lit and was in such a bad state that the gym instructors refused to open it, under health and safety regulations, and every morning told the governor as much, so he had to take responsibility instead. But although it was dark, half the class turned up wearing sunglasses, their shaved heads wrapped in scarves printed with the American flag. They looked like a group of reject Harlem Globe Trotters.

Our first activity was an experimental game of basketball, and after only twenty minutes my pulse-rate went through the roof – not, as one would expect, through physical exertion, but rather from the adrenalin surge of being in the middle of a group bundle. It was Stan's fault. One of the three white inmates on the course, he had the gall to dribble expertly through the defence zone of the Rasta team and score a three-point basket, only to collect a solid punch in the neck for his pains. Unfortunately they picked on the wrong man. Stan, not having completed his anger-management course, reacted with predictable ferocity. Within moments the gym was in action.

My nimble footwork found a way through the writhing mass of bodies and I made it to the far wall intact, where I turned and watched with fascination as Pete the instructor gave a blast on his whistle and waded in. I knew he was powerful, but I'd never seen him in action. He steamed in, literally picking up bodies, throwing them to one side and, only minutes later, the 'dirty dozen' sat having an enforced 'time out' in the shower area where Pete held court.

An ex-paratrooper who had seen action in the Falklands, Pete was about as tough as they come, and although his solid, sixteen-stone frame did not in itself dominate the group, menace exuded from his dark eyes and square, granite jaw.

'Right, you lot, let's get one fucking thing straight,' he said, in a quiet though riveting voice. 'This nick might let you get away with murder – shades, your own clothes and all that fucking music, but don't try any of that crap down here. Any bullshit and you answer to me – got it?'

He surveyed the group, dissent and sulkiness evaporating before his eyes. It was obvious that the PEI's in prison were not governed by the same constraints imposed on the normal officers, and I had no doubt that Pete would indeed sort out any troublemakers. More than ever I started to warm to his charm.

Initially the course was rife with racism, the blacks hated 'whitey', we hated the blacks. One particular black guy called Twister I disliked from the start, and I'm sure the feeling was mutual, as I represented everything he hated. Accepting the ref's decision was simply not on the agenda. Balls that landed in court were called out, deliberate fouls were the order of the day, and the concept of fair play was totally absent. However, as the course progressed, the atmosphere started to change.

The sportsmanship that emerged came mainly from the three gym staff, who led by example, demanding fair play and insisting we all take turns to referee, so that we could all experience firsthand the frustration of having decisions constantly questioned. However, a major influence on us all arrived one Wednesday afternoon, in the form of an outside 'special needs group' of mentally handicapped adults who were brought into the prison. They came every week and as part of our course we had to look after them.

I had never had any contact with people with disabilities before and, at first, was slightly apprehensive; but after a couple of weeks, having become acquainted with the group, I couldn't wait for our mutual therapy sessions. Over the weeks I built up such a rapport with the group that Pat, the outside organiser who brought them into the prison, asked permission for me to continue the work after the gym course had finished. But the benefits weren't just one-sided. Linda, Brian and the rest of the 'gang' (as they liked to be called) also helped me a great deal.

Throughout my life I had always been far too self-conscious, far too worried about what people thought of me, but suddenly, mixing with people who *did* have a right to worry, I realised how pathetic I had been. I admired every one of them. They suffered mainly from physical disability, their brains simply let down by a lousy communications system, but although slow, they were mentally 'all there'.

Each week, to enhance their enjoyment, I strove to come up with entertaining ways for us to pass the two hours – a curious game of bowls, hockey-stick putting and darts, which, apart from David, they all loved to play. He, however, less than five foot tall, only enjoyed standing onstage, microphone in hand, wearing dark glasses and singing along to his Roy Orbison tape.

As the weeks passed, though, it was not I alone who tried to get on with the group. I would never, *never* have put money on Twister making an effort, but I think we had all been humbled by the 'gang' and were becoming less self-obsessed.

One afternoon when Pete was away, Twister was sitting on a bench talking to Linda when she innocently asked why he was wearing sunglasses. A month before, the question would have led either to complete shutdown or volcanic eruption, but he could do neither to Linda. He reached up, took them off and, for the first time ever, I saw him smile.

David was still onstage singing along to his tape when he waved for me join him. With my confidence growing, the opportunity was too good to miss. Put this in a Disney script and it would be thrown out as too sickly-sweet, but I held out my hand for Twister's glasses – which he passed across – and I headed for the stage. Dave and I blasted through ten of Roy's greatest hits and, as we played imaginary guitars, I didn't give two hoots about looking odd in front of everyone. Our final rendition of 'Pretty Woman' brought the house down, and when I returned the shades to Twister his comment, 'Nice one, John', summed up the new 'entente'.

As the course came to a close I started to ask myself the question: where does sportsmanship come from? Is it hereditary or learned? I had been lucky enough to have a private education where sport was much approved, and where accepting the ref's decision was part of the ethos, but how would I have turned out without hour upon hour of supervised team games? By the end of the course, watching team spirit and a sense of fair play emerge through example, I decided that without education we would be reduced to basic, animal instincts – to getting what we could at anyone's expense. I felt sorry for the thousands, millions of young-sters who miss out on sport at school, who never learn 'how to win with grace, how to lose without bitterness'.

When the time came, I passed my exam with a 'best ever' remark from the local examiner from Guildford College. More signifi-cantly, I'll remember those two months for the impact sport had on our group. I promised myself that if I could ever use my expertise to help young people through teaching sport, I would do so. Unfortunately, back in the realms of peer pressure, 'whitey' was still unable to mix with the brothers, but I'd now seen the goodness that lay inside Twister and the whole experience put paid to my new-found racist views.

I was sorry that the course had finished. I had got on extremely well with the instructors and over the weeks had let slip more and more information about my past life. Nick, Pete and Dave were all sportsmen in their own right and at first I could see they had their doubts that anyone so small and frail could be a professional sports-man, but for the first time in prison I was not treated like a hard-ened criminal.

I explained how much weight I'd lost and, as my confidence grew, I even showed them a picture of myself in my playing days. So thin had I become they couldn't recognise me.

On the last day of our course, after our exam, Pete asked me to stay behind. When the rest of the class had drifted off I was left alone with the three instructors, and from behind his back Pete produced a gift. 'Present from us,' he said, and handed me an archaic golf club – an eight iron. It had a perished rubber grip, a rusted shaft and a leading edge so sharp it would have been the delight of any 'hit man'. It was the sort of club that in the past I would have thrown onto the rubbish tip without a second glance. But then, as I took hold of it, it was as though the club contained an electric charge.

Pete explained that the idea was to see me swing, so they could see what muscles needed building. I picked up an old shuttlecock from the floor, had a few swings and within minutes was facing my first shots for over six months. When I started to hit, I could have cried with the familiar sensations. The movements I had drilled into my body over thousands of hours of practice still seemed to be second nature. In that instant I knew that if I ever had a chance to play again I would be able to recapture my old form. After ten minutes of firing shuttlecocks accurately between the tram lines of the badminton court my three spectators were captivated.

'Deceptive little bastard, aren't you?' said Pete.

15

Michelin Man

When the gym course came to an end I found myself unemployed for the first time in my life. I didn't relish the prospect of a return to the metal shop but the only other apparent vacancy was for a toilet cleaner on my wing. That appealed to me even less and so, as a last resort, I headed up to the education department to see whether they could suggest any alternatives.

Apart from when I took the assessment test as a new inmate at Coldingley, I had been at work all day and had seen little of the department. It was situated above the main corridor of the prison and as I made my way along to see the head of department it was obvious it had known better days.

A woodwork room, where in the past carpentry had been taught, now lay dormant through the day and was only used by inmates in the evenings. Next to it was the 'sign shop' classroom. Inmates who worked in the sign shop itself were entitled to take a course in screen printing, but the point of letting them do so was really to help the industry in Coldingley become more efficient. There was also a pottery room, but I never saw more than a few inmates in there the whole time I was in the prison. The core of the department comprised two rooms, one containing computers, the other a standard classroom where a GCSE business studies course was taught.

There were two types of education available, full-time and 'day-release', and both were actively promoted by the enthusiastic staff. But they faced an impossible task. Their obvious commitment to helping to educate prisoners was in direct contrast to that of the prison, and the prison service in general.

It is a simple fact that a prisoner's ability to survive in jail is linked directly to the wage he earns at work. Every single penny is vital – and I mean *every* penny. Wages for a forty-hour week in the metal shop averaged out at about £10. For taking a full-time education course we were paid £4 a week. The £6 shortfall constituted three extra phonecards for those who wanted to phone home, or half a bag of heroin for those who didn't.

There were many inmates who desperately needed to be educated or learn a trade. There were many who wanted to enrol in full-time education, but very, very few could afford to do so. I myself was tempted into taking the business studies course when I walked into the department that day – but the cut in my prospective wages would have meant virtually severing communication with home.

'I can't do it, Paul. It's not that I don't want to, *I can't afford to*,' I said, when I was invited to enrol for the full-time course.

'What about putting your name down for the new computer course? It's only one day a week.'

'Brilliant. Put me down. Is there a waiting list?' I asked.

'Only four months,' he answered.

When I emphasised that I needed help *now* they were very sympathetic, but off the top of their heads they could think of nothing. They promised, however, to give it some thought and said that if they could find anything to help me with my predicament they would let me know. 'Come and see us again in a week,' they said.

I was actually quite hopeful, they were very caring people, but I had to make a decision there and then. Once inside the metal shop you had to stay for at least a month before being allowed to apply for a move. Trusting to instinct, I gritted my teeth and elected to clean the toilets for a week and give education time to make some enquiries.

*

Finding the right equipment to do the job had always played an important part in my life, particularly as a professional sportsman, when the right equipment could make the difference between success and failure. But never had I prepared quite so meticulously as I did before my new job as toilet cleaner. I had no idea what microscopic 'bugs' were lurking unseen in the 'pans' and urinals but looking at my fellow inmates there were bound to be some pretty dangerous ones. No longer was it a matter of success or failure. It was now a matter of life or death.

Ready for action I emerged for my first day's work. I wore two sets of rubber gloves and a face mask in the form of a plastic bin liner tied round my head, with only two holes cut out to see through. Two pairs of jeans covered my legs and three sweatshirts ensured that my best top would not become contaminated. I also wore my heavy industrial boots. With so much protective clothing moving normally was difficult and I walked down the landing feeling as graceful as the Michelin man. It was the first time I heard an officer laugh with genuine humour.

I hesitate before using the expression 'throwing myself into it', but I must say that, feeling adequately protected, I did do a good job that day. Almost too good in fact.

'Jesus, have you seen the bogs?' I heard one inmate say when he returned from work.

'What's up with them?' said another.

'They're fuckin' clean – that's what's up.' There was a moment's pause when obviously this anomaly was investigated.

'Who's the cleaner at the moment?'

'Dunno, but whoever it is, we wanna keep him.'

The next day, needless to say, I went about my job less conscientiously.

Since arriving in prison I had seen a phenomenal number of inmates transferred at a moment's notice, either to a new wing or out of the prison entirely, and rarely did I get to see them again.

Friendships that might have been forged over months were instantly terminated and rather than have to go through more hardship I made a conscious decision that I would not allow myself to become too close to anyone again.

Ahmed and Bill were no longer on the wing, and for some time I had felt quite lonely. Tommy, my 'lifer' friend, had been let back onto the drug-free wing, having served his punishment. With no inter-wing movement allowed, it meant I saw very little of them and I spent nearly all my time alone.

For much of the time I kept myself busy studying for my journalism course. After working late into the night I would often relax on the bed and let my thoughts carefully sift through the outer debris of the wreckage I carried inside me. More often than not when I went to explore anything sensitive I would immediately pull back. For the first time, prison and my former life became mixed up in my dreams.

It was the first time in prison I had nightmares.

Since the mandatory drug tests had been introduced in January there had been an appalling increase in violence on the 'bad boys'' wing, as users switched to heroin. The worst aspect of this was not the violence itself, but the worryingly phlegmatic response I had developed to watching my fellow man beaten to pulp. I was becoming brutalised. I became uneasy about this one evening after phoning Bronya. The ground floor was devoid of officers (they were sorting out an argument in the kitchen), when three guys, 'hooded and tooled up', came rushing down the stairs and headed for the television room. Poor Floyd was in debt.

'What's that shouting?' asked Bronya.

The room was only a few feet from me and through the window I saw Floyd's arm go up to protect his head.

'Oh, nothing really. Listen – I've got some good news.'

The chair legs rained down on him.

'What news?'

Floyd went down foetal-like on the floor.

'I've been made a "D" cat.'

The blades came out – ripped into his unprotected back and opened him up.

'John, that's brilliant!'

Then they slashed his face.

'Thanks – it's taken ages.'

Floyd's arm had just been broken in three places. He needed a hundred and forty-seven stitches to close him up. Two days later, Vinny got the PP2 battery in the face, but Geordie got the worst. I was told that the police even came in for that one while we were at work. They took photos of the cell two doors down from mine, after which Dave the wing cleaner had to wash it out. To get the blood off the walls was easy, he said, to get it off the ceiling: a nightmare.

Now that I was a 'D' cat I was looking forward to moving to another wing, but until then, apart from quick sorties to the gym, I spent most of my time in my cell. Rarely was my routine upset, but one particular night I was called down to the office. When I reached the ground floor I saw Twister waiting outside, looking slightly less macho than normal, and when he beckoned to me I followed him into a far corner.

'What's the problem?' I asked, wondering whether I'd done something wrong.

'I need some help,' he said quietly.

'What sort of help?' I asked, slightly taken aback.

'I need to write a letter,' he said, 'an important letter to my solicitor – and I can't do it.'

'I'd love to help,' I said, even taking myself by surprise at my enthusiasm.

Twister explained his problem, and after he handed me the rough drafts of his letter I knew what was needed. Two days later I had completed the task and gave him the letter rather furtively in the gym. No one else could hear what he said as he moved past: 'I owe you, John – thanks.'

There was very little opportunity of doing anything to make yourself feel good in prison and I really enjoyed helping Twister. It was particularly satisfying to do something positive for one of the brothers. It really was a shame so many barriers existed.

Because everyone I first knew in Coldingley had been transferred from 'C' wing, the only time I was able to shake off my tremendous feeling of isolation was on Saturday afternoons, when I had a firm appointment to see both Ahmed and Bill. Although I would have preferred to see much more of them, as least we enjoyed those times together. Mind you, the entertainment was top class.

Every Saturday afternoon an inter-wing football match took place on the pitch hidden round the back of the prison buildings. The captains, supposedly elected through a democratic vote, always seemed to be the drug barons (conveniently, each wing had one). They alone became responsible for choosing the team that would uphold the reputation of the wing, and they always chose the strongest side. But scoring goals was purely incidental. The match was a war of attrition, extremely tough to referee, but each week a new inmate was flattered into taking on the job. I had once been asked *and I'd almost said yes.* I think the longest a match lasted before the first punch was thrown was five minutes *before* kick off.

It was a time when the officers turned a blind eye. Someone had to take a drubbing and better for it to be the inmates than themselves. It reminded me of the Japanese office blocks where the workers are encouraged to vent their anger with baseball bats on dummies rather than their own bosses. Ahmed, Bill and I would take refuge at the far end of the pitch, in 'the neutral zone', refusing to recognise the voluntary apartheid that seemed to reign. But no one ever took any notice of us, once the action started. I saw broken legs, battered faces, 'groin strains', and a whole assortment of injuries. But the one who was invariably stretchered off was the ref. It could be the most definite goal of all time, no hint of offside, no hand-ball, but if the ref should blow . . . *POW!*

★

Unfortunately Saturday afternoons never lasted long enough, and after the matches we would make our separate ways back to the confines of our own wings. By this time I had been on 'C' wing longer than any other inmate. Not only had I virtually completed my first 'term' when I had been transferred to Downview, but on arrival back into the prison I had been treated as a 'new boy' and had had to go through the process again. My 'extended play' meant that I had spent longer than anyone else getting to know the officers, and there were several whom I quite liked. Certainly they were all better than those in Wandsworth.

One of the wing's Senior Officers, the one who moved me when Bronya had complained about the noise, was particularly kind. Over the months he had learned that I was a golf professional, and occasionally, when no one was about, he would ask questions about the game. In the privacy of his office he always called me John.

One evening though, both of us made a mistake. I was standing outside the gym waiting for it to open when the officer walked by. I had known he was going to play golf that morning and, as he passed, I raised my eyes. 'Any good today?' I asked.

'Yes, not bad, actually,' he said, with a smile on his face. 'Broke eighty for the first time.'

'Well done,' I said. I was pleased for him; he was very keen.

Moments later he disappeared onto the wing and within seconds I was grabbed from behind and thrown back against the wall. A white hand grabbed my chin in an excruciating grip. 'Don't ever let me catch you smiling at a screw again,' said one of the drug baron's henchmen. 'If I do, I'll cut you so fuckin' bad your bird will never want to set eyes on you again.'

It was a cruel warning and one I took very seriously. Prisoners are not meant to show anything but the utmost contempt towards officers. As the prison service takes no account of individuals, so the prisoners evaluate authority. Whilst that barrier of hatred exists, little can be achieved. But there is a solution. The hatred is born in prisons like Wandsworth, where the regime breeds malevolence. A more human approach, adopted from the start, would surely lead to greater harmony in other prisons. For the rest of my sentence, I was never able to further any friendship with an officer.

Up until that time, apart from the occasional lapse, I was in a relatively stable emotional state. Now, perhaps, everything was getting on top of me: my friends had moved, I was expecting to move myself, but didn't know where, and I was worried about my next job. One morning, at chapel for Sunday service, I suffered a setback.

At first the service took a slightly humorous turn. There were about fifty chairs set out but only eight inmates were present, plus a handful of official prison visitors. When everyone was seated the vicar, dressed in his cassock, stood before his small congregation. 'We'll now open with a hymn,' he said. He paused while everybody turned to the right page and in those few silent seconds the noise from outside began to invade. *Boom . . . Boom . . . Boom.* The vicar's head turned towards the walls. 'Let your voices celebrate Jesus,' he said. Then, raising his voice as though in defiance, 'Sing as loudly as you can. Carry the good news to every corner of the prison.'

As the organist started playing, the incessant pounding of the drums from the ghetto blasters put me in mind of a scene from the film *Zulu*. We sang as heartily as we could, but were soon overwhelmed by the fierce competition.

The vicar's jaw was set firm as he preached his sermon. His words, *Love thy neighbour*, were hard to take. By the look of some of the faces around me, it was almost 'mission impossible'.

When the service had finished it was time to mix with the visitors over a coffee, which I was looking forward to, as talking to anyone from the outside world had become a novelty. After most had drifted into the adjacent hall I found myself standing by the chapel door next to a pleasant-looking lady. There was only one other person near us, the chapel orderly, who was cleaning up. The lady took a pace towards me. 'Hello,' she said, smiling kindly. 'How are you coping?'

The words stunned me. Instantly my eyes filled with tears. I couldn't talk. I couldn't even nod. As I stood there, I wasn't even sure that I could pull myself together. I took a tissue out of my pocket and wiped my nose. 'Sorry,' I mumbled, with my head down. 'I've got a cold.' I fled down the chapel stairs, through the prison, and ran to the sanctuary of my cell, where I threw myself onto the bed. I was devastated. I *thought* I was coping well, but those few words of personal kindness made me realise how lonely I really was.

I hit the wall hard with my fist, hoping the pain would pull me out of my depression. One day at a time, I reminded myself, *one bloody day at a time.*

16

The Half-Marathon

The cell I moved to on 'A' wing was about the best you could get in Coldingley. Outside my window I could actually see the prison tree, which was sprouting fresh green leaves, as it was now late May. In fact, it was only two days till my birthday, which I had often spent at the PGA Championships at Wentworth, only a few miles down the road. Not for the first time, I felt like a captive animal.

I was becoming accustomed to the golf reports on Radio 'Five Live' and, up to that time, only the US Masters had been really traumatic for me, but the previous Friday, when I wandered innocently into the chapel area to see Mike Hart, the chapel orderly, there was live golf from Wentworth on the television, and I felt devastated. I cringed at the thought of Open Week in July. It was going to be a long, hard summer.

Six other inmates inhabited my section of the landing tucked away on the top floor: four armed robbers, a murderer serving 'life', and Eric, serving 'a ten stretch' for impersonating a police inspector. It was not by chance that I was privy to such a safe environment. Knowing the powerful sixball had a vacancy on their 'spur', my former neighbour on 'C' wing, Tommy the 'lifer', had put my name forward. Although one normally couldn't choose, I received the nod from the 'A' wing SO and moved in. It was a great compliment, as they really knew little about me except that I was quiet and could help with crosswords.

Since arriving at Coldingley I had been at pains to keep my past life quiet, and even though I whacked shuttlecocks around the gym once a week, I felt comfortable keeping this perceived middle-class activity to myself. I had often witnessed how an inmate, boasting of comfort in the outside world, would be subjected to bullying and blackmail. 'Transfer money into this account by tomorrow, or you'll be cut,' was the usual threat. Few, therefore, knew I used to be a professional golfer. Early one Saturday morning however I made the mistake of having a practice swing on what I thought was a deserted landing. I was in a classic follow-through position when Paul, one of the armed robbers, came out of the toilet area and spotted me.

'Fuckin' 'ell – I didn't know you played.'

I was completely taken aback. 'Er, I don't any more,' I managed.

'Got a handicap?'

'No, haven't had one for years,' I said. It wasn't exactly a lie: a professional doesn't have one.

'Jesus, I can't wait to play again – worst thing about the nick, no golf.' He proceeded to have a couple of practice swings that looked as if he would slice the ball in two. I didn't mention it, though.

I made my way to the toilet hoping it would prove to be a suitable point to end the conversation but he followed me, stood next to the three-foot piece of wood that constituted the door and gave me an all-too-detailed account of his last round, six years before. Unfortunately he had a remarkable memory.

'Yeah – great fun,' he said. 'Came off the eighteenth green with the guys, then headed straight for the bank – got arrested with the sawn-off stuffed in my Ping bag – cosser bastards never did give the clubs back.' I smiled as I pictured some rules official trying to work out the penalty for carrying the extra 'club'.

Over the next few days I was bombarded with golfing stories and details of his rarely worn Faldo golfing sweaters. For once I had to appear interested. Whereas at my golf club I could tell a friend to belt up if he started to drone on, I found there is only one thing worse than a golf bore – and that's a golf bore with an anger management problem. But one day the irritation of living in the company of a fanatic turned to fear, when he invited me into his cell. To my horror, on his table was a stack of golfing magazines, the top one of which contained an instruction article, with pictures, that I had had published the previous year. Whilst I had told no lies I had been economical with the truth, and I wondered what the hell he would say if he found out that I was a professional.

Apart from this little conundrum I was very pleased with my new cell and neighbours. I was also content with my new job. For a month I had been working in the chapel area as the new job orderly: I had to collect all the forms filled in by the inmates requesting job changes. My new boss was the vicar himself. Not only was he responsible for the spiritual wellbeing of the prisoners, he also organised the whole prison workforce. He was as powerful as the governor and without his help you got nowhere fast. As a shepherd, he was the classic vicar; as the minister of labour, he reminded me of the vicar in the Monty Python sketches, and I half-expected him to turn up wearing shades and smoking a fat cigar.

I had introduced myself to him after a chapel service when I first arrived in Coldingley, but it was two weeks after the gym course had finished that I was summoned to his office.

'Sit down,' he said. I sat. I watched, as he finished signing some papers, deciding he would make the most perfect villain in a Bond movie, another Dr 'No' – the vicar's reflex answer.

'Got a job for you,' he said, swinging dramatically round in his chair to face me. 'Been told you're the man I need to hire.'

My name had been put forward by the education department as someone who could help run the labour division (God bless them). Not wanting a return to the workshops, I regarded the opportunity of working in the clean and peaceful surroundings of the chapel office as literally a godsend, and I leapt at the chance. OK, so I lied a little, told him I was computer fluent, and, yes, I suppose the hierarchy was a little peeved when I crashed the software in my first week; but I was very polite to the fuming head of industries and somehow held on to my job.

Almost overnight, as a member of the 'God squad', I became a major influence in the allocation of jobs and very definitely climbed a rung up the prison ladder.

I liked working in the chapel area: it gave me access to a man who knew my ever-present smile hid a troubled mind. Mike Hart worked in the chapel as the orderly and was the most respected inmate in the prison. He was a 'lifer' who had already spent twenty years inside for a bank raid that had gone wrong in the seventies when someone had been shot. An 'A' category prisoner for ten years, he had lived with the Krays, the IRA and the worst possible criminals, but through it all he had emerged a humble, kind and generous man. Mike worked harder and longer than anyone else in the prison, not only with his duties in the chapel, which he kept meticulous, but also way beyond the call of duty with his 'Youth Project', an idea he had conceived years before whilst an inmate of Maidstone prison.

The 'Youth Project' was a drama production, staged by a group of fifteen inmates, and shown to youngsters between the ages of twelve to sixteen who were contemplating a career in crime. Every month sixty or so came into the prison where they could see at first hand the end-result of a life of crime. The idea behind the project was not to shock, but to educate, and the project was so highly regarded by police, youth leaders and teachers, that its audience was growing every month. Unfortunately, letting the public see that prisoners were trying to make a positive contribution to society didn't fit into the government's desired image of prison inmates and they seemed to take every opportunity to block publicity for the project. A video of the drama and testimonies of several inmates depicting the horrors of prison life had been sent out to local police forces and youth clubs. It was highly praised by all who saw it, but with the election coming up, the Home Office had refused to give it a press release – it would have been too embarrassing.

Having spent so long in prison, Mike had himself experienced every conceivable emotion, and he was looked upon by the inmates as a father-confessor. Although he never referred to the incident, it was Mike who had witnessed my breakdown in front of the lady visitor in the chapel and, looking back, he must have known that I was very confused. I had tried to deal with my emotional experience in my usual way, by burying it as deep as possible. But more and more I was finding that I couldn't bury my feelings deep enough.

One day, during a work break, we were sitting at a table in the chapel office, having a cup of tea, when, with deadly precision, he exposed a nerve.

'I'd like you to come onto the Youth Project, John – give your testimony, tell the kids what you're in for, what it's like inside. Maybe you can make some of them think twice.'

I cringed at the idea. They were honest and good sentiments but I could hardly face what I had done myself, let alone talk publicly about it. 'Sorry, Mike, I can't,' I said, fidgeting uneasily in my seat. 'I could *never* make a public confession.'

He stared at me unwaveringly and seemed to understand. 'Can you tell me about it, then?'

Mike had spoken openly to me about his crime but he knew little about why I was in prison. I thought back to the first time I had seen him running round the exercise yard, and the fear I felt when I found out he was a 'lifer' who had already served over twenty years: the last sort of person I would ever have wanted to meet, yet now the one man who was getting close to helping me. I tried to picture telling him, but immediately my eyes filled with tears and I knew it was impossible. I looked at the floor to cover my embarrassment.

'Have you talked to anybody about the way you feel, John?' he asked me.

'No,' I said, quietly.

'Listen to me,' he said, leaning forward to catch my eye. 'It takes a lot of courage to face up to these things. But the longer you delay the harder it becomes. You've got to fight your instincts to hide everything. You've got to confront your feelings. If you keep bottling things up you'll be history. You need to give your testimony, if not for the others, *for yourself* . . .'

That night I lay on my bed in the darkness and tried to digest Mike's advice. He was right – I had been hiding away. There was a huge difference between the front I displayed on the wing and my inner feelings. The strategy I had employed of surviving from day to day had been specifically designed to avoid confronting the pain inside me, and had become second nature. Mike was right when he said I would have to *fight* my instincts to stop hiding. It would be the first step towards confronting the pain – but therein lay the problem.

Competitiveness had been a way of life for me when I was a professional sportsman. There was nothing I enjoyed more than a real challenge, but for some reason (I would need a psychologist to explain it) I had lost my will to fight, both physically and emotionally. I can't explain it; it was as if the pressure of the last two years had fundamentally changed me. Since the accident, I hadn't had the stomach to fight anything.

Several weeks before, an incident had taken place that typified my attitude. Early one Saturday morning I had gone into the nearly deserted gym to find Chris, one of the 'lifers' in Coldingley, waiting for an opponent at badminton. He asked me for a game. With so few people about, if I turned down his offer, it would have looked downright rude, and I had no intention of antagonising a 'lifer'. For fifteen minutes I enjoyed a knockabout, then he suggested a game.

Chris was a very good player, probably the best in the prison, and I could see he was a natural athlete; but I had played tennis to a high standard as a boy and I was equally competent on the badminton court. I could cope with his shot-making. What I wasn't ready for was his unbelievable tenacity. He chased down every shot and fought for every point – a born competitor, someone I would have relished taking on in the past. But when I went to stretch myself and make that all-out effort, something held me back. All I could do was tamely go through the motions, expose my neck and wait for the axe to fall. It was the first time in two years that I had been asked to fight for something, and I had capitulated without resistance. We played two games and I hardly won a point. We didn't even shake hands afterwards – I don't think Chris respected me very much.

As I lay on my bed I realised that one day soon I would be ejected from the protective bubble of prison back into the real world. I had no idea what awaited me, what form the future would take, but one thing was certain – I was going to have to fight for it. If I continued to hide, it was possible that my most basic instinct would lie dormant for ever. If I wanted a decent future it was time to change my strategy.

Living from day to day was a luxury I could no longer afford. If I could learn to fight again, and then fight my instinct to hide, perhaps I would be in a position to address the pain inside me and take my first steps towards building a future. As John Wayne would have put it, I had to 'get back on my horse'.

Since entering prison I had run almost every day – in fact in Coldingley I was known as 'the runner'. As such, when the annual Coldingley Half-Marathon was due to be run I was almost an automatic entry. But what started out as a fun exercise, just another part of my training, suddenly took on new meaning.

It was a Saturday in early June, the day of the big race, and I was sitting in my cell receiving my pre-race motivation talk.

'Don't let us down, Hoski – we've bet a month's tobacco on you.'

'Thanks for the encouragement, guys – you might try good luck.'

'Bollocks,' said Eric. 'You don't need good luck. Just make sure you fuckin' win and beat that black bastard Bowler.'

At least they weren't into wishy-washy tactics, hoping some sub-liminal message would get through. This was the full-frontal, 'Get your finger out or you're history!' lecture and by the time I hit the starting line I was very much aware I had to win. But I had my own motives driving me.

THE COLDINGLEY HALF–MARATHON
(Journalist Course Lesson 6)

Controversy clouded the thirteen-mile race on Saturday when first past the post Andy Bowler was disqualified for cheating.

Bowler was said to be 'destroyed' by the decision, but race organiser Dave Watson had 'no option' after runners and spectators reported Bowler for missing out part of the course.

On an ideal morning for long-distance running, over forty inmates set out to complete twenty-one laps around the prison grounds, but the 'hot money' was on three regular runners, Hoskison, Thorpe and Bowler.

Covering the first two miles in eleven minutes the favourites opened a gap of four hundred yards over the main group. However at the halfway stage the uneconomical action of Thorpe proved too much to sustain and the race turned into a classic dual between Bowler, 'tall, rangy, with a good turn of pace', and the steady style of Hoskison.

Bowler piled on the pressure and by the sixteenth lap had opened a gap of two hundred yards, but Hoskison, who regularly took on water, doggedly stuck to his task and gradually closed on the leader.

With two laps to go Hoskison caught and passed the visibly tiring Bowler, a move overshadowed by unruly behaviour from the gathering crowd. But on a part of the course hidden from the main body of spectators Bowler stopped, walked across the 'loop' and carried on running to finish in front of Hoskison at the line. Unknown to Bowler the short cut had been spotted, and, after carefully assessing reports, Mr Watson made his decision and disqualified him.

Hoskison was 'delighted' with his win, claiming it to be his first victory in two years. Thorpe came in second with Smith winning the bronze medal.

The awards ceremony was held in the board room with prizes presented by the area manager of prisons, Mr Welleby.

It was half an hour before detonation occurred. 'I'll show you fuckin' disqualified!' shouted Bowler, as the chair flew across the gym, smashed into the far wall and disintegrated. I'd seen some pretty powerful club throwers in my time but Bowler would have been right up there with the best of them. But it was all hollow bravado – he must have been scared stiff. Half his wing had bet a month's tobacco on him, and they were none too pleased with his tactics. The new book had him odds against surviving till morning. As he stormed off to meet the seething punters, their annoyance exacerbated by 'whitey' beating their brother, I felt sorry for him. The race had been intended as fun, but there had been a lot of unwelcome pressure for both of us. Twice I had been warned against winning and, even since I'd finished, I had been told I was 'for it'. I was only mildly concerned: I felt confident my friends would protect me.

When it was time for prizegiving I received my trophy from the area manager of prisons. He presented it to me in the administration block, away from the other prisoners, which surprised me as I thought it a natural opportunity to boost the morale of the troops.

For ten minutes I was allowed to stand and talk to him but during those minutes I became more and more annoyed. This was the man in charge of every prison I had been in. He was responsible for the motivation and morale of every prisoner and officer, including those in Wandsworth. Yet he seemed embarrassed to talk to me. I tried continually to open up some sort of discussion but he would not enter into a conversation.

'Wouldn't it be a good idea to encourage more events like this?'

'Mmmh.'

'You're in charge of Wandsworth, aren't you?'

'Mmmh.'

'I spent some time there. I was with some inmates who really looked after me. I was so lucky.'

No response.

After ten minutes, absolutely livid, I left the room and waited outside. My reaction was 'over the top' but I was bitterly annoyed. How could such an apparently ineffectual man be in charge of so many men? I had to walk out. Had I stayed I would have said something I regretted.

Back on the wing my legs felt like lead. I had pushed myself to the limit to battle my way back into the race and I was very tired. My thighs were already stiff after standing around while they had been sorting out the result and, crab-like, I slowly climbed the stairs. When I reached the top, I paused for a moment. It was unusually quiet and as I looked around I realised the landing was deserted. I didn't mind in the least. In my golfing days I had never been worried about receiving congratulations. Most of my battles had been against myself and the pleasure I got was from knowing internally that I had put up a good show. I remember one day at West Surrey when the secretary of the golf club thought I carried this philosophy too far. He had just walked into the shop as one of my assistants was rummaging around underneath the workbench.

'What are those?' he asked, pointing to the array of silverware usually hidden from sight.

'Oh,' I said, taken aback. 'Just bits and bobs.'

'*Just bits and bobs?*' he said, aghast when, moments later, he held in his hand the PGA National Club Professional Championship trophy. It had been my proudest moment as a professional. Going into the last round I had doubted I could win. Yet somehow I had hung on to beat a potential field of three thousand. The trophy may well have been gathering dust on the floor, but the memory of that victory was unforgettable. The secretary would have none of it, though, and half an hour later the three championship trophies I had won that year were proudly on display in the club house trophy cabinet. I had to smile as I remembered my feeling of pride at winning those tournaments.

I was outside my cell door, when suddenly, the silence was shattered in a cacophony of noise, as all the cell doors flew open and, simultaneously, steel-capped industrial boots hammered against the solid steel plates in the standard victory ritual. Had it been the nineteen-forties, perhaps they would have sung 'For he's a jolly good fellow', but instead I was subjected to a few verses of a rude little number, presumably learned on the terraces. What a welcome!

Anything was mine, I was told, and Paul my golf bore was particularly kind. 'You've got balls, mate – bloody great big balls.'

I'd been worrying about Paul and the fact that soon he was bound to see my golf article, so while he was steeped in the euphoria of collecting an extra month's tobacco I headed for his cell.

'Paul, can I come in?'

'Sure, want some burn?'

'No, no, I need to talk,' I said, sitting down on the end of his bed. 'Listen, Paul, I've got a confession to make.'

He looked at me with a puzzled look. I didn't quite know what to say so I reached forward, picked up the magazine and turned to the six-page article where my face stared out from the pages.

'I should have told you straight away – I was a pro,' I said, holding out the article. 'That's me.'

For a moment he just looked at the pictures. 'This really you?' he asked in amazement.

'Yes,' I said, waiting for the backlash.

'Fuckin' 'ell – you're a pro.' I nodded.

'Jesus, can you cure my slice?'

Later that night I lay in my bed and thought back to what the race had meant. I thought I was going to be sick on the last few laps, but I gritted down and somehow found the strength to fight back. No longer would I have to live from day to day. With a newfound willingness to accept a challenge I was on the road to recovery. But no individual battle wins a war, and although I was determined not to hide from anything, I knew there would still be difficulties. The end goal of being able to confront my problems still seemed a long way off.

17

Crossing the Line

When Tom Lehman holed his last putt to win the 1996 British Open, it put an end to four days of torture and I breathed a sigh of relief. It evoked such powerful memories that I had to fight to suppress my instinct to hide – which was a good job, since there was no escape. Mike Hart watched it in the chapel hall, the officers had it on downstairs, and Paul, my next-door neighbour, listened to it in his cell. Radio blasting, he didn't miss a shot nor a chance to fire questions. It was like being in the Mastermind chair for four days.

'Why don't you go and watch it downstairs?' I asked.

'You're kidding – when you're here?!'

Confronting my emotions, as well as getting to grips with the daily troubles of prison life, enabled me to get closer to facing my own problems, while at the same time making me very aware of all around me. Before, when I had switched off my feelings, I remained in one monochrome mood for most of the time. Now I was exposed to a whole spectrum of disturbing emotions. When Ahmed was finally released, though happy for him, I felt personally devastated. Even though I had seen very little of him recently, I considered him a kindred spirit. Just knowing that he was in the prison I had found comforting. He is one of the very few people

I met inside whom I would consider meeting again.

At least we had a laugh before he went. When called down to sign his discharge papers, his personal officer realised that his sentence plan had never been filled out. You couldn't blame the officers, though. Since inside probation had been discontinued, the burden of paperwork had fallen on them. It was a bit disconcerting, though, to see your personal officer, head in hands, in despair.

Massive cutbacks had meant that no department was safe. On the catering side, the quality of food had continued to decline. The new kitchen Senior Officer, ironically a twenty-four stone giant, had introduced 'portion control', which gave a new meaning to the word 'stingy': 34 pence per meal was budgeted for each man. Every prisoner's fat reserves were rapidly depleted, and I plummeted down to nine stone three, my Wandsworth weight.

It gave Pete the gym instructor a headache: he was trying to build me up. 'John, you've got to eat,' he badgered, but one day I showed him the amount we were given and from then on he left me alone.

In fact my lack of muscle was one of the reasons I became injured on a run. My hip was excruciatingly painful and although apprehensive about seeing the doctor, ominously nicknamed the 'Butcher of Bisley', I had to go. He was not a popular man, hardly surprising when it was his job to get inmates to work, not dish out sick-notes, but I found he'd developed a rather cynical approach. No blood – no protruding bone – no injury. (Michael Howard would have loved him.)

'You're fit for work,' he said, in dismissal. *Bloody hell, and the dentist was meant to be worse!*

I played my joker. 'I don't want a sick-note, doctor – just help.'

He eyed me for a second, smiled, then scribbled something almost illegible which he gave me and pointed to a door down the corridor. Nice guy. I hobbled along, found the door was ajar, and, after knocking, entered the room to find an oriental woman sitting neatly on a chair. She looked at me in a way that dispelled any thoughts of her being an orthodox osteopath; 'I'm a healer,' she proclaimed. I was asked to 'disrobe' and lie on the couch.

For half an hour I had the most marvellous head and body massage, which ended up with her hands slipping under my back and holding my buttocks. I began to wonder if she had misread the doctor's note, but I decided not to say anything – *sod the hip*. A week later I returned and, amazingly, had the same treatment – but a tad firmer.

In my final session, looking into my eyes, she explained: in prison, one had to be careful. But once again the healing hands returned to my buttocks. I did wonder whether she had escaped from Holloway, but no. Apparently, the healing was complete. I thanked her, disappointed I was not to reach the fourth week, and hobbled away.

Not many people passed the 'Butcher' to get to this inner sanctum, so there were few I could tell my story to. I told Paul but he thought I was exaggerating. However, a few weeks later I was vindicated.

I was sitting in the chapel area waiting for the vicar to turn up when the conference to raise funds for a new holistic clinic began. At first, when people started to arrive, I thought some form of theatre production was being put on. An oriental gentleman came up, carrying a shepherd's crook and looking just like a character out of a Kung Fu series. Following him was a man with gold leaves in his hair.

'Is this the place of the gathering?' the first asked me. He spoke like a druid out of a fantasy film.

'This is where the believers meet,' I said, taking the mickey.

'You have Karma indeed,' the man with gold leaves said.

I had to get the guys: this was too good to miss. I dashed back to the wing where I found Paul and Eric. 'Come on, you've got to check this out.'

For the next hour we watched the biggest bunch of weirdos I've ever seen, all talking this mystic language, drinking herbal tea and looking 'oh, so serene'.

It was the beginning of the Stress Clinic in Coldingley. On offer were cranial osteopathy (head massages), transpersonal counselling (conversation), and stress management crisis intervention (animated conversation). Brochures distributed onto the wings also offered the silver star therapy, which involved healing by 'crystal power'. Crystals placed on the angry inmate would apparently absorb all evil thoughts. *Oh yeah?*

I learned from the vicar, who looked as though he wanted to machine-gun the lot, that Coldingley was the first in a national project. Fourteen prisons were to have the same facility by the end of 1997. By the year 2000 it would be nationwide.

We had lost inside probation, education was all but non-existent and the food was appalling, yet this débâcle, incredibly sanctioned by Howard and the Home Office, was given £120,000 funding. Inmates were crying out for practical help, instead we were given a collection of witch doctors. We thought it farcical, we wanted it publicised and although the *Observer* picked up the story, little was made of it. Yet disconcertingly, other people whose help was more immediate took some fearful criticism.

Take, for example, drug addiction. The criminal world revolves around drugs. Cure an addict and there's a chance he'll go straight. There are only four rehabilitation units for a hundred and thirty prisons – the staff and their work are vital. Coldingley is one of the four. Yet one of the drug counsellors, an ex-con who did a fabulous job, was 'exposed' in a Sunday paper: 'EX-CON WITH KEYS', the story ran. The day before, a helicopter had flown over the prison to take pictures. It was a double-page spread.

I knew the counsellor. He was a man who had virtually been in the gutter, who had clawed his way out and was respected by everyone. His success at breaking the drug habit meant everything to those who wondered if they could do the same. The furore caused by the article, written to fire public opinion, galvanised action from the top, and only the governor's fighting spirit saved this man from the rabid reaction of the Home Office. He only just survived. And since then he has continued to save many from heroin addiction.

Crossing the Line

*

Since I was less introverted than I had been, I started to look around. I was 'D' category security, the lowest risk, and as far as good behaviour went, at the top of the tree, so where was this 'easy-touch' prison the tabloids were so outraged about? So far I had sampled four: Brixton, Wandsworth, Downview and Coldingley, housing between them over two thousand inmates. There was one television set per forty inmates, insufficient money to buy shampoo and toothpaste, and a diet that left me almost skeletal. This did not fit in with my perceived view of a holiday camp.

I didn't give a damn how hard prison was, I'd grown used to it, but prison is meant to be a deterrent. All the youngsters out there contemplating a life of crime should be given clear messages as to what prison is *really* like, yet biased newspaper reports, written to fuel reaction from the public, are so wide of the mark. The public perception of prison means that it is no deterrent at all.

There are 60,000 prisoners in one hundred and thirty jails, and every day thousands of decisions are taken. Some obviously back-fire – and these, unfortunately, are what fuel media coverage. It is such a pity that this minute percentage is perceived as representative of the prison service. And so young tearaways get the impression that prison is a 'breeze'.

I found it all very depressing, but at least it provided plenty of material for my journalists' course. In August the early release of prisoners was a well-publicised event, and although it turned out to be a major cock-up, it gave me something to write about while I took refuge in my cell.

PRISONERS REACT AS HOME SECRETARY STEPS IN
(Journalist Course Lesson 14)

Chaos reigned in HMP Coldingley over the weekend when the expected release of prisoners was suspended by the Home Secretary Michael Howard.

Notice boards explaining the new way sentences are to be calculated were torn down and prison officers who had all but lost control had no option but to close off all wings in an attempt to split mob rule.

The previous week over five hundred inmates nationwide were released early, due to the new interpretation of the way time spent on remand is taken into account. Richard Tilt, head of the prison service and responsible for the new rules, was away on holiday in Italy.

On the advice of the prison service, many inmates had informed families of their imminent release, but hope turned to bitterness with the news that this week the courts would halt proceedings.

Tony Simmons, head of the prison union responsible for 27,000 officers, said, 'Right or wrong, the way it was handled caused total confusion and has put my members in the front line of violence.'

HMP Coldingley, a 'C' category prison, holds many dangerous criminals, and the governor agrees that the situation has been handled badly. 'When inmates who have a year left to serve are told to expect release, only to have the decision overturned, no matter how many anger management courses they've attended, they're liable to react.'

Two prisoners have already received treatment in the medical centre but it is hoped that control is soon re-established.

Tom Parker, a senior officer on 'A' wing, said: 'I feel sorry for some of them, but this is not the way to carry on – many will be spending even more time inside after this.'

Any vestige of hope that crystal healing might work disappeared that weekend when Paul returned to the wing, after 'losing it' downstairs. He had been led to expect early release, and when he was then told he still had a year to serve, he was understandably upset. In the medical centre, crystals were placed on his shoulders to absorb his violent thoughts, but when he got back upstairs, he smashed up half the landing. That weekend Adrian's Stress Clinic took the test but failed.

Throughout the summer months I continued to train but had to concentrate on upper body strength as my hip made it too painful to run. In my spare time, I worked at producing articles for my journalists' course. I began to find getting my ideas down on paper very therapeutic. At the end of long evenings, as before, I would lie on my bed and let my mind go back to the past. I was getting closer to facing up to what had happened, and could now sift through nearly all the wreckage that lay deep inside me, but bringing it to the surface still seemed a long way off.

Occasionally, the guys on my spur would wander into my cell to see what I was up to, but in the main they left me alone. Fortunately Paul had not suffered too badly from his fit of temper and remained on the spur. I hadn't realised how powerful he and Eric (the landing leader) were until they hurled the cupboard from the top landing. One day a heroin addict was walking along our spur, hoping to borrow some 'burn'. I thought he was going to follow the cupboard. Eric and the 'magnificent seven' kept the incoming tide of heroin at bay with a determination that would have had King Canute gasping for breath.

The weeks drifted by, a mass of blurred days, and I often found myself having to think what month we were in. Without any regular input of information from papers and television, I tended to lose my bearings.

My feelings of loneliness and isolation were exacerbated when I saw other prisoners welcoming new inmates to the jail. If they didn't know them personally, they often came from the same background or even the same street. It's a lot easier to survive prison when you are surrounded by people you can relate to.

Summer brought stale heat and boredom; weekdays were painful to get through. What made life acceptable were the weekends, in particular Saturday evenings, because Saturday evening was my night on the tiles.

It was one of the benefits of being 'in' with the 'lifers'. Votes had been cast before I was invited to join the group, but once accepted, we gathered every week like a secret society and headed for the chapel. It was our safe haven, the only place in the prison not affected by weekend drug and hooch orgies. Every week, it was the same routine, the same programmes we watched on television. Oh yes, Cilla Black's *Blind Date* is about as good as it gets in prison.

'I'm going for a smoke,' Geoff said.

'Me, too,' I said, joining him. I couldn't stand the show at home, couldn't stand it in prison either – all those cringing lines. But compulsive? Not half! We stood outside pretending not to listen. It was the one thing I allowed myself to hide from.

'He's got to pick number one – fuckin' 'ell, she's a cracker,' said Tommy, his comments drifting out to us.

'No! Number two's much better,' said Mike.

'Half-ounce he'll pick number one,' said Steve, who always ran a book.

Our own seats, coffee and biscuits – but it was the camaraderie that really made the nights. When the commercial breaks came I would hear stories of the old days – of gangs and bank jobs, trials and 'hit men'. Most of the guys had spent over fifteen years inside and had seen little television in that time. Having recently been in the modern world, I was a great source of information.

'Do they still have red telephone boxes?' – a typical question.

The adverts with all the modern computer graphics totally blew their minds. When hair grew quickly, or cars fell off buildings and stopped before hitting the ground, they watched open-mouthed. 'How the fuck do they do that?'

We laughed, clapped, cheered and argued our way through like a bunch of kids, and those two hours, each week, became the highlight of my life inside.

It was a good job I had something to smile about. The increase in violence over the summer period had left me gasping with horror. Apparently it's a seasonal phenomenon in prison. As the heat rises in the poorly ventilated cells, so do tempers, particularly after the weekend 'hooch' binge when trails of blood can be found all over the jail. One week one hundred and twenty gallons of the 'brew' were found fermenting in the kitchen.

And it was not just the level of violence that rose according to the season. When Ramadan, the Moslem daylight fasting period, came round, the number of practising Moslems in the prison increased by a thousand per cent. A goody-bag of food was handed out for night-time consumption to all believers, and from nowhere all these prayer mats appeared.

The Roman Catholics also experienced a rise in attendance. When the priest changed the time of the Sunday service from morning to night – when 'C' wing were locked up – suddenly the chapel was inundated with inmates who, desperate to avoid the early 'bang up', had obtained permission to attend the service. True, all the candles were taken by the heroin users, but at least the numbers looked good. As summer came to an end, spirituality was really on the increase.

Symbolically, as the days started to draw in, so my chances of being transferred to a less secure environment diminished. In September, seven months after I had been interviewed by a visiting officer from Latchmere House, a jail in Richmond which allowed inmates out into the community to work, I was given a 'knock back'. Initially I had been promised a place in April. Then it was May. When my third transfer date was rescheduled, I started to suspect that something was wrong, but after voicing my reservations to the governor at Coldingley, who had suggested the move, I remained full of hope. Little did I know that the eligibility rules had changed and I was no longer on the list. (*Thanks for telling me, guys.*)

It was an article in the press that had crushed my chances of a move. An incident had occurred in Latchmere House that had caught the imagination of the tabloids. A 'lifer' had been caught on camera innocently standing in a bus queue when on his way to work. He was standing next to a woman whom the press then interviewed. They explained to her that the man was a 'lifer' and then asked her how she felt – a somewhat loaded question. Over night, Latchmere House became Michael Howard's least favourite institution.

Slowly the knife was being turned on any institution that offered hope. Plans were proposed to cut the number of 'open' prisons from twenty-two to six, and to dispense with many outside rehabilitation programmes. Latchmere was particularly hard hit. Yet inmates who have spent maybe ten years in jail desperately need to experience at least a 'taste' of the outside world before they are released. Without some form of transitional period between incarceration and freedom, long-term prisoners are often scared witless about getting out and, in many cases, are only too happy to return to the safety of jail. It must be like coming up from the bottom of the sea without stopping on the way. A diver gets the bends – inmates overdose on space.

As for me, I wasted hours of anguish waiting to hear about a transfer to Latchmere. In the end, I never did manage to get out of a 'C' cat prison. Like many others I was simply exposed to more and more of the criminal mind. I was lucky though: I had a caring family and friends to go back to. Most didn't.

Throughout summer I kept my emotional batteries topped up by phoning Ben and Bronya. Ben was due to start a new year at school, and I hoped there would be some sort of organised sport. Bronya battled away at work, coped with life at home, and visited me every week. God knows how she survived, standing outside, waiting in the long queues each week, only to be treated like a criminal herself by some of the reception officers. But she still kept coming and, more than anything else, her regular visits helped me to survive. Like other visitors she was searched more thoroughly after a gun and ammunition were found in the grounds, but cuts in staff and a huge increase in the prison population made it inevitable that one day security would be breached. Anyway, according to Paul, it was only a 'peashooter'. No self-respecting blagger would be seen dead with such a puny weapon.

Another, major problem was the amount of drugs pouring into the prison. I simply couldn't see why the authorities didn't do something about it. Anyone who says that it's impossible to stop drugs getting into prison is adopting an extremely apathetic stance. Of course it's difficult – *but it is possible.*

It needs only discipline, limited funds, and determination, to stop 'importing' in its tracks. A sniffer dog allocated to every prison would make an enormous difference, but even that's *too expensive* (though the £120,000 given to the whackos in the Stress Clinic was presumably not). Seeing drugs in daily use and the effect that they had on those around me, I couldn't help but feel strongly about the issue. Everybody agreed how deplorable they were, yet no one did a thing to stop them being imported.

Apart from standing on my soap-box and banging my drum to some of the officers about the evils of heroin (yes – that was brave), I survived the summer pretty well. I hadn't hidden from much and I could feel myself almost jockeying for position to unload my problems. I saw a lot of Mike Hart, and he continued to try to persuade me to give my testimony on the Youth Project. But I still held back – I couldn't quite commit myself. Then, one day, something happened that forced the issue.

It was Wednesday night and I went to the chapel for the Christian fellowship. The meetings took place every Wednesday and were open to all, irrespective of belief. That night about thirty of us sat round to watch a slide-show given by Harold, a landscape gardener and occasional prison visitor. It was a good show, hardly exciting, but some of the long-term prisoners hadn't seen many flowers during their twenty-odd years inside and it made a pleasant change from the drab uniformity of prison. On the downside, it was a sad reminder of what we were missing.

After the lecture we had coffee, which I helped serve, and it was during those twenty minutes that I came across Thompson. He was standing on the edge of the group, looking very timid, and he immediately struck a chord in me. He was small and thin, he even looked a bit like me – just younger, without the greying hair. I wandered across to offer him coffee.

'Like one?' I asked, but he shook his head. He was very pale. 'Are you OK?' I persisted, concerned.

'Yes,' he said quietly. He looked like a lemur with those huge staring eyes and I guessed he had recently come from somewhere like Wandsworth. He was a classic example of a young man who had no idea what prison was like. Although he looked pretty forlorn, so did many others in the prison, and with an encouraging smile I moved off to serve others.

After the meeting he went back to his cell like the rest of us, but once he was alone, he passed the point so many get near, but few cross. At the end of his tether, he broke up a disposable razor, took out the blade and, in an attempt to end the torment, slashed both wrists. Two hours after leaving the meeting he lay dying in his cell.

No one had known that he was being bullied at work, or that his Mum was ill. Normally, inside probation would have picked it up, but they were no longer there, and the landings were no place if you had problems. It was only through a quirk of fate that an officer happened to look through Thompson's peephole and spotted the blood. After an emergency dash to hospital they managed to save him.

I was told the next morning, when the metal shop needed to fill a vacancy. I realised that I must have been one of the last people to talk to him, but I had been unaware that he was so close to the edge. It left me shattered. For two weeks I walked around trying to understand how I seemed to be coping, asking myself why I never suspected the depths of his turmoil, but at the same time wondering whether my turn was only round the corner. Had I been younger, I don't think I could have coped.

One morning, in mid-September, I was sitting in the deserted chapel area waiting for the vicar to turn up, when the door below opened and an officer came upstairs.

'Is the vicar around?' he asked.

'No, not yet – can I help?'

He hesitated. 'Someone from the block's being transferred; wants to pray in the chapel.'

'Who?' I asked.

He knew me well enough to answer. 'Thompson.'

'*Thompson!*' I said, aghast. 'I thought he'd already been transferred.'

'No prison would have him – he's been here since he came back from hospital. No one wants a suicide risk – he needs watching all day.'

'How is he?' I asked, concerned.

'Bit of a mess. His mum's just died of cancer. I'll go and get him.'

For two weeks I had thought about Thompson, hoping he was managing to cope, only to find he had been sleeping within yards of us, suffering his problems alone. I wanted to disappear. I'd never witnessed so much pain – *I was scared.*

A few minutes later the door opened and I heard footsteps on the stairs. When they arrived at the top the officer went to unlock and check the chapel, and I was left looking at the young man. His hair was lank and his eyes bloodshot. His face was deathly pale, his body slumped forward devoid of tension – it screamed capitulation. I had always thought myself a good motivator, but as I looked at the figure before me, at the two plaster casts on his wrists covering his wounds, I was dwarfed by hopelessness.

'Where are they sending you?' I asked, trying to force a sympathetic smile. He looked at me and I could see his bottom lip start to tremble.

'They mentioned Broadmoor . . . the hospital unit,' he said, his voice quavering.

There was nothing I could say, no last-minute tactics, no advice. He was crossing into territory I just couldn't imagine. We both knew it was the end of the line.

'I've . . . come . . . to . . . pray,' he said. 'Will . . . you . . . pray . . . for . . . me?'

I was trying to keep my composure. 'I'll pray very hard for you,' I said. 'People care, you know.'

He stood rocking gently back and forth and then he started to cry. I couldn't speak – I stepped forward and hugged him, trying to convey sympathy. My instinct told me that he needed comfort, and I held him, trying to pour some hope into his empty shell.

For twenty minutes I knelt with him in the chapel. His plastered wrists kept slipping off the edge of the pew, and eventually he let his forehead sink to the wood, his hands gripped between his thighs as if in a position of execution. His tears dripped onto the floor, his breathing was racked with sobs.

The officer came down the aisle and I watched as he gently put his hand on Thompson's shoulder. 'Time to go,' he said.

I looked at Thompson for the last time. I didn't know what to say, but threw everything into two words: 'Take care,' I said.

I found Mike Hart waiting for me outside. 'OK?' he asked.

I wiped my eyes; I couldn't answer.

'John, come onto the Youth Project. Stop people like Thompson coming in here. If he'd been warned what it's like . . .'

I thought of the young, wretched man. 'OK,' I agreed.

18

The Youth Project

Coming face to face with Thompson in the chapel had a lasting effect on me. For him prison was the very worst nightmare. Being subjected to bullying and then hearing those devastating words from the chaplain, 'I'm sorry but I have some bad news for you,' had been more than he could cope with. I realised I'd been lucky to survive unscathed so far. And it *was* luck. Had I found myself in the wrong cell in Wandsworth, with inmates less supportive than Guido, or had something devastating happened at home, it's possible that I would have crumbled in the same way.

I was determined to make my testimony in public, for my own sake, but also to speak to others about the realities of prison, in the hope of making one or two change the direction in which they were heading.

The next Youth Project production, however, was only a week away and had been carefully organised and rehearsed. After discussing my role with Mike, we agreed that my testimony would best be given a month later, and that on Tuesday I should just watch and listen. I was quite happy with that. I had made a commitment to speak, and that in itself had brought me an element of peace.

A week later, dressed in my smartest prison shirt, I was escorted with three other prisoners (who constituted the 'welcoming committee') to the visiting hall where we were to meet the sixty young-sters, their teachers and youth leaders. The youths had been picked to experience a day 'inside' as a last resort. Many were already in serious trouble with convictions for theft and drug-taking, but their day in court and the leniency shown had had little effect. Without a change of direction, the next stop could be prison, not as a visitor but as an inmate.

It took about twenty minutes for all the kids to be searched by an officer before they sat down. It wasn't altogether necessary but it added to the atmosphere of discipline, something that seemed to be sadly lacking in all the youths congregated in the hall. Most of them were boys, some as young as twelve, but the average age must have been fifteen. I hadn't considered the possibility of girls being present, but there must have been about ten, dotted around the room. It was only later I learned that two of the girls were already taking heroin and had convictions for shoplifting. They reminded me of the kids who always seemed to be hanging around outside the supermarket, or in the bus shelter, in Cranleigh, where I once lived, a sleepy town similar to hundreds of others around the country.

Some were dressed in school uniform, most were in casual clothes, but they nearly all wore the same surly expressions. From their body language alone, as they slouched casually in their chairs, it was obvious they felt hard enough to cope with prison – prison, it seemed, was a joke.

After a few minutes to allow them to become accustomed to the atmosphere, Terry got up to make his introductory speech. He had been handpicked for the job. Terry was one of the biggest men I've ever seen – six foot six and twenty-two stone. His low gravelly voice contained as much power as Clint Eastwood at his most menacing, and he gave the impression that if you were foolhardy enough to mess with him, it would be the last thing you would do. His sheer physical presence made the youths sit up and listen. They could not have seen many such powerful men, and they must have been shocked to hear his story.

Incredibly, Terry had been bullied inside. He explained how he had been 'housed' on the wrong landing, amongst the wrong inmates, and the daily persecution had started when he complained that the toilet hadn't been flushed. After several other incidents five inmates crashed into his cell and pinned him to the floor, where another took out a tin lid and with the serrated edge slashed his face from forehead to chin. The ugly jagged scar that we could all see bore testimony to the event.

The power of his quiet testimony was awesome and anyone who had ever contemplated surviving in prison through their own physical power had their illusions immediately dispelled. It was a brutal story to open up with, but unless the bravado of the youths was broken down, little impact would be achieved.

Dave then got up and gave a short speech specifically aimed at the girls. Dave and his wife had been convicted of theft and were both sentenced to three years' imprisonment. His wife was pregnant at the time and had to give birth to their son handcuffed to a hospital bed. He read out a letter she had written, depicting the squalor of Holloway and the dreadful depression she went through after their baby was taken away.

Finally Ted spoke about the rules and regulations that the prisoners have to abide by and the general lack of privacy. He pointed to the prying cameras. 'You're being watched already,' he said. He explained that in prison they would have to do exactly what they're told *when* they're told. There would be no excuses. Anybody who broke the rules would be in serious trouble.

After these welcoming speeches, the group moved through to see the punishment area: 'the block' where violent prisoners are constrained with 'body belts'. It was impossible not to imagine the screaming and the pain that would go with the sometimes necessary but dreadful treatment. What made the scene particularly shocking was the detached, clinical way the officer described the punishment, as though he were dealing with a piece of contaminated meat. As we finally made our way across to the chapel, the surly, macho swaggers were becoming a little less confident.

It took about twenty minutes for the group to move from one side of the prison to the other. Seven large iron gates had to be opened and relocked as we passed through, and every time the bolts slammed back into place it brought home how distanced we were becoming from the outside world. Friends stayed closer together and the one macho boy who thought he could taunt the officer by lagging behind was now firmly attached to the group. It must have been the worst place they had ever seen.

When we eventually arrived in the chapel, stern-faced inmates greeted the children at the door, cruelly separating them from their friends and leading them individually to a semicircle of seats around a makeshift stage. Police officers, teachers and youth leaders sat in the back row. Conversation had died, and it wasn't long before Mike Hart walked round to the front of the stage and faced the audience. I thought the youths were adequately stunned and wondered how Mike would greet them. His silver grey hair, pale blue eyes and kind smile immediately reassured the youths that the day was not meant to frighten, it was a warning from Grandad.

'Good afternoon,' he said, his eyes taking in every one of the children. 'My name's Mike Hart, and I want to explain what the Youth Project is all about. Today's event has not been organised by the prison, but by the inmates themselves,' he said, pointing to the fifteen standing at the far end of the hall. 'We're here because we care so much about you that we never want you to come into a place like this again. Some of us are serving sentences as long as twenty-five years, and yet we started off our lives of crime by doing exactly what you're doing now: petty theft, causing trouble, playing truant. We're not your teachers or parents, we can't tell you what to do. All we *can* do is warn you not to make the mistakes we made.'

Mike's brief explanation was perfect. We did care about them more than they could possibly know. Knowing what awaited them 'behind bars', the thought that some of these baby-faced youths could one day end up in prison, was an appalling one, and the next two hours reflected that. Every effort was made to force them to sit up and think.

The drama production was very poignant. The simple plot revolved round two young lads who one day steal some sweets from the local shop but aren't caught. This leads them to take greater risks, where they do get caught. The ensuing community service order has a positive effect on Joe. His friend, however, returns to crime, and eventually gets eight years for armed robbery. The drama was good on its own, but the contained message was made additionally powerful when the action stopped and the audience was given an opportunity for role-play.

'Joe's friend has just persuaded him to go and steal some sweets,' Mike said, looking expectantly at the audience. 'We want one of you to come out here and re-enact the scene, but this time say "no".'

At first there wasn't a great deal of enthusiasm, but eventually, with a little help, a young boy put his hand up. 'I'll do it,' he said.

Joe's mate, supposedly a ten-year-old boy, was played by Frank, an inmate well over six foot tall. 'Come on, we'll go and nick some sweets,' he said to the child looking up at him. We all waited for the answer.

'No,' said the boy.

'What d'you mean, "no"?' said Frank, raising his voice. 'Come on, we won't get caught.'

'No, I don't want to,' the boy said, sounding slightly less sure of himself.

'*Don't want to*. Call yourself a mate?' said Frank, applying the pressure. 'Come on, don't be such a chicken.'

The boy looked round. No one moved. Everyone was holding their breath, hoping he could say 'no' one more time.

'No, I'm not doing it,' he blurted out. 'If you were my mate, you wouldn't ask me to do it.' The room erupted into applause. It sounded as though it was the first time the boy had ever said 'no'. For his pains he received a T-shirt proclaiming, 'I've been to prison – I know what it's like.'

The rest of the drama was equally successful, but at certain points where Joe's friend was struggling to come to terms with prison, the action again paused as an inmate delivered his experiences 'inside'. Many were gruesome and horrific – but all were true.

Hearing the brief speeches had an amazing impact on me. It was almost as though I was seeing the true picture of my environment for the first time. I had survived in prison because I had switched off my mind and my senses. When someone described what I had gone through and survived, I was left open-mouthed.

When the drama came to an end, as a finale, the inmates sang a song written by Mike, called 'It's Better Out than In'.

It was nearly the end of the day, but first there was a ten-minute period when the youths were split into small groups with an inmate allotted to each group, so that he could answer any questions the youngsters had. I thought I was to play no part, but Mike led a small boy to one end of the hall, sat him down and then headed in my direction.

'John, I've been talking to one of the teachers about the boy over there,' he said, nodding towards the end of the hall. 'He's got involved with a group of older boys who're stealing cars. He used to be good at sport, but no matter how much the teacher tries to get through to him, he can't. Have a go, will you? Get him to open up a bit,' he said, taking me by the arm and leading me across the hall.

'Jason, I want you to meet John,' he said. 'Talk to him, tell him what you're doing.' The boy looked at me cautiously.

'Hello, Jason,' I said, giving him a reassuring smile. Mike drifted away and I was left with the youngster, who could not have been more than fourteen.

'Mike tells me you're good at sport,' I said, trying to steer him onto neutral ground, but he sat looking at the floor. I wasn't quite sure where to take the conversation and we didn't have long. 'I used to be a professional golfer, played for England once or twice before I came in here.' He continued to stare at the floor, but after a few seconds he spoke. 'I've played golf once or twice with my dad,' he said. Then he lifted his head. I suppose it was a bit like hitting the jackpot. Almost immediately the common ground was firm enough for me to begin to get through to him, and when we parted I hoped my message about keeping on the straight and narrow would be remembered. Certainly his attention was focused on me more closely than if we shared nothing at all.

From then on, my past career was almost a signature tune, and I like to think that the youngsters I've spoken to since have at least remembered what the 'golfer' said. The game itself, the fact that I'd been a professional sportsman, had opened many doors to me in the past. I like to think that none have been more important than the ones it has opened recently.

Throughout the day I had watched Mike constantly trying to get through to the young people who had come into the prison. His energy was fantastic and at the end I was left with an overwhelming impression of a man totally dedicated to helping mixed-up children. I knew then that, given the opportunity, I would do the same if I could. It could possibly be the one positive thing to emerge out of the last two years.

Two days later I was in the chapel with Mike when one of the officers came up to deliver a letter. It had come from the Metropolitan Police. Apparently six youths who had attended the project had turned up at the police station and handed in six flick-knives, a crowbar, and several other bits and pieces that were tools of the house burglar and car thief. The police were delighted. They praised the boys and immediately wrote to Mike to tell him the good news and congratulate him on yet another success. They regularly sent their problem youngsters to see the project and they also had the video that they could show at their station.

The lack of publicity that the project was getting, though, was frustrating. 'World in Action' wanted to film it and one day the ITV news team came down, but it was such a political 'hot potato' without Home Office backing, that there was no way it would get a media launch. Mike had great hopes of extending the project nationally with the use of the video, but without the necessary backing, only the local area was benefiting. He also felt strongly that prisons throughout the country should be participating in similar projects, and I knew he was prepared to travel to other jails to show the prisoners what to do.

At the time, the then Home Secretary Michael Howard, in response to public opinion, was proposing much tougher prisons, boot camps and fewer privileges for inmates. But those conditions were already in existence. To have a video bandied about showing the realities of prison was not on the agenda, particularly when it was a 'lifer' who was doing all the good work.

However there was one piece of good news. So many important people were behind Mike and his project, that he had been invited to go to London to speak in front of nine hundred people at a conference on crime and punishment. I was thrilled for Mike when he told me, not only because the Youth Project, at last, might attract some deserved publicity, but also on a personal note: it would be his first day outside for twenty-two years, albeit under escort, and handcuffed to two officers.

As the day drew closer all those involved in the project came into the chapel to wish Mike good luck, knowing it was going to be the biggest day for the project since he had conceived the idea ten years previously.

The morning before he was due to go I wandered into the chapel to find him sitting in a chair. It was unusual to find him sitting anywhere. Normally he was busy working away, and instinctively I knew something was wrong.

'What's the matter, Mike?' I asked, walking round and sitting next to him. He seemed to have to collect himself and paused before answering. 'The Home Office has stopped me from going, John.'

What?! I was aghast 'Why?'

'They don't want me to go – that's it.' Mike knew the Home Office. There was no arguing.

'Mike, I'm so sorry.' I felt absolutely sick for him.

'Forget that. Look, I need someone to speak and the only person

I can trust to do a good job is you. I've asked the vicar to speak to the governor and clear it with security. You're a 'D' cat, they should let you go.'

I was stunned. My initial instinct was that I couldn't possibly go – not to replace Mike like that. It was his day, his baby, and anything said about the project he should say.

'John, I need you to go,' he said, trying to convince me that it was the right thing to do. 'I need you to speak about the project and I want you to go for another reason. My speech was to last for twenty minutes and it also involved some of my experiences inside. I want you to use this opportunity to give your testimony – you *need* to.'

I argued for a while, but Mike was stubborn and, what's more, he'd asked me to do it as a personal favour. Within the hour, the vicar had returned with authorisation that I was to go to London the following day – *unescorted*. A wave of emotions hit me. I was so disappointed for Mike, it seemed grossly unfair that he couldn't go. But what dwarfed every other emotion was fear. Not the fear of speaking in front of so many people. One person or nine hundred – it made no difference. It was fear of finally confronting the pain inside. I had fought hard for this chance, and I hoped, beyond hope, that it would be a crucial step towards a future.

19

The New Bridge Conference on Crime and Punishment

The next morning, after a fretful night, I woke up at four o'clock and thought about the day ahead. I knew I was looking pathetically thin and scrawny but at least I'd made an effort to make myself look presentable.

From reception, I had been allowed to collect a leather jacket that had been left for me by Bronya. I had phoned her during the afternoon to tell her the news, and, knowing full well the only overcoat I had was prison issue, she had left work, collected my jacket from home and delivered it to the prison.

This really threw the reception officers. It was against regulations to receive goods into the prison without permission from the governor. They *thought* it would be all right but they had to check. The reception SO *thought* it would be fine, but he also had to check. The PO had no objections but it *was* against regulations, so he was unable to make a decision and the deputy governor was called. The prison was so afraid of upsetting the Home Office, that everybody was paranoid about making decisions.

Finally, though, I had been allowed my jacket. With the shampoo I had borrowed from Eric and the new razor I had collected from the downstairs office, I would go out looking my best.

One cloud hung over my trip. News that I was going out to London had spread like wildfire, and it wasn't long before one of the drug barons came for a chat. He was one of four major sources of drugs in the jail and he constantly needed supplies. The thought that a trusted inmate was going out was an opportunity too good to miss.

'I want you to go to this address, collect a parcel, swallow it or sew it into the lining in your jacket and bring it back to me. I'll give you two hundred quid for your troubles.'

Mickey was white, aged about thirty. He was hard, had a dreadful reputation and employed several thugs to carry out his threats. But it was no temptation to me – all I wanted to do was refuse in the politest way.

'Sorry, Mickey – I'm just not into that.' He looked at me and slowly spoke the address where I should go. 'Remember it,' he said, winking. 'I'll see you tomorrow when you get back.'

When I went to borrow some shampoo, I mentioned the little chat to Eric. 'Jesus, you do get yourself in the shit, Hoski. You should give up all this honest crap – too much trouble. Look, you bugger off to London. Enjoy your day – you lucky bastard – and if I get the chance, I'll have a word with Mickey.'

'Tell him I'm not doing it,' I said.

'You'll owe me, big time.' I nodded. *Thank God I have friends*, I thought.

As soon as my cell door opened at seven-thirty I dived out, grabbed a shower and, when dressed, made my way along to reception.

'Say hello to Soho for me, Hoski.'

'Give her one for me, kid.'

'Send us a postcard when you get to Spain.' The comments rained down as I walked past the wing.

I was given a travel warrant from Woking station to London and £2.20 so that I could buy lunch. The senior security officer looked at me as he handed it over. 'Be back by six, not a minute later. And Hodgkinson,' he said, giving me a stern look, 'don't do a runner.'

I was then escorted to a part of the prison I hadn't seen before. It was the visitors' entrance, the hallway to the front door. The security was phenomenal. Two huge electric doors slid open to let me through, and it crossed my mind that my son had passed down this same corridor when he came to see me. For a seven-year-old boy it must have been pretty daunting.

Finally I came to the entrance hall and, with all my paperwork completed, I was free to step outside. Before I did so I looked round at the two officers watching but they didn't shout, or call me back, and moments later I took the step that brought me outside the walls of the prison.

Almost immediately the taxi booked for me pulled up alongside. 'Woking station, is it?' he asked – but I was in a daze.

'Yes, Guv,' I answered.

The first thing that struck me was the fear I had of travelling in the car. The driver was a lunatic, the speed he was driving was ridiculous – but when I looked at the speedometer it was only showing forty miles an hour.

When I reached the station I walked to the ticket office to show my travel warrant, but six people bustled past me to the front of the queue. They appeared to be set on fast forward. I was amazed. In just a year I had adapted to the pace of prison, which was obviously considerably slower than that on the outside.

After collecting my ticket from the man behind the counter whom, like the taxi driver, I also called Guv, I went out to stand on the platform. There were a few minutes before the train came, and I decided to buy a Mars Bar from the sweet shop, as I hadn't had time for breakfast. I felt quite ashamed when I stuffed it deep into my pocket and walked to the far end of the platform. I tried to tell myself that there was no way any of the commuters would mug me, but I ate it with my back turned to the crowd.

The platform was packed as it was still only 8.15, and when the train came I found the only seat available was next to a business-man. I felt PRISONER was stamped across my forehead and that everyone would instantly know. I put my hand up to my brow in the 'thinking man's' position. Apart from an occasional glance out of the window I pretended to be asleep for much of the journey. Finally the train pulled into Waterloo and I headed towards the underground and Bedford Square, my destination.

Even the smallest things, like looking up which line I had to take, I found complicated. My whole metabolism, both mental and physical, had slowed down to such a degree that it needed all my concentration to work out the simplest things. In that respect, prison was definitely a protective bubble.

Eventually I arrived at the correct station and wandered out to find my way to the university hall where the conference was to take place. In the back of my mind I knew what I was going to say. I was well aware of the importance of preparation. I had made many important speeches in the past after winning golf tournaments, twice in front of Prince Andrew when I had won the Nelson Trophy in consecutive years; but twenty minutes is a long time to stand and talk in front of nearly a thousand people. As I walked the final few hundred yards once again I rehearsed the main points in my mind. It was going to be an emotional time.

At ten o'clock I climbed the steps to the imposing building, took a deep breath and went inside. The hustle and bustle was unbeliev-able, and I had to stop myself from thinking that flight was the best option. Holding my head up and taking a deep breath, I summoned all my courage and made my way to the reception desk where I had been told to report.

'Good morning,' I said to the woman. 'I'm meant to register here, I believe.'

'Name?'

'Hoskison – I'm one of the guest speakers.'

She went straight to a small pile of badges laid out in one corner but then found mine in an envelope tucked to one side. I could see her mouth open slightly in surprise as she took out the badge and slowly handed it to me. It was probably my paranoia but suddenly I felt like an animal at the zoo.

I was pointed in the direction of a small room where the panel of speakers were gathering, and before I could change my mind I walked across and opened the door. But my bravado almost crumbled and I tried to slide in unnoticed. Almost immediately a voice seemed to rise above the rest, 'Ah, you must be John Hoskison from Coldingley.' All eyes turned towards me. It was almost the first time since my court appearance that someone other than prison officials, fellow inmates or family had spoken to me. I was so embarrassed. I willed the ground to swallow me up, but the man who had organised the conference was very experienced, and within a few minutes, during which he spent time reassuring me, I was feeling a little more confident.

After what seemed an interminable wait we were led through to the hall where we took up our places behind a table on stage. On my right was the Right Honourable Lord Justice Brooke, on my left, Chief Inspector Peter Golding of New Scotland Yard. Nine hundred students, lecturers and dignitaries packed the hall. I looked at the sea of faces. I sat, quite frankly, in terror.

I don't remember much about the conference over the next hour until Sir Peter Lloyd, MP, finished speaking and began introducing the next guest-speaker. 'It's now time to listen to someone who's currently serving a prison sentence.'

I was so nervous it took a second to realise that he was talking about me. I stood up on trembling legs and made my way to the podium which was bathed in spotlights. The audience, who had appeared slightly fidgety during the previous hour, suddenly fell completely silent. I adjusted the microphone, took a deep breath and then let my soul pour out.

'I've been asked here today to give my personal testimony and speak of the harsh realities of prison.' My throat was dry, but there was no going back. 'I've agreed to speak in the hope my story will stop anyone from making the same mistake I made.

'I'm currently serving a three-year prison sentence for a car accident in which someone was killed,' I heard my hoarse voice say. 'I'm serving that sentence because, for once, I didn't listen to my conscience warning me I was about to do wrong . . .

'The choice I made was "just this once – I'll take the risk". The choice I made has inflicted untold suffering.

'For twenty years I was a professional golfer. Not only did I enjoy playing tournament golf but I also sat on many committees, gave my time freely to charities and actively encouraged junior golfers. I was respected by friends and colleagues. I had a most wonderful life. Then one day I went to play in a golf match. After we finished we went to the bar for a drink. I'd always been very careful not to drink and drive, a discipline I'd maintained over all the years of travelling to tournaments, but I'd been ill, hadn't eaten for three days and although inside my head alarm bells rang, I was sufficiently distracted not to listen to the warning. I drank no more than the others but on an empty stomach I was over the limit when I left the club.

'My drive home took me down a dark country lane with no street lights and at a bend by a bridge, described at a parish council meeting only nine days before, as "narrow and causing a hazardous situation", a car came towards me with headlights full on. I was dazzled. I put my left hand up to shield my eyes. The speed limit was forty, I was travelling at thirty-four.

'A split second later when I regained my sight, a cyclist, unseen till now, was only a yard in front of me. There was no time to react, no time to move a muscle, and my car hit the cyclist . . . My mind was paralysed by the staggering shock, and with all thought and reason blocked I left the scene of the accident.'

I looked at the audience while I gathered myself. Inevitably in my thoughts I was reliving those dreadful moments. I had seen the cyclist at the very last second. There had been no time even to take my foot off the accelerator and, frozen in position, I had driven on. When my mind stopped reeling I found I had already left the scene. The only thing I can remember clearly is that I wanted to die. There is no rational way to behave in such circumstances. In the pitch blackness of the night, animal instinct shut the system down and I panicked. Had anyone told me beforehand that I could possibly have reacted the way I did, I would never have believed them. It was something I had avoided thinking or talking about – the most difficult thing for me to come to terms with.

I went on to explain to the silent audience that my car had been damaged in the accident and that within the hour I was at the police station, where I was breathalysed and found to be over the limit. It was there that I was told the cyclist had been instantly killed . . .

For the next few minutes I managed to continue with my speech, all the while experiencing a mix of emotions so concentrated that I doubt I will ever taste the like again. Remorse for the accident and my reaction to it; grief at the loss of life; sadness for everyone touched by the tragic affair; and humility at the compassion and forgiveness shown to me by the victim's wife. Finally, when I spoke of Mike Hart's project there was hope. Crossing from one emotion to the other with such speed left me literally gasping for breath. But, even as I spoke I could feel relief sweep through me. Somehow I managed to get through to the end without breaking down but when I returned to my seat, I was sweating, weak and shattered. I sat down listening to the applause. I couldn't believe that my speech had been met with a positive reaction.

I longed for peace and quiet at that very moment, so that I could reflect on my speech and what it had meant to me. But the conference continued and I knew my thoughts would have to wait until the evening when I could be alone in my cell.

Throughout the rest of the day, various experts stood up and voiced their opinions, backing up their views with hard facts. Britain now stands third in the world league when it comes to handing out custodial sentences. The rest of the conference looked at how other countries dealt with those who broke the law. It seemed that the less severe policies of many countries eventually led more convicted criminals back into society without reoffending.

But in Britain it was Catch 22. During his speech Graham Wilson, head of prison services, explained the frustration felt by his department when the press blew up a story involving a degree of leniency, and publicised it as the norm. It was understandable, he explained, that the public should get annoyed if they only hear one side of the story. What was not understandable, as far as the prison service was concerned, was when the government, there to provide a lead, simply adopted policies to give them a quiet life.

At the end of the conference one of the organisers stood up and gave an impassioned speech. He gave an example of the damage that could be done by not following the experts' advice, but it had nothing to do with prison. It was regarding an old oil platform in the North Sea that was due to be sunk at sea. 'Greenpeace' had got on the bandwagon and protested so vehemently that, after much press coverage, public opinion was fired. It has been proved beyond doubt that the safest place to bury the platform was at sea. But the government had crumbled under the pressure, halted the process and insisted that the platform be dismantled on land.

He made it clear to everyone present that it was they who would help shape the future of the country, and their decisions should be based on facts, rather than swayed by media reports intended to inflame public opinion.

When the discussions finished all the panel congregated in the waiting room for a cup of tea and it surprised me how relaxed I felt, socialising once more with normal people. Although I would have liked to stay longer I was very time-conscious and couldn't stop looking at my watch. I had no intention of arriving back late and after a short while I made my apologies and left.

Lunch had fortunately been provided at the conference and when I finally arrived at Waterloo I could feel my loose change burning a hole in my pocket. I sat down in the cafe opposite the huge arrival and destination board and bought myself a coffee.

I had grown used to prison over the last year, but a day outside, living and mixing in a normal environment with normal people, was enough to make me realise what a terrible and violent place jail is. For the first time in a year I had been with people who wouldn't stab me if I said the wrong thing. I still had six months to serve and I was voluntarily going back. As I looked up at the destination board, for just a brief, fleeting moment I considered absconding.

A train was shortly due to leave that I had taken in the past on my way to Cornwall, a place I considered a second home. Beautiful beaches, a marvellous coastline and all that space. It would be great to visit. Maybe just a short break. Just a few days . . . Shocked by the direction my thoughts were taking I got up quickly, left my coffee half-finished and headed straight for the Woking train, though it was not due to leave for another ten minutes. In my compartment I sat gripping the sides of my seat as though at the dentist's, telling myself that I was 'definitely doing the right thing'. It seemed an eternity before the train eventually departed.

As we headed towards Woking, the fear that had evaporated during my 'away day' slowly descended like a dark mist to dominate my instincts completely. All I could think about was Mickey and his bloody drugs parcel. He was a hard, unforgiving man and the main fuel-tanks of my imagination fired simultaneously. When the train pulled into the station, I made my way back to the prison with gritted teeth.

It took ages for me to get through reception. I was strip-searched and questioned in depth. They couldn't believe that I had travelled straight there and back without any 'dodgy' detours. Eventually when they couldn't find any proof (which they looked hard enough to find) I was allowed back onto the wing. But no sooner had I entered my cell when a message was passed along and I was summoned downstairs. It was question time.

Mickey the drug man and his henchman took me along the corridor. I looked round to see if any of my allies were around but there was no one. 'Well, where is it?' he asked.

'Listen, Mickey, I didn't have the time, and I couldn't do it anyway – it's just not me.'

He looked at me closely and I met his eyes. 'If I find you've collected, I'll cut your fuckin' throat.' His hand gripped my chin for a few seconds, then, playfully, he slapped me across the cheek. 'Eric said you wouldn't bring it back, too much of a straight goer – but there's always next time,' he said, with a wicked smile.

I was left in the corridor and for a while didn't make a move to go – it had been an emotional day.

Later, although tired, I lay on my bed and released my mind to wander freely. At first it was hard reflecting on the consequences of that fateful night after such a long time, but as the emotions and memories I had hidden from for so long came flooding back, I tried to absorb them, rather than continue to turn away.

The year on bail had almost crippled me. Nothing had been harder than trying to carry on as normal, while knowing that things would never be normal again. I thought back to the endless hours I had spent alone in my flat trying to find a reason to carry on. I thought of Ben. I thought back to the day when I had received a reply to the letter I had sent the victim's wife. I had sunk to my knees when I had read her words of forgiveness.

I still felt immense guilt when I found myself thinking about the devastation to my own life but I realised finally that it had to stop. There and then I got up, switched on the light and from out of my personal box, stashed underneath my bed, I got out the *Golf Monthly* articles that I had had published. Someone had kindly sent them in to me but until then I hadn't had the strength to read them. I opened up the first six-page article, entitled 'Building Good Foundations'. I stared at the main photo in which my son Ben stood next to me, sticking out his chest and looking so proud. I made myself look at all the other articles and thought about the plans *Golf Monthly* had had for making an instruction video of my ideas, that was to have been released nationally. My life had been so rewarding, there were never enough hours in the day. Yet, now there was little of that left. I had held a sparkling jewel in my hand and it had turned into a pebble.

*

My memories took me down a hard road that night, but somehow I managed to survive. Delivering my personal testimony to so many people had been the right thing to do. Whatever the problem, whether it be alcoholism, drug addiction, or denial, it seems that a frank admission is the first step to recovery.

I knew there would be problems ahead, but Mike Hart had been right. I could now allow the healing process to start.

20

The Last Hurdle

In October, having completed two thirds of my sentence, I was allowed to apply for 'home leave': a period of four days away from the prison when you can stay at home. For months Bronya and I had dreamt of the chance of spending some real time together. Not only would home leave allow the luxury of freedom away from the problems inside, but it also represented a hurdle. Once passed, it would be the beginning of the end of my time in prison.

Everything suggested that I would be given the go-ahead. I was a 'D' cat prisoner and I had returned safely from my trip to London, but even so, I still couldn't believe it when the security department passed me as acceptable. It was something we had dared not rely on, particularly at a time when so many privileges were being refused. It was a week after I handed in my application form before I received a reply, but when I read the confirmation slip, a grin lit my face and I made a beeline for the phone.

Bronya had been so strong for me throughout the year. She'd taken all the heartache and frustration without complaining once, but for all her support there had been little I could do in return. I had earned the privilege of home leave through good behaviour. It was the first gift I was able to give her since arriving in prison. When I told her the news she burst into tears.

Inside the prison walls I tried to keep the news quiet. Not only did I feel sorry for the men whom security turned down, but I also didn't want the likes of Mickey, the drug baron, asking me for favours. But inevitably news like that travels fast, and, for the next week, I was subjected to a fair amount of flack. Nothing serious however, until one evening, when I was waiting in the canteen queue with about thirty other inmates.

A solidly built white man, known as a trouble-maker, was making his way back to the wing when he paused in front of me in the narrow corridor. 'You're a fucking grass, aren't you?' he said loudly. Everyone stopped talking. I didn't know what to say – or do. It was the worst thing you could ever call another inmate. He obviously couldn't see how anyone could earn the privilege of home leave without being an informer.

With the speed of lightning, a black fist flashed past me and crashed into the side of his head, flooring him instantly. The man who threw the punch then bent down. 'He ain't no fuckin' grass,' he said, sticking a finger into the face of the dazed man. 'Don't ever say that again.'

The man on the floor slowly stood up and moved off. I turned round to my saviour. 'Thank you,' I said, looking at the black face. Twister simply nodded back. The incident was over before it had started, with my reputation intact. As we continued to wait in the queue, I couldn't help but think back to the time I had virtually written Twister off as a no-hoper. I had to revise my conviction that my first impressions were accurate.

The following days dragged interminably. Never had I looked forward to anything quite so much, and I knew Bronya felt the same. Eric and the guys on my landing were really good about my going. I was even given a tin of tuna that Eric had bribed off one of the kitchen staff. 'Better get this down yer neck,' he said. 'You'll be needing plenty of energy, you skinny runt.'

It was four days before my scheduled trip that one morning I was called down to the office on the ground floor. I thought I had been summoned to sign my temporary release licence but when I entered the office I saw the deputy governor sitting behind the table, obviously waiting for me. He didn't beat about the bush. 'Latchmere House have offered you a place,' he said. 'You're getting shipped out tomorrow.'

'What?' I said, aghast. 'Tomorrow?' I couldn't believe it. I had waited months and months to go to Latchmere, but every time I was notified of imminent transfer it had been cancelled. Eventually, I had been told that the eligibility rules had changed, and only prisoners serving over four years were accepted. Yet now I was being given twenty-four hours' notice before a move.

'Guv, I'm due to go on "home leave" on Friday. Can't I go after that?' I asked.

'It's now or never,' he said. 'You're not really supposed to go at all, they've just got a spare place that needs filling.'

'Will they honour my "home leave", Guv?'

'No,' he said, shaking his head. 'You've got six weeks' induction before you get any privileges at all – you've got to prove to them that you're trustworthy.'

'But I've done that here. I've spent a year proving I'm trustworthy.'

'That makes no odds – you've got to start again.'

I asked for ten minutes to consider my position, but deep down I knew I would turn down the offer. I had secured myself a niche in Coldingley, I was on the best 'spur' in the prison, Eric and the guys ruled with a rod of iron, and somehow kept it heroin-free. Although the prison was one with a fearful reputation, I felt safe. More importantly there was no way I could sacrifice my home leave. If I phoned Bronya now to tell her I was being transferred to Latchmere and that my leave was cancelled, unquestionably she would take the blow. But it was one I was not prepared to hand out.

'Sorry, Guv,' I said, facing the deputy governor, 'but I'm not prepared to forgo my home leave. If it means staying here, I'll do so.'

In one fell swoop I was committed to spending the rest of my sentence in Coldingley.

*

Four days later I emerged from prison into the outside world: a dress rehearsal for what was to come in five months' time. At eight o'clock in the morning and in a state of intense joy, we drove away for four days of bliss.

I had already discussed with Jane, Ben's mother, how much I should see of my son during my break. He was doing so well that neither of us wanted to disturb the equilibrium, but it was also a vital opportunity to reassure him that, eventually, things would be back to normal. We decided on a happy medium – I saw him twice. The first time, my parents and I took him swimming at the local pool in Guildford. Over the course of the last year one of my friends had taught him to swim and Ben delighted in showing me his large repertoire of underwater stunts. Then, one evening, we took him out for a pizza. We didn't have to do anything exciting, just being together provided all the entertainment we needed. No one could possibly know how proud I was of him. When I finally waved goodbye he left smiling, happy and content, and I knew he would survive until my eventual release. That alone would have justified my home leave.

My brief return was vital for my relationship with Bronya. We both needed to be alone to talk, free from time restraints. She was able to reassure me that she hadn't found a boyfriend. I was able to reassure her that I was getting used to Coldingley's way of life and that *I* hadn't found a boyfriend. It seemed everybody's preoccupation with prison had been the rape and sex that went on 'inside' and the constant questioning by well-meaning friends was wearying. I told her that there were only two gays in Coldingley and they kept themselves to themselves and were tolerated. 'Next time someone asks you how I'm coping with all the rape that goes on, tell them to bugger off,' I said. We both laughed about it. Thank God we had managed to maintain a sense of humour.

I had no idea what the future held for us. At the back of my mind there was a nagging fear she had stuck by me out of kindness, worried what I would do if I received a 'Dear John' letter.

Whatever the future holds for us, there is no one to whom I owe more. I hope that one day I will be able to make it up to her.

There was only one surprise that she had in store for me during the break. On the third day, without previously warning me, she announced that within the hour I was due on the first tee at the local golf club to play a round with my two closest professional colleagues. It was as well that she hadn't told me – I would have backed out.

Since being given a golf club by the gym staff in Coldingley, I had nurtured a dream that perhaps, one day, I might return to golf. Hitting shuttlecocks in the gym once a week was a far cry from the real thing, and I had no idea what my form would be like. For twenty years I had worked at my game to make it professionally competent. Nothing would make me more depressed than to find I had lost my ability, possibly for ever. As we headed for the club I was more than nervous.

The course was nearly deserted when we arrived, which was a good thing, as I had no intention of letting anyone see me playing golf. All it would need, I thought, would be for a journalist to be told what a prisoner was doing and I would be swiftly recalled to Coldingley. With my clubs slung over my scrawny shoulder I dodged round the clubhouse and headed for the first tee. Everything seemed so alien. The only grass I had seen for a year was on the football pitch in Coldingley which was more mud than anything, and the well-manicured tee looked like a green carpet. I took my bag off my shoulder, stood it on the ground and then in my customary way, almost a ritual ingrained through years of pressure golf, I reached for a club. Like drawing Excalibur from the stone, I took out my driver.

It was like meeting up with an old friend from the battlefields – we had bonded under fire. I waggled the club back and forward in my hands, felt a deep-rooted sensation of familiarity and thought back to the drives we had nailed, over the closing holes of my championship victories. It was now time to test that friendship.

I teed my ball up with trembling fingers. There had been no

time for any practice hits and after only a few swings to loosen up, I faced my first golf shot for over a year. Out of the corner of my eye I could see my friends and Bronya watching closely. I think they must have been as nervous as me.

I took up my stance, glanced up towards the distant fairway, which seemed an impossibly small target; then, focusing on the ball I took a swing. *WHOOSH!* I looked up after contact but my unpractised eye lost the ball in flight. I looked to my friends for a reaction.

Bronya was grinning. Nick and Peter were staring, open-mouthed. It must have been a fluke, but somehow, I had caught the shot perfectly, sending the ball, like an arrow, hurtling towards the intended target. Minutes later, my second shot was just as accurate and landed only a few feet from the flag. The ensuing putt from five feet never looked like missing. A year in prison, without hitting a shot in practice, and the first hole I play – I make a birdie. It was an amazing feeling. But even while feeling overjoyed that I *could* recapture my old form, I also felt an overwhelming sense of sadness that I might never be given the opportunity of competing again. It was a bitter taste of emotions.

Knowing my son was surviving, that Bronya was coping and our relationship was good, and that my form on the golf course was better than in my wildest dreams all helped me enormously over the next few months but my home leave alerted me to a deeply worrying problem. Throughout the four-day period, with the exception of swimming with Ben, I did not once smile in public. With Bronya and close friends I was able to lighten up, but as soon as I went out into the public eye, I felt it wrong to be seen looking happy. Every other facet of my behaviour suggested I would adapt quickly to the outside world, but deep down I suspected there was still a significant step for me to overcome before I would feel at all comfortable in society. I hoped that, before being released, I could come up with an answer.

The following day at four o'clock, Bronya drove me back to the prison. It is impossible to put into words how much we had enjoyed the freedom. It was hard to say goodbye. We sat in the car waiting for the minutes to pass until it was time for us to part. I felt like a marine waiting to be dropped from a transport plane over enemy territory. Finally the moment arrived. I gripped my overnight bag as though it were a parachute, took a last glance at Bronya to receive the nod. Then, without looking back, I opened the door and dived out. As I walked into reception, I heard the engine scream in frustration.

I had to serve one last term. Another one hundred and fifty days behind the lines.

Within hours of returning, I slipped back into the tense world of prison with surprising ease. An inmate was stabbed in the toilet area of my landing. I didn't hear him scream, but half an hour after the incident occurred I wandered into the room to wash my hands. On the floor was a large pool of congealing blood, and I almost retched. It was a stark contrast to the past few days but with determination I knew I could cope with the five remaining months. I had survived before, I could again.

But to give substance to what I had been through, to *prove* to myself that I could survive, I decided to write down my experiences 'inside'. It would be my therapy. In black and white I would record incidents that would prove me tough enough to cope with anything, inside and outside. It would also help to pass the time. I was well aware that I was on course for a bout of 'gate fever', an unfortunate ailment that causes time to stand still.

Over the next few days I planned out chapters and worked out a time schedule so that the last chapter would coincide with my release date. If I disciplined myself to write a predetermined amount each day I would finish it the night before I walked out of prison for ever. Every day, as normal, I would work for the vicar in the chapel; every night I would work in my cell. (It was a good arrangement in theory.)

However, the schedule proved hard to stick to. My desk was small and often I found myself kneeling on the floor, resting the paper on my bed. The light in the cell didn't help and after long periods of squinting at words, my eyes became strained and blood-shot. I also developed a small sore on my little finger where it skimmed across the page as I wrote. I spent hours and hours behind my door.

The guys on my landing took my antisocial behaviour well. They had become used to my spending most of my time alone, and rarely troubled me. At first they were a little concerned that I was writing an exposé of all their dodgy dealings, but when I explained it had nothing to do with their past capers, they left me alone. Ironically, among some extremely hard and dangerous individuals, I considered myself to be entirely safe. It was a paradox. Paul tended to be in charge of anyone who caused trouble regarding hooch. Eric, who had a blind hatred of anyone involved with heroin, kept the addicts at bay with a subtle blend of terror and intimidation. Anyone who brought heroin into our spur risked being tossed off the landing. The safe oasis in which I lived, though, was one day put into jeopardy.

For some time Eric (king of all he surveyed) had been working in the gardens. It was a much sought-after job, but he was very conscientious and held off all opposition. One day, a new officer to the prison took over the duty of looking after the garden workers. Almost instantly he clashed with Eric's outgoing personality, and within a short time Eric was out of a job.

One Saturday morning, a week after the sacking, I had just finished a run and was going back to my cell when I saw Eric looking slightly dejected. 'What's up?' I asked.

'I've been nicked,' he said.

'What for?'

'Someone shouted out of the window this morning at the garden screw. The bastard's nicked *me*.'

'Was it you?' I asked.

'As if!'

'What's the punishment?' I asked.

'A move back to bloody "C" wing. I couldn't cope with that,' he said. My mind reeled. The thought that the cell opposite me would suddenly become vacant, only for some animal, more than likely a 'smack' addict, to take up residence was too much. I had turned down a move to Latchmere partly because I felt safe. Another five months with a junkie for a neighbour would be intolerable.

'Can I do anything to help?' I asked.

'You could tell them it wasn't me.'

'I can't do that, I wasn't there,' I said, looking him in the eye. 'Someone could prove I was out running.' But I owed Eric a favour. What's more, he was responsible for keeping heroin off our spur. He'd certainly done more to protect our landing from the drug than all the officers put together. A petty charge might well be held against him but the whole of our landing, and possibly the wing, would suffer if he had to move. Surely I could make one hell of a plea on his behalf, at least make them think twice. I hesitated before suggesting my solution. 'Why not let me be a character witness?' I said.

'A *character witness!* That'll never work,' he said. He had to smile. So did I.

'Trust me – I owe you.'

A week later, I was summoned to the Coldingley court. I had never been put on report during my sentence, so I had no idea what to expect. It all seemed a bit grand, considering the charge. To have an officer spending time making a ruling about a fairly common-place event seemed more than over the top. I stood outside the room for what seemed like ages but all the time I rehearsed my plea. Eventually I was called, and let in. I couldn't believe the scene. At one end of the room, sitting behind a large table, was the deputy governor. On either side of him were two officers. To the right of the chair in which I was instructed to sit was the officer who had brought the complaint. To the left of me, behind another large table, was Eric, hemmed in by two more officers.

There were men in the prison desperate for decisions to be made about parole, home leave and transfers. Yet one of the main cogs in the decision-making machine was tied up with this pathetic adjudication.

In the silence that followed, the deputy governor explained the charge brought against Eric and pointed out that I had been called in his defence 'as a character witness' (I detected the sarcasm).

Eric had been imprisoned for impersonating a police inspector and from what I'd heard of his performance, had it been on the stage, it would have earned him an Oscar instead of an ten-year sentence. He stood up and adjusted his bifocals so he could peer at me over the rim. This was his day and he was going to milk it for all it was worth. 'Mr Hoskison,' (he actually got my name right), 'or could I call you John,' he said, majestically, sounding more and more like Rumpole of the Bailey. I managed not to laugh.

Thoroughly enjoying himself and going *well* over the top, he eventually got to the crux of the matter and turned round to the officer who had brought the charge, but the question was directed at me. 'Do you think', he said, letting his voice build to a crescendo, 'it was me who shouted at this . . . officer?' he asked, then looked directly into his eyes and enunciated with absolute precision, 'You pig-faced cunt!'

Eric had had his fun. The floor was now mine.

That night, when the celebration party for Eric's exoneration had calmed down on the landing, I returned to my cell and continued my writing. I was behind schedule and my release date was looming. At least for a while, it seemed that our landing would remain intact.

21

Ready and Waiting

And so to the last chapter.

My writing has been timed to perfection. It has been a struggle to discipline myself to work over the last few days but, at last, I only have this one section to write. In ten hours, my five hundred and thirty-five days of prison will be over and I'll be walking out of the gates for ever.

An hour ago, my leaving party finished. I was called every name under the sun when I refused the hooch specially brewed for the occasion, but Eric and the guys must have known I would refuse. 'No' is a word that has become easier for me to say over the last eighteen months. Judging from the lack of noise outside, none of the hooch went to waste. By the sound of it my friends are sleeping peacefully.

For the first time in my sentence I think I'm going to make it. God knows how I've avoided being stabbed, beaten up or becoming a drug addict, but now, behind a locked door, I'm pretty certain I'll go the distance. The only thing that could get me now is a cock-up in administration. Considering the officers still can't spell my name right it's a possibility. I think Bronya would have something to say about that. I spoke to her earlier this evening, my last call from prison. She'll be waiting at the gates at eight, probably at the wheel of a JCB. If they keep me a minute longer than they should,

I wouldn't put it past her to come crashing through the front door. I once told her not to wait for me – yet she has.

So, to work. I'm sitting at my small desk with a stack of paper and little else. I've packed nearly all my possessions. On the desk, however, next to the paper, is a small alarm clock that Ahmed gave me when he was released. The way time has slowed down over the last few weeks, it will take a long time for the hands to move to eight.

Above it, stuck to the wall, are my two most treasured possessions. Pictures of Bronya and Ben – the ones I showed to Guido so very long ago when I first arrived in Wandsworth. There was not a mark on them then. Now, after holding them close for comfort thousands of times, they are creased and worn. Every night they've watched over me. Throughout this long night they will keep me company one more time.

Mike Hart has my other valuables. I have asked him to give my radio to any new inmate on 'C' wing who is lonely and needs company. I also gave him five phonecards, which I bought at my last canteen. I'm so sick of seeing young inmates beaten up for being in debt that, as a last resort, Mike will use them to bail one out. It's the least I can do. He's done it enough times himself.

One of the few positive aspects of my life inside has been the Youth Project. Over the last few months I've become much more involved in it. Apart from my own testimony, I give one of the welcome speeches to the youngsters when they first enter the prison which helps set the scene, and I'm a mean backing vocal on the songs.

Inviting sixty children into the prison each month is logistically difficult. Twice this year the project has been cancelled at the last moment, because of staff shortages, yet the demand to send youngsters into the prison is growing by the day.

Several times over the last few months, when requested by the police, Mike has obtained permission for me to go out to schools and talk to some of the worst cases. I'm particularly pleased to hear that a fourteen-year-old I spoke to recently, who was already on the 'heroin-theft roundabout', is responding to rehab. I like to think I was of some influence.

Whatever direction my life will take I'm determined to carry on helping vulnerable kids. I can certainly warn them about drugs and prison. Perhaps it will help some of them to say 'no'. It's a good feeling when you can help. That's why I'm so disappointed for Mike. He's done so much to warn youngsters about the dangers of drugs and crime but they still won't let him extend the project. *What a waste.* I'm determined to keep in touch with him. God knows how he keeps sane with the frustration. God knows how anybody keeps sane in here.

I've just had to take a break from writing, my hand is painful from a knock it took this afternoon during my final game of badminton against Chris the 'lifer'. It took a while for me to persuade him to play against me again after our first, disastrous match, but since then we've had some amazing battles. The last one this afternoon ended with me crashing into the benches at the far end of the court in a near-suicide bid to return his cruel, mocking lob.

I've tried not to become too close to anyone these past few months but I've gravitated naturally towards Chris. He shows some of the same qualities I've seen in many champion sportsmen: talent, determination and a born competitiveness that drives him to make that all-out effort. I have often laughed at his fanaticism. Pete the gym instructor, however, said we are as bad as each other.

Over the last few months Chris and I have pushed each other to the limit training in the gym and, as I came to know him better, I found out why he was in prison. Chris grew up in south London and attended a school with few sporting facilities, but worse, for a young man like Chris, a school with a complete aversion to any form of competition. He therefore honed his battle instincts as a member of a local gang who vied for supremacy in his area. One day there was a fight with another gang and although Steve didn't deliver the fatal blow, someone was stabbed. Instead of a future picking up championship trophies, he received a life sentence inside prison. Had I not been blessed with my background and been sent to a school where all my excess energies were channelled into competitive sport, I could well have drifted down the same road.

There are a lot of fundamentally sound young people in the community with an abundance of energy who are only just managing to keep themselves out of trouble. That's where I'm determined my background in sport will help. Not just golf – sport in general. I hope I can show wayward youngsters a way to help pass the time more constructively and distract them from temptation. With little sport available at school nowadays, what else is there to do except hang around in gangs outside McDonalds?

Talking of schools, I shall always be indebted to the teachers of the education department. When they realised what I was doing, after weeks of scrounging paper, they came up with a way that I could get access to the computer room and use one as a word processor. Early in the mornings I've been meeting them at eight o'clock and they've been letting me in to type. I owe them a debt of gratitude. They've been really kind to me and will no doubt continue to try and influence as many as they can in a world that seemingly does little to reward the conscientious.

There are other people whom I'll miss. Every week on Wednesday afternoons I've continued to see the 'Mencap' group. I was thrilled to hear last month that Linda and Brian have just been employed by Sainsbury's. The 'gang' helped me a lot when I was very low, and I shall miss them. Perhaps one day I'll pop into the supermarket to see them. They always liked surprises.

True to form, the authorities didn't spring one on me. I have received not one word of advice regarding my release. The only thing I'll be taking from here is my £46 discharge grant, which won't go far. I've got to start to earn an income quickly, no doubt the bills will start mounting, but in the present climate anyone with a criminal record is unlikely to get a job. I cling desperately to the hope that I can get back into the PGA. Fortunately everyone I know wants to see me back. They say I've served my punishment, but I'll have to wait and see. Coupled to a five-year driving ban it'll be hard, no matter what. I'm not even sure where I'll live. When I lost my job, I lost my flat. Fortunately, I have some good friends around who will protect me. I myself would never consider using my diploma from the university of crime. But I now know many who would.

The one hope I had of immediate employment was shattered the other day. An old friend of mine wrote from abroad offering me a job in the world of sport. I was thrilled. Even though I didn't want to leave England, I had never been unemployed and I didn't want to start now. At least, temporarily, it would keep me from the dole queue. When I contacted my probation officer to let her know the good news I received a letter back stating that no matter what the reason I would *definitely* not be allowed abroad for nine months. I was staggered. I went to see the governor and chaplain to explain my problem and see if there was any way that an exception could be made, but they said the matter was completely out of their hands and they could only confirm the probation officer's words.

For the next nine months I have to report to the probation offices every two weeks to show that I'm not causing trouble and under no circumstances am I to go abroad. Apparently it looks bad in the press if an ex-prisoner is seen travelling.

The guys in here though say probation appointments are a good thing – it's the easiest place on the outside to get hold of drugs and 'dodgy' work. It seems a criminal influence will continue for a while. How ironic.

It's been a real eye-opener, prison. Perhaps it's now time I made some sort of comment. One thing's for certain – prison is essential. There are some dangerous people in here; the public (of which I'll shortly be one) has a right to be protected. But it's no good putting everyone in the same boat. There *are* good prisoners around and they need protecting. They're the ones who (if serving under four years) should be let out after half their sentence *if they earn the privilege*. If an inmate shows no intention of turning over a new leaf he should not get a day off. In the present system both walk out on the same day. That's wrong.

And someone has got to do something about the problem of drugs. There are only three ways that drugs can get into prison: when a visitor smuggles them in at visiting time; when prison officers (responsible for twelve per cent of all drugs inside jail) bring them in during the course of work; and (the main source), when inmates leave the jail, swallow a parcel, then bring it back in. They're the crucial ones to stop. If an inmate wants to go out to see his family and has earned the privilege, he should be allowed to do so, but there's got to be somewhere where inmates are held while their digestive system eventually gets rid of the drugs. It may be a pain in the arse (excuse the pun) for the prison to organise such a thing, but they should do something about it now.

Speaking as a prospective member of the public – I'm frightened of what the future holds. The streets are being swept clean, the prison population is exploding and currently society is enjoying a (relatively) crime-free period. Unfortunately an ever-increasing proportion of the 60,000 angry men in prison will be getting out hooked on heroin and looking for revenge. Recently I heard the expression 'tie ups' used for the first time. Apparently traditional housebreaking is now too dangerous with all the alarms. The simple solution is to go in during the day, tie up the occupants, beat them until they divulge the whereabouts of their wealth, then beat them senseless and do the burglary. You don't stop heroin addicts just with more security. They will keep coming . . . and coming . . . and if you simply lock them up without trying to cure them, they will go back into prison, learn new techniques in the most active think-tank in Britain and come out yet more devious.

Come on, let's have some action! I've lived with the authority's attitude towards heroin for eighteen months *and I'm fed up with the apathy*.

Only four days ago, knowing the results wouldn't be here until after my departure, I was drug-tested. They know I'm clean so it was a good chance to cook the books. If a drug addict can admit he's got a problem, so the prison service should admit theirs. I've kept my temper pretty well in check these past eighteen months, *but sometimes my blood really boils when I see the general lack of effort. . .*

Being able to write has really saved me, these last few months. Many things have happened, of course, but only the usual ones: a few stabbings, nothing much out of the ordinary. It's true what everyone says in here – once the initial shock of prison is overcome, it really is just a question of helping time pass as quickly as possible. The concept of 'too much of a good thing' can work in reverse. 'Too much of a bad thing' leads to indifference. And there's plenty of that in here.

Fortunately I'm surrounded by some pretty decent men who have now had enough of prison and want to lead normal lives. My custom has been to spend as much time as possible in the chapel area, but now, needing to write has meant a premature return to my cell each evening, and I have come to know the guys on the landing a bit better. I constantly remind myself that they are hardened criminals, and that I shouldn't find anything they do amusing, but there are some genuine characters in here. Take away the violence, albeit mainly directed towards the drug addicts, and there are some honest guys on my spur. Some of them, not many, but some of them I'll miss.

Well, the minutes are ticking by, and there's not much longer for me to go now till I take those final steps from here. I am pretty apprehensive about being released. I've tried to do everything I can to prepare myself, but I still have nagging doubts about some things.

Certainly giving my testimony at the New Bridge Conference really helped me. It took a long time after I returned from London to be able to think deeply about the night of the accident and the terrible suffering it caused, but I can think about the consequences now without breaking down. If I hadn't spoken out and learned to face up to my feelings, my release would be the start of a nightmare.

I know that I'm not fully recovered, I never will be; but, worryingly, I still feel my reaction will be to move impassively amongst society. Since returning successfully from my first 'home leave', I've been allowed out every eight weeks for the same privilege and every other week I've been allowed a day release on Sundays. Each time I've come up against the same problem. I don't know how long it will take for me to smile again in company, but life won't be worth living if I don't learn how to. Smiling, of course, is just a beginning. I worry that any positive gesture on my part will be misinterpreted. I'm not sure if there's an answer: perhaps it just requires discipline. Certainly I have always been too concerned with what people think of me, it's an intrinsic part of my character that even prison hasn't been able to change. I must endeavour to keep my chin up and look the world in the eye.

In my spare time recently, I've done a lot of thinking. When I was a little boy I used to think it would be great to live for a thousand years. As a young man my philosophy changed (I think it coincided with starting to smoke) and I came to the conclusion that in the same way literature contains only a certain number of plots, life contains only a certain number of emotions. It therefore seemed to me that the success of your life was not how long you lived, but how much of the emotional spectrum you could experience. Now, my attitude has changed again. The emotional journey I've been on this last two and a half years is one I would not wish on any man.

I can't say I'm sorry that my prison experience is nearly over, but it's an experience I had to go through. There's no way I could have continued my life in the outside world without being seen to be punished. The irony is, prison is no punishment at all compared to the pain I've felt inside. A pain, I know, that will never go away but

I'm learning to live with it. I now owe it to those closest to me to try to find a way forward and get on with my life.

Well, zero hour approaches. I don't know what I'm going to do with all this writing. Part of me says that I should give it to somebody who could help publish it – maybe it could do some good. There does seem to be a discrepancy between the realities of prison and the general perception of it. Maybe my account could scare a youngster into changing his ways. Perhaps if Thompson had read it, he wouldn't have ended up in here trying to commit suicide. On the other hand, will I want this around my neck in the future? The decision will have to wait. This has to be my last sentence.

Outside a new day is dawning. The future now beckons and I want to be first in the queue.

Epilogue

I n my golfing days, sometimes I would be called to the first tee knowing that my swing wasn't quite right. Yet, I would have no option but to look positive and get on with the job. In a similar way I emerged from prison knowing that emotionally I wasn't completely healed.

Over the following weeks, when I met people I used to know, I struggled to relax in their company. Often I would find myself walking down the street, looking at the pavement. Never did I smile in public. I tried to tell myself that things would get better, but the future looked bleak.

One day I received a letter. It had been sent from the wife of the man who had been killed in the accident. In the kindest words she suggested that it might be a good idea to meet up – for both our sakes.

Not long ago, on a sunny summer day, we met in the beautiful surrounds of Wisley Gardens, near Guildford. At first we walked among the blossoming flowers but eventually we found a deserted wooden bench and sat down. It was so peaceful.

I had already witnessed her compassion when she pleaded for leniency at my trial. But that afternoon she went a step further. In a voice that was so calm it took me aback, she explained that she and her family were now coping well. She said it was time to look to the future. Turning towards me, with a look of absolute sincerity, she asked me to do the same. The warm and reassuring smile she bathed me with became the gateway to my future.

For all the effort I had put in, over the long months, to get better, in the blink of an eye my life was given back to me. I was, and am, truly humbled.

I write these words as a free man.